THE ACCURSED TOWER

The Fall of Acre and the End of the Crusades

ROGER CROWLEY

BASIC BOOKS
New York

Basic Books
Hachette Book Group
1290 Avenue of the Americas, New York, NY 10104
www.basicbooks.com

Printed in the United States of America

First Edition: October 2019

Published by Basic Books, an imprint of Perseus Books, LLC, a subsidiary of Hachette Book Group, Inc. The Basic Books name and logo is a trademark of the Hachette Book Group.

The Hachette Speakers Bureau provides a wide range of authors for speaking events. To find out more, go to www.hachettespeakersbureau.com or call (866) 376-6591.

The publisher is not responsible for websites (or their content) that are not owned by the publisher.

Print book interior design by Trish Wilkinson.

The Library of Congress has cataloged the hardcover edition as follows:

Names: Crowley, Roger, 1951– author.
Title: The Accursed Tower : the fall of Acre and the end of the Crusades / Roger
   Crowley.
Other titles: Fall of Acre and the end of the Crusades
Description: First Edition. | New York : Basic Books, 2019. | Includes
   bibliographical references and index.
Identifiers: LCCN 2019019102 | ISBN 9781541697348 (hardcover) | ISBN
   9781541699724 (ebook)
Subjects: LCSH: Acre (Israel)—History—Siege, 1291. | Crusades—13th–15th
   centuries.
Classification: LCC D171 .C66 2019 | DDC 956.94/032—dc23
LC record available at https://lccn.loc.gov/2019019102

ISBNs: 978-1-5416-9734-8 (hardcover), 978-1-5416-9972-4 (ebook)

LSC-C

10 9 8 7 6 5 4 3 2 1

For Richard and Sophie

And it is worth noting that they say that Our Lord, when he travelled beside the Syrian sea, did not enter this city, but cursed one of its towers, which today is called Accursed by the inhabitants. But I believe rather that it took its name from another source. When our men laid siege to the city, this tower was the most strongly defended of all; whence they called it the Accursed Tower.

—WILBRAND VAN OLDENBURG, VISITOR TO ACRE, 1211

Contents

The Crusader States in the Thirteenth Century.

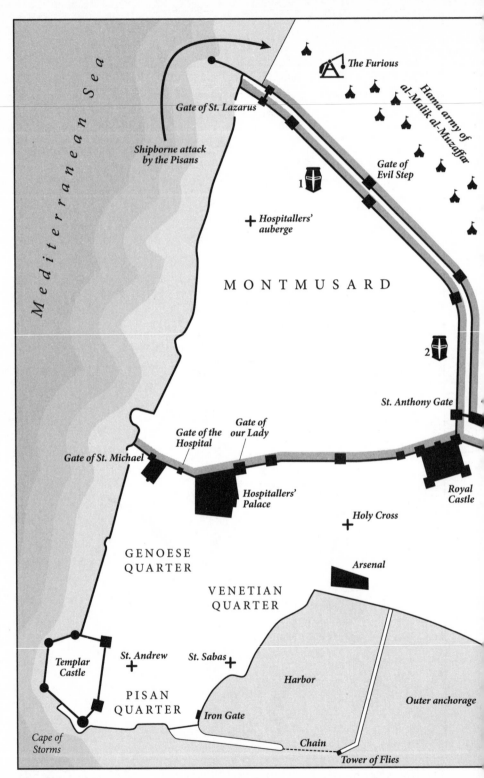

The Siege of Acre, 1291.

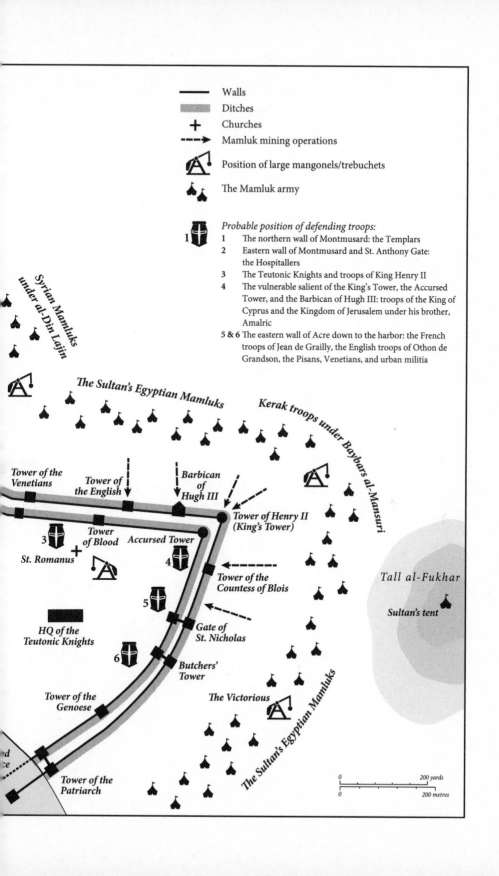

Walls

Ditches

Churches

Mamluk mining operations

Position of large mangonels/trebuchets

The Mamluk army

Probable position of defending troops:

1   The northern wall of Montmusard: the Templars
2   Eastern wall of Montmusard and St. Anthony Gate:
     the Hospitallers
3   The Teutonic Knights and troops of King Henry II
4   The vulnerable salient of the King's Tower, the Accursed
     Tower, and the Barbican of Hugh III: troops of the King of
     Cyprus and the Kingdom of Jerusalem under his brother,
     Amalric
5 & 6 The eastern wall of Acre down to the harbor: the French
     troops of Jean de Grailly, the English troops of Othon de
     Grandson, the Pisans, Venetians, and urban militia

Syrian Mamluks under al-Din Lajin

The Sultan's Egyptian Mamluks

Kerak troops under Baybars al-Mansuri

Tower of the Venetians

Tower of the English

Barbican of Hugh III

Tower of Henry II (King's Tower)

3   *Tower of Blood*

St. Romanus

Accursed Tower

4

Tower of the Countess of Blois

Tall al-Fukhar

5

Sultan's tent

HQ of the Teutonic Knights

6   *Gate of St. Nicholas*

Butchers' Tower

Tower of the Genoese

The Victorious

The Sultan's Egyptian Mamluks

Tower of the Patriarch

| 0 | | 200 yards |
| 0 | | 200 metres |

A BRIEF TIMELINE OF THE
HOLY LAND CRUSADES

1095	Pope Urban II preaches crusade in France.
1096–1099	The First Crusade.
1099	The crusaders besiege and sack Jerusalem.
1104	King Baldwin captures Acre.
1147–1149	The Second Crusade.
1171	Saladin becomes ruler of Egypt. Start of the Ayyubid dynasty.
1171–1185	Saladin consolidates Ayyubid rule over Palestine and Syria.
1187	Saladin defeats a crusader army at Hattin, takes Acre, and regains Jerusalem.
1189–1192	The Third Crusade, led by Philip Augustus of France, Frederick I (Holy Roman Emperor), and Richard I of England.
1189–1191	The crusader siege of Acre.
1192	Treaty between Richard and Saladin, and departure of Richard.
1202–1204	The Fourth Crusade sets out from Venice but deviates to capture Christian Constantinople.
1217–1219	The Fifth Crusade attacks Egypt but is defeated in the Nile Delta.
1228	Frederick II regains Jerusalem by treaty.

1239–1241	Small crusading ventures by Theobald of Champagne and Richard of Cornwall.
1244	The Khwarazmians sack Jerusalem. The city is finally lost.
1245	Pope Innocent IV sends an embassy to the Mongols.
1247	Louis IX plans a crusade.
1248–1254	The Seventh Crusade.
1248	Louis invades Egypt, his army is defeated in the Nile Delta, and Louis is captured.
1248–1250	The end of the Ayyubid dynasty. The slave Mamluks gain control of Egypt.
1250s	Baybars emerges as leader of the Bahriyyah Mamluks.
1258	The Mongols sack Baghdad.
1259	Qutuz gains control of Egypt.
1260	The Mongols under Hülegü sack Aleppo and take Damascus. The Mongol army is defeated at Ayn Jalut. Qutuz is assassinated, and Baybars becomes sultan of the Mamluks.
1260–1264	Baybars tightens his grip on power and reforms the army.
1265–1271	Baybars embarks on systematic destruction of crusader castles. Acre is repeatedly raided.
1268	Baybars takes Antioch.
1270	The Eighth Crusade. King Louis IX attacks Tunis and dies there.
1271	Edward of England's crusade to Acre. Baybars captures Krak des Chevaliers.
1277	Baybars dies. Qalawun gains the Mamluk sultanate.
1289	Qalawun takes Tripoli.
1290	The massacre of Muslims at Acre provides the excuse for Qalawun's attack. The Mamluk army is mobilized. Qalawun dies, and Khalil becomes sultan.
1291	Khalil attacks and destroys Acre. All remaining crusader outposts in Outremer fall.
1293	Khalil is assassinated by a group of Mamluk emirs.

PROLOGUE

THE ACCURSED TOWER

IN THE SPRING of 1291, the largest army that Islam had ever assembled against the crusaders in the Holy Land was moving toward the city of Acre. It was, by all accounts, an extraordinary spectacle—an immense concourse of men and animals, tents, baggage and supplies, all converging on Christendom's last foothold. The aim was to deliver a knock-out blow.

Forces had been drawn widely from across the Middle East—from Egypt five hundred miles to the south, from Lebanon and Syria as far north as the banks of the Euphrates, from the great cities of Cairo, Damascus, and Aleppo—a gathering of all the regions' military resources. The elite troops were enslaved Turkish-speaking warriors from beyond the Black Sea, and the army included not only cavalry, infantry, and specialist supply corps, but enthusiastic volunteers, mullahs, and dervishes. The campaign had inspired a popular fervor for holy war—and a less pious one for booty.

Visible in this panorama, a vast array of outfits, devices, and armor: lordly emirs in white turbans; foot soldiers in conical metal helmets, chain mail, and leather scale tunics; cavalry armed with short bows, their animals covered in colorful cloths and saddles embroidered with heraldic insignia; camel-mounted musicians playing kettledrums, horns, and cymbals; fluttering yellow banners and weapons of all kinds—maces, javelins, spears, swords, siege crossbows, carved stone balls, naptha for the manufacture of Greek fire and clay grenades. Oxen strained to haul carts laden with timbers from trees felled

A schematic map of Acre from the 1250s. The round Accursed Tower is prominent on the walls, reflecting perhaps its psychological importance, even if by this date the city was double walled with the Accursed Tower now protected by an outer line of defense. The map shows the suburb of Montmusard to the left separated from the old city by an inner wall as well as prominent buildings. (The Parker Library, Corpus Christi College, Cambridge)

in the mountains of Lebanon and fashioned in the workshops of Damascus. These timbers were the prefabricated components of stone-throwing catapults—known in the Islamic world as *manjaniq* (mangonels), to Europeans as trebuchets. The rumbling carts were bringing an unprecedented number of such devices, some of enormous size, to batter the walls of Acre. They represented the most powerful form of artillery weapon before the age of gunpowder.

THE CITY THIS army had come to attack was very ancient and its role in regional power politics continuously significant. It has had many names: Akko in Hebrew, Akka in Arabic; Ptolemais to the Greeks and the Romans; Accon in crusader Latin; St. Jean d'Acre to the French. It has been recorded in Egyptian hieroglyphics, the chronicles of Assyrian kings, and the Bible. Bronze Age people occupied the nearby hill that would later be the base for Acre's besiegers. It was captured by the pharaohs, used by the Persians to plan attacks on Greece. Alexander the Great took it without a fight, and Julius Caesar made it the landing place for Roman legions; Cleopatra owned it. It fell to Islam in 636, just four years after the death of the Prophet Muhammad.

Acre's long habitation and value lay in its site and strategic location. The city backs onto the Mediterranean Sea, on a hooked and

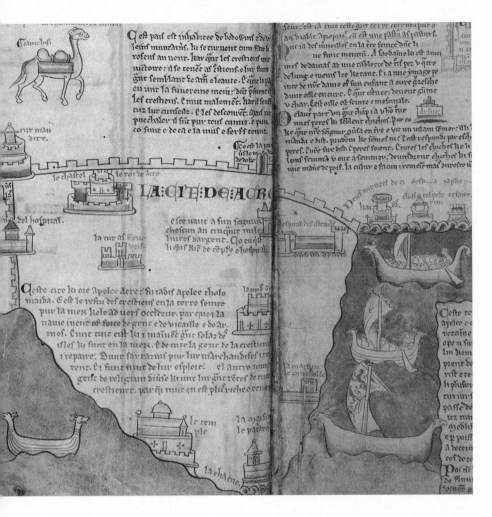

rocky promontory that provides a small but reasonably sheltered harbor. To the south lies a coastal plain and a long sweep of bay of the finest sand, valued from the time of the Phoenicians for glass making, through which runs the river Naaman, watering the city's hinterland. Visible on the next headland, ten miles away, is the equally ancient city of Haifa. Acre's position midway along the shores of the Levant has rendered it a natural halting place—a hub for maritime trade, south to north from Egypt to the Black Sea and east-west across the Mediterranean. Acre has been an entrepot for the exchange and transshipment of goods, linked by land as well as sea to routes along the coast and into the heart of the Middle East. In the process, beneath the surface of war, it has been a door through which crop species, goods, industrial processes, languages, religions, and peoples have passed and enriched the cycle of trade and the development of civilization.

To the crusaders, Acre always mattered. When, in November 1095, Pope Urban II preached his incendiary sermon in a field near Clermont in France, calling for the salvation of Jerusalem, the city where Christ had lived and died, he ignited the imagination of Western Christendom—with astonishing results. The First Crusade saw ordinary people set out spontaneously for the East in large numbers—and perish miserably—and then a more professionally organized expedition under the great barons of Europe. Thousands of soldiers slogged the 2,000 miles round Europe into the Middle East. Against all expectations, they captured Jerusalem in July 1099, trampling over the corpses of Muslims and Jews on their way to the Temple Mount. But despite this achievement, the first long march to the Holy Land had been massively attritional. Of the army of 35,000 that left Europe, probably only 12,000 saw Jerusalem. This quickly taught military planners the need to transport armies by ship, and the necessity of ports such as Acre to receive them. Acre was initially taken in 1104 by Baldwin of Boulogne, the first crusader king of Jerusalem, and then became the chief landing place for pilgrims and the armies to protect them. It was so valuable that when a leading crusader lord, Gervais de Bazoches, Prince of Galilee, was captured in a raid four years later, the ruler of Damascus tried to exchange his prisoner for the city, plus Haifa and Tiberias further down the coast. Baldwin chose to sacrifice the man. Gervais's scalp, tied to a pole, became an Islamic banner, his skull the emir's drinking cup.

Holding Acre proved critical to the continuation of *Outremer* ("Overseas"), as the French called the principalities on the shores of Palestine, Lebanon, and Syria they had established during the First Crusade. But almost a century later, in 1187, Islam regained the city. It came off the back of the destruction of a crusader army at the battle of Hattin a few days earlier. In the aftermath, Acre was quickly surrendered, its inhabitants allowed to depart unharmed.

This formed the prelude to the most exhausting military encounter of the Holy Land crusades. For 683 days, between 1189 and 1191, a Christian force struggled to regain Acre. The contest for the city involved the champions of the age: Saladin, prince of the Ayyubid dynasty, pitted against the crowned heads of Europe, Philip Augustus of France and Richard I of England, Guy de Lusignan king of Jerusalem, and the forces of the Third Crusade. This was a titanic struggle, in which the besieging crusaders were at times themselves besieged. It involved naval battles, open-field warfare, sorties, and skirmishes. The walls were pummeled by catapults and battering rams, assaulted from siege towers, undermined by tunnels, defended by counter-bombardment with stones, arrows, and incendiary devices. Men were hacked to pieces with swords, maces, and spears, and burned alive by Greek fire. Each side in turn was brought to its knees by starvation, disease, and despair.

Eventually, the struggle narrowed to one particular point. Medieval visitors came up with vivid analogies to describe the city's layout. It was pictured variously as being shaped like an axe or like a crusader's shield, or more crudely as a triangle, with the sea its base. The other two sides were formed by the north and east sides of the city's single wall, punctuated by gates and towers and fronted by a low fore-wall and ditch. These met at the triangle's apex. This was both the most vulnerable and most heavily fortified sector, and it was here that the contest for Acre was at its fiercest. The apex was guarded by a formidable tower—the keystone of the defense, which the crusaders called the *Turris Maledicta*, the Accursed Tower. There is no clear explanation for the origin of this name. Legends surrounded the ill-omened tower: Christ had cursed it as he traversed the Holy Land and so never entered the city. Or that it was complicit in his betrayal: the thirty silver coins for which Judas Iscariot sold him were said to have been minted there. The name may have predated the siege, but the churchman Wilbrand van Oldenburg, who visited the city shortly afterwards, expressed a healthy skepticism for apocryphal explanations. He believed simply that "when our men laid siege to the city, this tower was the most strongly defended of all; whence they called it the Accursed Tower."[1]

The fight for this bulwark had been brutal. During the spring and summer of 1191, its walls were subject to terrific bombardment by powerful stone-throwing catapults. The defenders responded in kind. The tower was undermined and countermined; men fought in pitch-black tunnels, then agreed a subterranean truce. When a section of wall adjacent to the tower collapsed, the French sought glory with a frontal assault over the strewn rubble and were massacred; one of the great nobility, Albéric Clément, lord of Le Mez and the first Marshal of France, was killed in the attempt. And it was here, when miners finally brought down the tower on July 11, 1191, that the city's Muslim defenders bowed to the inevitable and surrendered.

At enormous cost, the crusaders had retaken the city. Perhaps the tower embodied the whole ordeal, its name simply giving expression to all the frustration, pain, and suffering the armies had endured before Acre's walls. Its capture ensured that the wars between the Franks and the Saracens, as each side called the other, would go on for another century.

THE AFTERMATH OF the siege left a bitter legacy. On August 20, 1191, shortly after the surrender, King Richard I of England—the Lionheart—bound the Muslim defenders of Acre with ropes, marched them onto the plain outside the city, and beheaded them. There were probably around 3,000 of these men, and according to an agreement reached with Saladin, they were due for exchange. In the moves and countermoves in the contest for Acre, mistakes were made on both sides, but Saladin missed a golden opportunity to sweep the infidels into the sea once and for all. He had been finally forced to seek a deal and surrender the city. When he was considered to have reneged on the agreed terms, Richard, in a decision taken in council, called his bluff and acted ruthlessly.

The Third Crusade, of which this siege of Acre was the prologue, failed in its objective of retaking Jerusalem. Richard turned back from the ultimate prize fifteen miles short, having judged the risks too great, just as Saladin was preparing to evacuate the city. The contest between these two great adversaries ended in stalemate: the City of God unrecaptured, the crusaders clinging tenaciously to the coast of Palestine. In the aftermath, Acre became the hub and the heart of successive crusading ventures. After 1191, the survival of Outremer rested on it heavily. The city was swiftly repopulated by the crusaders and, by a linguistic fiction, on it was conferred the title of capital of the Second Kingdom of Jerusalem, while Jerusalem itself remained, for all but a short time, in Muslim hands. Acre's monarchs gloried in the all-important and frequently contested title of King of Jerusalem and similarly the city's supreme religious authority, who answered only to the pope, was titled Jerusalem's patriarch.

The execution of the Muslim garrison remains a controversial episode in the history of the crusades, one for which no clear explanation has been reached. "God knows best," reflected Baha al-Din, Saladin's adviser at the time.[2] Exactly one hundred years later, the fate of the executed garrison would be remembered. In 1291, it would be an Islamic army battering Acre and the Christians defending a reconstructed Accursed Tower. This book is an account of the road that led back to the city's gates that spring and what happened there—the final act in the two-hundred-year struggle known to Arabic historians as the Frankish wars, to Europeans as the Holy Land Crusades.

1

THE SECOND KINGDOM
OF JERUSALEM

1200–1249

WHEN THE FRENCH churchman Jacques de Vitry landed at Acre in November 1216 to take up his position as bishop, he was appalled. He had come to rejuvenate the spiritual fervor of its Christian people in advance of a new crusade, but instead of the pious city of Western clerical imagination—gateway to the land where Jesus had walked and died—he found it "like a monster or a beast, having nine heads, each fighting the other."[1] There were deviant Christian sects of every persuasion: Arabic-speaking Jacobites (Occidental Syrians) who circumcised their children "in the manner of the Jews" and crossed themselves with a single finger; the Eastern Syriacs he considered "to be traitors and very corrupt," some of whom when bribed "revealed the secrets of Christianity to the Saracens" and had married priests, "who dressed their hair in the manner of the lay people." Meanwhile, the Italian merchant communities—Genoese, Pisans, and Venetians—simply ignored his attempts to excommunicate them; rarely, if ever, listened to the word of God; and "even refused to come to my sermon." Then there were the Nestorians, the Georgians, and the Armenians, and the Pullani (Syrian-born orientalized Europeans), who were "utterly devoted to the pleasures of the flesh." Doubtless the unfamiliar appearance of the Eastern Christians, often heavily bearded and robed like Muslims, was additionally disconcerting. Their daughters were veiled, and when he attempted to correct their doctrinal errors, he had to resort to an Arabic interpreter. Vitry was experiencing all the disorientation of arriving in the Middle East—yet in a city whose churches, houses, towers, and palaces looked puzzlingly European.

It was not just divergent Christian practices that sent Vitry reeling with culture shock. It was the place itself: "When I entered this horrible city and had found it full of countless disgraceful acts and evil deeds, I was very confused in my mind." He conjured a dreadful den of vice, full of "foreigners who had fled from their own lands as outlaws because of various appalling crimes," where black magic was practiced and murder rife, where husbands strangled their wives and wives poisoned their husbands, where "not only laymen but even churchmen and some members of the regular clergy rented out their lodgings to public prostitutes through the whole city. Who would be able to list all the crimes of this second Babylon?" This was his anguished cry.

Vitry might well have exaggerated Acre's reputation for sin, but it certainly confounded his expectations. This sense of bewilderment among newly arrived Christians with crusading expectations was a repeated theme—and one that would have tragic consequences in Acre's final crisis seventy years later.

AFTER THE FALL of Jerusalem to Saladin and Richard the Lionheart's failure to retake it, the crusader states had shrunk to three small footholds, pushed to the edge of the Mediterranean Sea: the isolated principality of Antioch to the north, the County of Tripoli, and the so-called Second Kingdom of Jerusalem—a long, narrow coastal strip that stretched some 180 miles, from Ascalon and Jaffa in the south to Beirut in the north. It was Acre that now became effectively the capital and political center of this displaced Holy Kingdom, and on it was conferred all secular and religious administration. Acre was home to the royal court and castle of the kings of Jerusalem and later the seat of the kingdom's patriarch—the pope's appointed representative. The powerful crusading orders of the Templars and the Hospitallers also transferred their headquarters to Acre, where they constructed impressive and formidable palaces and strongholds. Immensely wealthy, the military orders now comprised the most effective defense of the Latin East. During the early thirteenth century, the orders redoubled their castle building and development as forward positions for ensuring the safety of roads and protection of the remnant territories. In Acre, they were joined by a number of other, smaller orders—such as the knights of the Order of St. Lazarus, originally founded to provide care for lepers, and newly formed imitations, some of which had sprung out of the Third Crusade, including the Germanic Teutonic Knights and the English-inspired order of St. Thomas of Canterbury. At the same time, many of the religious orders, driven out by Saladin or fearful of insecurity, relocated their churches, monasteries, and nunneries within Acre.

Vitry had not only arrived in the fictitious replacement of the holy city of Jerusalem; he had stepped groggily ashore, disoriented and horrified, into a highly dynamic, colorful, ethnically diverse and bustling Mediterranean port with all the varied activities and attractions that this implied. Acre was an emporium for the exchange of goods over a vast area and the most cosmopolitan city in the medieval world. The city was a multilingual hubbub of peoples, cultures, and languages, each with its own quarters and religious institutions. Among its eighty-one churches, there was one dedicated to St. Bridget of Kildare, in Ireland; another to St. Martin of the Bretons; yet another to St. James of the Iberian Peninsula. At the forefront were the merchant communities of the Italian maritime republics—Genoa, Venice, and Pisa—fiercely competing for Mediterranean markets, as well as traders from Marseille and Catalonia. Many of these merchant groups had been granted their own judicial and commercial independence from royal authority. There was a small community of Jews, Copts from Egypt, and visiting Muslim merchants from Damascus, Antioch, and Alexandria who came regularly to do business. The main language of communication was Old French, but German, Catalan, Provençale, Italian, and English could all be heard in the streets, mingling with the languages of the Levant. Traveling merchants from Constantinople, Antioch, and Egypt came regularly to do business, and in spring and autumn, with the arrival of merchant ships from the west, the harbor was crammed with vessels, and the population of the city could be further increased by the arrival of up to 10,000 pilgrims intent on traveling to see the holy sites. Touts and tour guides and lodging houses benefited from these throngs of visitors. When the instability of the Palestinian hinterland made further progress to Jerusalem impossible, Acre, despite having no connection with the life of Jesus, became a pilgrimage site in its own right. Under the guidance of local clerics, Acre had a circuit of forty churches to visit, each with its own relics and holy souvenirs, and permission granted by the papacy to bestow remission of sins.

Swelled by refugees from throughout Palestine and with the city's attractiveness to European merchants and pilgrims, Acre at the start of the thirteenth century was booming. As an important harbor of the Latin Levant, it not only traded with the western Mediterranean but was an axis of commercial exchange for all the eastern Mediterranean, from the Black Sea and Constantinople to Alexandria and Egypt, which involved accommodation with the Islamic world and paid little attention to the barriers of faith. To the outright displeasure of the papacy, Acre employed the monetary system of its Muslim neighbors. It minted gold and silver imitations of Fatamid and Ayyubid coins, with inscriptions in Arabic, and when, in 1250, the pope banned the use of Islamic inscriptions and style of date, the city's mint simply replaced the words on its coinage with Christian ones— but still in Arabic and with added crosses. The interdependence of Christian and Muslim merchants ensured that neither had a strong interest in disturbing a status quo.

In the thirteenth century, Acre came to rival and even overtake the great port city of Alexandria in the volume and variety of goods that passed through its port. The Earl of Cornwall, who came here in the early 1240s, estimated that the city brought in £50,000 a year, a sum equal to the royal income of a monarch in Western Europe. Textiles, either as raw materials or as finished cloth (such as silk, linen, and cotton), passed from the Islamic world into Europe, along with glassware, sugar, and precious stones. Back came European wool, which Latin merchants took to Muslim Damascus to trade, along with iron work, food (spices, salt, fish), war horses, and various other supplies to support the crusading effort. Pottery entered Acre from as far away as China and from across the European world as ballast in the hold of ships, and daily through the city gates came camels and donkeys laden with produce to support a large population: wine from Nazareth; dates from the Jordan valley; wheat, fruit, and vegetables grown locally by Eastern Christians and Muslims. It was an industrial center too. The Templars and the Hospitallers manufactured glass and refined sugar at their own mills and furnaces outside the city. Among the crowded covered markets, there were also workshops specializing in glass, metal, ceramics, and pilgrim souvenirs, alongside tanneries and soap makers.

IF SUCCESSIVE POPES were scandalized by Acre's Islamic-style coinage, they were more deeply troubled by another highly profitable trade: many of the war materials sold to the Ayyubid sultans in Cairo—wood and iron for shipbuilding, weapons and war machines, and naptha for incendiary devices—passed through the hands of Italian merchants via Acre. Even more significant to the Holy See was the trade in human beings. Turkic military slaves from the steppes north of the Black Sea came via Constantinople on Byzantine or Italian ships, and Acre was a stopover and a slave market. Repeated papal bans were regularly flouted. In 1246, Pope Innocent IV was blaming all three Italian trading communities in the city for transporting slaves from Constantinople, who were then shipped on to Egypt to swell the sultan's armies. The acceleration of this trade from the 1260s was to have unintended consequences for the rump crusader states. Acre was destined to be besieged by armies recruited through its own port.

Vitry may have exaggerated the iniquity of Acre, but the city did serve as something of a penal colony: courts in Europe sometimes commuted criminal sentences by transporting the guilty for settlement in the Holy Land. And he was accurate about the disputatious, nine-headed nature of the place. Under the very nominal authority of the largely absent king of Jerusalem—a title that was to lead to endless factionalizing and internecine warfare throughout the thirteenth century—Acre consisted of a jostle of different, and largely independent, interest groups contesting access to the port and property rights. Communities within the city had their own historic privileges; a considerable measure of autonomy; and often their own legal systems, hindering any effective administration of justice. The rival military orders, answerable only to the pope, comprised the wealthiest and most militarily effective sector of the community—the Templars and Hospitallers, each occupying large areas of old Acre with their spacious palaces and walled complexes, were the most visually dominant presence in the city.

The layout of the city reflected the close proximity of the many different factions and religious communities to one another. Acre's plan consisted of a tightly packed urban center, in which the merchant groups occupied their own densely inhabited quarters. These came to resemble tiny fortified Italian towns, barricaded against their neighbors, protected by gates and watch towers, and containing warehouses, shops, and residences. Networks of narrow, winding streets (probably derived from a more ancient Arab layout) led to small market squares, the nuclei of each community with its own church, and religious houses and institutions. Activity was most dense around the port, where goods were unloaded. Direct access to it was a source of fierce competition.

Acre may have been a den of vice. It was also extraordinarily filthy. Visitors and pilgrims were struck by the sheer unhealthiness of the place. The Greek pilgrim John Phokas, coming in 1177, complained that "the air is being corrupted by the enormous influx of strangers, various diseases arise and lead to frequent deaths among them, the consequence of which is evil smells and corruption of the air."[2] The Arab traveler Ibn Jubayr, who came from the vastly more civilized world of Moorish Spain and had little good to say about Christians, thought the place a pig sty: "The roads and streets are choked by the press of men. . . . It stinks and is filthy, being full of refuse and excrement."[3] The Hospitallers, within their magnificent compound, possessed an extremely efficient latrine and sewerage system, the effluent of which, along with much of the rest of the city's ordure, including

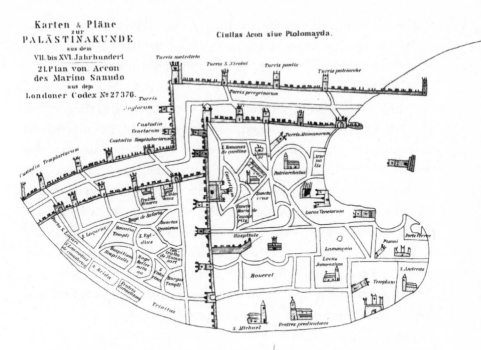

A medieval map of Acre, redrawn with modern lettering, showing the layout of the city, the double row of walls, the suburb of Montmusard on the left, and the harbor. The building in the sea is the so-called Tower of Flies, which guarded access to the inner harbor. The map marks key churches and buildings, the Templars' castle (*Templum*) by the sea, the Hospitallers' compound (*Hospitale*) and the areas occupied by the Venetians, Genoese, and Pisans. It gives a sense of the warren-like nature of the city. Curiously, it still places the Accursed Tower (*Turris Maledicta*) at the right angle of the outer wall, though by this time its actual position was at the same point on the inner wall. (*The Maps of Acre, an Historical Cartography*, Acre, 1973)

refuse from the fish market and slaughter house, was channeled into the enclosed harbor, nicknamed "Lordemer"—the filthy sea. The Venetians were compelled to block off the main window of their church of St. Demetrius, which faced the port, to prevent filth blowing onto the altar.

Out toward the city walls, there were gardens and more open ground, though these spaces shrank during the thirteenth century. In the fertile plains beyond, vineyards, orchards, and cultivated fields provided not only food for the town but also relief from its clenched and often tense environment. As the population grew, a second residential suburb, known as Montmusard, developed to the north of the old town and later became an organic part of the city.

When the crusaders retook Acre in 1191, the city was enclosed by a single wall, with the Accursed Tower collapsed and the sections adjacent to it severely damaged. Richard the Lionheart carried out repairs, but in 1202, substantial stretches were again flattened, this time by an earthquake. There must have then been concerted reconstruction because within a decade the walls had been rebuilt and extended to enclose Montmusard. The wall was now an impressive line of defense—more than a mile in length, locking the whole city in from shore to shore. The Accursed Tower itself was buttressed by substantial outer works. Wilbrand van Oldenburg, who came on a fact-finding mission in 1211 in preparation for the launch of a new crusade, was impressed by the city and its defenses:

> This is a good rich strong city, sited on the seashore, such that, while in its layout it is a quadrangle, two of its sides forming an angle are girded and defended by the sea. The remaining two sides are enclosed by a good ditch, wide, deep and walled from the very bottom, and by a double wall, fortified with towers in a fine arrangement in such a way that the first wall, its towers not exceeding the height of the parent wall itself, is overlooked and guarded by the second, interior wall, whose towers are tall and very strong. . . . This city has a good and stable harbour, guarded by a fine tower, in which the god of the flies, whom we call Baalzebub but they called Akaron, was worshipped among the deviant heathens; from which the city itself is named Accon or Accaron.[4]

From out of Acre's gates, roads led to the remnant crusader kingdom—the coastal route to Upper Galilee and to the Templars' castle at Safad, and to Tyre and the castle of the Teutonic Knights at Montfort.

THE WARREN-LIKE NETWORK of walled compounds reflected the lack of social cohesion and the disunified political rule. Fragmentation of political power paralyzed decision-making. The endless contests for the title of king of Jerusalem, splitting both military orders and Italian merchant communities into rival factions, ensured that for sixty years there would be no resident king present in Acre's royal citadel. In 1250, the populace temporarily declared the city an independent commune from the rest of the kingdom. Its one potential unifier was the patriarch of Jerusalem, whose Church of the Holy Cross was effectively Acre's cathedral and rallying place.

The discord within the kingdom of Jerusalem and the weakness of the remaining crusader enclaves in the first half of the thirteenth century raised the possibility that any further determined strike by Islam could be terminal. It never happened. Saladin, a Kurd and an outsider, briefly created a shared sense of religious purpose within the Islamic world and a consolidated Sunni empire that stretched from Egypt and the shores of North Africa through Palestine and Syria to northern Iraq and the banks of the Tigris. Under Saladin, who issued gold coins with the legend "Sultan of Islam and the Muslims," the spirit of jihad burned brightly: it was Muslim holy men who were offered the chance to behead the captured crusaders at Hattin in 1187—a task they performed with horrifying ineptitude. But this commitment to religious war, by which Saladin had managed to unite his feuding family, fell away at his death. The Islamic Middle East splintered into a quarrelsome group of Ayyubid principalities, with Egypt the only unified state but no will to expel the Franks. Individual rulers each negotiated their own treaties with the intruders from the West, sometimes even forming alliances with them against rival princelings. Appeasement and the fear of fresh crusading ventures replaced aggression. Jerusalem, whose image as a holy city had unified Islam, became strategically unimportant. Remarkably, in 1229 it was simply handed back to the Christians by treaty and without a blow struck—an unthinkable betrayal of Islamic pride. Although regained by Muslims in 1244, Jerusalem remained a potential bargaining chip. The last of the Ayyubid rulers of Egypt, al-Malik al-Salih, would give his son Turanshah worldly advice: "If they [the Franks] demand the coast and Jerusalem from you, give them these places without delay on condition that they have no foothold in Egypt."[5] The Ayyubids had seen off the Fifth Crusade to Egypt in 1221 and were determined to make almost any concession to avoid a reprise.

Among the pious, this craven realpolitik led to fierce condemnation. The historian Ibn al-Athir deplored the fact that "amongst the rulers of Islam we see not one who desires to wage jihad or aid . . . religion. Each one devotes himself to his pastimes and amusements and wronging his flock. This is more dreadful to me than the enemy."[6] The crusader states became just another player in the pattern of alliances and feuds. The kingdom of Jerusalem even sided with Damascus in the Ayyubid civil wars and suffered a crushing defeat for its pains at the battle of La Forbie in 1244, in which the Hospitaller and Templar detachments were almost wiped out.

Trade also fostered détente. The crusader states were economically useful to the Islamic world; Acre and Tyre particularly profited hugely from these interchanges during the first half of the thirteenth century, for which they were as roundly criticized by the papacy as were their Islamic trading partners by pious Muslims. However, at no time did the disunity of Islam enable the Franks to regain the substantial territory lost to Saladin. Periods of truce were interspersed with small-scale crusading ventures from Europe. The Fifth Crusade had ended in failure in the Nile Delta. It was followed by a string of other piecemeal initiatives that failed to shift the balance of power. The Holy Roman emperor Frederick II, under excommunication by the pope, came to the Levant in 1228. Despite negotiating the short-term recovery of Jerusalem, he stirred up deep opposition in the kingdom. When he sailed away from Acre the following year, the townspeople pelted him with offal. Theobald, count of Champagne, led an inconsequential crusade in 1239–1240, Richard of Cornwall another shortly after.

The functional inadequacies of both the Ayyubids and the Crusader States ensured a status quo. Without a more unified Islamic response, the Franks were impossible to dislodge; without unity among Christian factions, the goal of retaking Jerusalem remained a dream. In the West, attention to Outremer was also slowly waning. Europe was witnessing a consolidation of empires and nation-states. The papacy's long-running feud with Frederick II and his successors over the rule of Sicily was diverting energy and funds from the Latin East. It had become possible for the faithful to fulfill their crusading vows elsewhere—in Sicily, or Moorish Spain, or the forests of Prussia, or even by purchasing remission for their sins. The Templar poet Ricaut Bonomel complained:

> *For he [the pope] pardons for money people who have taken our cross*
> *And if anyone wishes to swap the Holy Land*
> *For the war in Italy*
> *Our legate lets them do so*
> *For he sells God and Indulgences for cash.*[7]

WITHIN THE HEART of Asia, however, the tectonic plates of power were starting to shift. At the beginning of the thirteenth century, the Mongols embarked on their sweep west, and before their advance, other nomadic people were being displaced. Soon the repercussions were felt in the Islamic world. The Mongols destroyed the existing Persian dynasty and pushed its Turkic tribal rulers, the Khwarazmians, into Palestine. (It was this warlike people, of similar central Asian origin, who sacked Jerusalem in 1244.)

Among those buffeted by the Mongol advance were another tribal people from the central Asian steppes, the Turkish Kipchaks. Like the Mongols, the Kipchaks were restless nomadic tent dwellers who lived by grazing flocks and raiding their neighbors, animists who worshipped the earth and the sky through the intermediation of shamans. Similarly, they were also horse people, highly skillful fighters, expert in the use of the powerful composite bow and the mobile tactics of cavalry warfare. Pushed ever westward into an area north of the Black Sea, young Kipchaks were captured in raids by rival tribes and shipped to the slave markets of Anatolia and Syria, converted to Sunni Islam, and sold to appreciative buyers.

The fighting qualities of the nomadic peoples had been quickly recognized. The caliph of Baghdad was recruiting tribal fighters into his army as military slaves as early as the ninth century. They were praised for their unique skills in mounted warfare: "raiding, hunting, horsemanship, skirmishing with rival chieftains, taking booty and invading other countries. Their efforts are all directed towards these activities, and they devote all their energies to these occupations." Kipchak boys probably started to learn archery skills from the age of four. "Thus," it was said, "they have become in warfare what the Greeks are in philosophy."[8]

These first-generation Sunni Muslims still retained many of their tribal practices, but they brought to their new religion the zeal of converts. Looking back from the fourteenth century, the Arab historian Ibn Khaldun saw the appearance of the Turkic peoples as providential in reviving a decadent Islam: "Sedentary people," he wrote, "have become used to laziness and ease. They find full assurance of safety in the walls that surround them, and the fortifications that protect them. [Nomadic people] have no gates and walls. They take hurried naps only . . . when they are in the saddle. They pay attention to every faint barking and noise. Fortitude has become a character quality of theirs and courage their nature."[9] Ibn Khaldun saw them as a providential blessing sent from God "to revive the dying breath of Islam and restore the unity of Muslims."[10] Saladin, a Kurd, had led armies that were Turkish in ethos. Within the insecure dynasties of the Middle East, there was a long tradition of recruiting such slaves, known in Arabic as *mamluks*, "the owned ones." With no hereditary ties to competing factions, they owed all their loyalty to their master. One statesman put it thus:

One obedient slave is better
than three hundred sons;
for the latter desire their father's death,
the former long life for his master.[11]

The concept of military slavery in the Islamic world was radically different to the understanding of slavery in Europe. The Mamluks were more like elite mercenaries than bonded serfs. They could rise through the ranks to positions of power as emirs, they were paid, and their occupation could not be handed down—their children could not inherit a place in the sultan's corps. There was always a demand for fresh conscripts from the grasslands beyond the Black Sea.

When the Ayyubid prince al-Malik al-Salih came to power in Egypt in 1240, he began buying Kipchak military slaves and importing them into Egypt. These soldiers became his loyal imperial bodyguard and crack regiment. Al-Salih acquired a corps of about a thousand Mamluks during his reign. Many were garrisoned on an island in the Nile, from which they gained their name the Bahriyyah—"the regiment of the river." Another smaller corps, the Jamdariyyah, served as al-Salih's personal bodyguards. Isolated in barracks and subject to intense training in skills of horsemanship, hand-to-hand combat, and archery, the Mamluks developed a strong group spirit that served them well in battle—but potentially rendered them a threat to masters increasingly reliant on them.

IN THE WAKE of the 1244 loss of Jerusalem, there was a fresh call in Europe for crusade. The response came from the king of France, Louis IX. Louis set about organizing the best-planned and most deeply funded military expedition ever mounted for the recapture of Jerusalem. This grand mission was destined to have unintended consequences. It would see the collapse of the Ayyubid dynasty; the Bahriyyah Mamluks would move from slaves to sultans. And it would set in motion a chain of events that would lead back to the gates of Acre in 1291.

2

DEATH ON THE NILE

1249–1250

A T DAWN ON Saturday, June 5, 1249, a crusader fleet prepared to land on the coast of Egypt, near the eastern tributary of the Nile and the town of Damietta. The army of the Fifth Crusade had alighted at the same spot thirty years earlier, and this new expedition was not unexpected. "We found there all the sultan's forces lined up on the seashore," wrote the French knight Jean de Joinville, surveying the scene before him. "These were very fine men to behold, for the sultan's coat of arms were golden and they glittered where the sunlight fell on them. The noise of their kettledrums and Saracen horns was terrifying to hear."[1] With the sun rising, thousands of men waded ashore from small boats.

A beach landing against organized opposition was dangerous in the extreme, but the level of discipline was exceptionally high, and the knights and foot soldiers were covered by fierce crossbow fire. Joinville landed to confront a band of Muslim horsemen. "As soon as they saw us land, they advanced towards us spurring their horses. When we saw them coming, we planted our lances in the sand with the points towards them. Once they saw the lances ready to impale their stomachs, they turned and fled."[2] To his left, the knight could see a magnificent galley rowed by three hundred men, studded with shields bearing brightly painted coats of arms and pennons fluttering in the breeze. "As it neared the shore, the rowers propelled it forward with all the force of their oars, so that it seemed as if the galley was flying. Such was the cracking of the pennons in the wind, the thunder of kettledrums and Saracen horns that were in the count's galley that it sounded like thunderbolts crashing from the heavens. As soon as the galley grounded on the sand, riding up on the shore as high as it could, the count and his knights leaped from the galley, very well armed and wonderfully equipped, and came and formed themselves up alongside us."[3]

Up and down the beach, the standards of the great noble families of France were being planted as a rallying point for the troops in the face of mounted attacks. Prominent among these was the oriflamme, the red and orange banner of the French kings, the color of the blood of the martyr St. Denis. When the leader, organizer, and financer of this expedition, King Louis IX, watching from his magnificent ship, the *Montjoie*, saw his standard planted on the beach, he could restrain himself no longer. He leaped into the sea—the water up to his armpits, his shield slung over his shoulder, his helmet on his head—and stepped ashore. With his blood up, he leveled his lance, armed his shield, and was preparing to charge into the enemy ranks. He had to be held back.

KING LOUIS'S PREPARATIONS had been detailed and thorough. The crusade was French in inspiration and composition, and consisted of some 25,000 men——mounted knights and sergeants, foot soldiers and crossbowmen. It included three of the king's brothers and the flower of French chivalry, and had been four years in the making. This was a completely professional force: Louis had left behind the volunteers who turned up at the departure port of Aigues-Mortes on their own initiative. He was driven by a rigorous sense of duty toward his men and devout Christian ideals, inspired by a vow he had taken when he had been near death in 1244. The campaign's initial objective, however, was not Jerusalem, but Cairo.

SHREWD MILITARY THINKERS, such as Richard I, had understood that Saladin's victories in Palestine and Syria depended on the wealth of Egypt. "The keys of Jerusalem," as he put it, "are to be found in

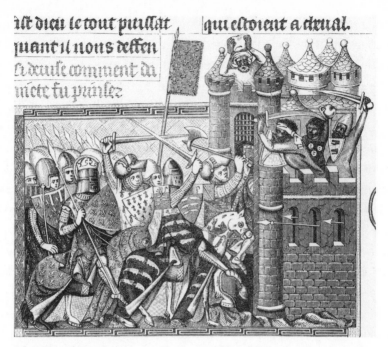

The crusaders advance on Damietta. The defense as shown in this medieval manuscript never happened. The town was abandoned. (*Jean, Sire de Joinville*, Paris, 1874)

Cairo."[4] This thinking had held currency for half a century. The disastrous Fourth Crusade, which had ended in the sacking of Constantinople in 1204, had been covertly intended to make a strike on the Nile Delta. A decade later, when Jacques de Vitry arrived in Acre to prepare for a new crusade, the objective was quite explicit: "We planned to proceed to Egypt, which is a fertile land and the richest in the east, from which the Saracens draw the power and wealth to enable them to hold our land, and after we have captured that land, we can easily recover the whole kingdom of Jerusalem."[5] This Fifth Crusade had also ended in abject failure. It took eighteen months to capture the coastal city of Damietta, a hundred miles north of Cairo. The crusaders had spent another indecisive eighteen months there, had twice refused to accept a peace treaty with the Ayyubid sultan (who even offered to return Jerusalem), and had then been ambushed among the complex seasonal flows of the Nile and the labyrinth of its channels. Blockaded, trapped, and forced to wade waist deep in muddy water, the army had surrendered ignominiously.

Louis's crusade came with the same strategic objective, greater clarity of purpose, and whatever knowledge it had garnered from its predecessor about the unique hydrology of the Nile. It all started so promisingly. According to Joinville, the defenders of Damietta sent urgent carrier pigeons to Cairo, but they received no reply. The sultan al-Salih was dying. "They thought the sultan was dead and they abandoned Damietta," was the confident explanation in the Christian camp.[6] Where it had taken their predecessors nine months and a long and horrific siege, Louis's troops entered the town in a single day to find its commander, the emir Fakhr al-Din, and the garrison gone. The panic-stricken population had followed. It seemed providential—a sign from God that Louis's crusade would succeed—and it imbued the king with a disastrous sense of confidence. The planners were aware of the vulnerability of the Ayyubid regime, torn apart by factional feuding and in slow decline. This had provided some of the rationale to go for Egypt. Damietta had been provisioned and garrisoned to withstand a long siege, so its capitulation seemed to confirm that they were pushing at an open door. It was in the Islamic annals both "a terrible disaster, the like of which had never happened before" and a disgrace on the part of the emir and his regiment.[7] But what the crusaders did not know was that Fakhr al-Din had only abandoned the town without a fight in order to mount his own bid for power upon the sultan's death.

What followed was a slow motion and much ghastlier reprise of the Fifth Crusade, whose events were recounted in vivid detail by Jean de Joinville. Louis demanded unbending discipline from the troops, but in the early skirmishes, the desire to fight led to individual knights charging at the enemy and losing their lives. He himself had set an intemperate example at the beach landing, and the chivalric code of personal valor in single combat was a recurrent problem: the nobility proved difficult to restrain from reckless acts of bravery.

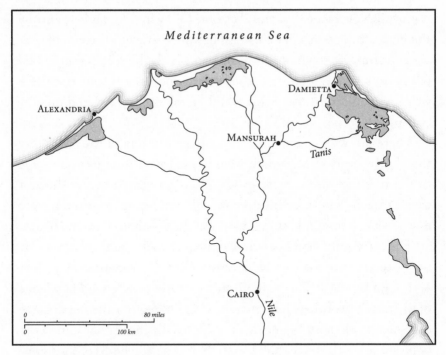

Egypt and the Nile Delta.

A grimmer reality quickly set in. Despite the collapse of Damietta, the crusader camp was stalked nightly by Bedouin horse thieves and murderers. "They came and killed the sentry of the lord of Courtenay, and left his body lying on a table, having cut off his head, and they made off with it. They did this because the sultan gave a golden bezant for each Christian head."[8] For the same reason, the Bedouins were said to have also cut off the heads of hanged men and dig up buried bodies. The crusaders were quickly compelled to entrench their camp outside Damietta and guard it round the clock. They debated their next move: consolidate by taking the strategic port of Alexandria 120 miles to the west or march on Cairo. Louis's brother, the count of Artois, was adamantly for Cairo, reasoning that "he who wishes to kill the serpent must first crush the head," but the army was forced to wait for the Nile's seasonal floodwaters to recede.[9] It was not until November that they set out, following the path traced by the Fifth Crusade in a march south up the river, with the aim of seizing the strategic town of Mansurah, to which the sultan's army had fallen back. Buoyed up by the disarming success at Damietta, there was a feeling that if this town could be taken, Egypt would quickly collapse.

There was widespread alarm among the Muslims at the possibility that "if the army at Mansurah were to be driven back just one stage to the rear the whole of Egypt would be conquered in the shortest time."[10] Cairo was thrown into panic. The troops at Mansurah were dug in for a determined stand, with the dying sultan in attendance.

The forty-mile march south was a combined operation, the army progressing along the east bank of the Nile, accompanied by galleys with food supplies. The expedition had reasonably good knowledge of the river's hydrology but crucially failed to register the importance of a stagnant-looking waterway, the Mahallah canal, that joined the opposite side of the river halfway to their goal. It seemed too insignificant to consider blocking. This canal had played a key role in the defeat of the Nile crusade thirty years earlier, and it was about to again. As Louis's men approached Mansurah, they found their way barred by another side river, which the Christians called the Tanis; their adversaries were encamped on the opposite bank, and the crusaders were halted in the fork between the Nile and the Tanis.

While Louis was on the march, the sultan died, on November 22. Al-Salih had harbored suspicions about Fakhr al-Din's retreat from Damietta, and he had hanged the whole deserting garrison. Now these fears seemed confirmed. In conjunction with one of his widows, the sultan's death was concealed from the people, and a power struggle for the succession was underway. Fakhr al-Din forged al-Salih's signature on documents and called on people to come to the cause. Amid the rumors and counter-rumors, he dispatched Aqtay, the leader of the Mamluk Bahriyyah regiment, on a mission to distant Hisn Kayfa, a town on the Tigris in southeastern Turkey, to invite the late sultan's son, al-Muazzam Turanshah, to take up the throne, perhaps with the hope that he would never arrive.

Despite the secrecy, the news of al-Salih's death leaked out, but people were too frightened to voice what they suspected. It was believed among the emirs that "Fakhr al-Din was aiming at sole and arbitrary rule, should al-Malik al-Muazzam [Turanshah] find it impossible to come."[11] In any case, Turanshah, the sultan's youngest and only surviving son, did not inspire confidence. He was, by inclination, a scholar rather than a military leader, and al-Salih was reported to have harbored deep fears over his succession: "When death comes upon me, do not summon Turanshah from Hisn Kayfa and do not entrust the country to him, for I know that nothing good will come from him."[12]

MEANWHILE, THE TANIS was posing a serious obstacle for the crusade. Crossing it was critical but the river was fast flowing and apparently too deep to ford, and the Ayyubid army was determined to resist any attempts. Louis and his commanders decided to construct a causeway across it, and to protect the men tasked with building it, two "cats"—moveable wooden towers—were constructed, and catapults positioned to bombard the Egyptian camp. From the Muslim side, a similar torrent of catapult shots and Greek fire was directed at these towers. To overcome the protective screen provided by the cats, the Muslims also took to firing their arrows "straight up into the clouds so that their arrows fell right down among our men."[13] Guarding these wooden structures became fraught with danger, from both the fear of being burned alive and the shower of arrows that their enemies were launching over the water. Confronted by a "great hedge of flaming fire coming towards our cat castle,"[14] Joinville and his men were forced out into the open in an attempt to extinguish it, "so the Saracens hit all of us with the arrows they were firing across the river."[15] He was openly relieved when the tower he was assigned to guard was set on fire before his next turn of duty: "God granted a great favour to me and my knights, as we would have undertaken guard duty that evening in great peril."[16]

Over and beyond the attacks, constructing the causeway was proving tricky. The speed of the river kept washing it away, and their opponents dug back the bank on the far side, so as to continuously widen the channel. No matter how fast the crusaders dumped earth and stones, it made no difference. Louis was compelled to realize the futility of the strategy. Morale sank. If they were unable to cross the Tanis, the crusade was over. At this point, a Bedouin arrived in the camp with the offer to show the crusaders a ford where they could cross in return for suitable reward. A new plan was hatched: to ford the river, draw up in good order on the other side, and then attack the enemy camp. The bridgehead would be established solely by horsemen, as it was harder to get infantry across in the first phase.

On Shrove Tuesday, February 8, 1250, "with daybreak we prepared ourselves in every way," Joinville recounted. The ford was deeper than the Bedouin had promised. "When we were ready we went down into the river and our horses had to swim. . . . Once we reached the middle, we found the bottom where the horses could set their hooves." Some of them lost their footing and drowned their riders. They were watched by three hundred mounted Saracens, "and as soon as we made it over the Turks fled."[17] The aim was for the Templars in the vanguard to hold the ring on the south bank while the king and the main force crossed over and regrouped.

At this juncture, discipline broke down; the king's brother Robert d'Artois decided to lead a reckless charge against the Muslim camp. The Templar commander, Brother Giles, was unable to restrain him. Robert and his men bore down on an unsuspecting foe. "They attacked the Saracen forces encamped there, who were expecting no such attack. Some were still fast asleep, others lying in bed. The Saracens on sentry duty were defeated first and almost all put to the sword. Our men charged in through the Turks' quarters killing all and sparing none; men, women and children, old and young, great and small, rich and poor, they slew and slashed and killed them all. . . . It was sad indeed to see so many dead bodies and so much blood spilt, except that they were enemies of the Christian faith."[18] Among those cut down in the slaughter was the emir Fakhr al-Din himself, taken by surprise at his morning ablutions. Carrier pigeons hurried news of a great battle at Mansurah back to Cairo. "This information alarmed us, as it alarmed all Muslims," wrote one chronicler, aware of its critical importance. "Everyone imagined the ruin of Islam."[19]

If the advance guard had stopped with the destruction of the camp, all would have been well. Brother Giles tried again to restrain Robert from further pursuit, but in vain. Tempted by the lure of total victory, and perhaps remembering the ease with which Damietta had fallen, Robert accused the Templars of cowardice. "My Lord," Brother Giles answered, "neither I nor my brothers are afraid. We shall not stay behind, we will ride with you. But let me tell you that none of us expect to come back, neither you nor ourselves." Even explicit orders from the king failed to restrain his brother from charging into the town. Waiting for them in Mansurah were the formidable Mamluks of the Bahriyyah regiment.

Robert's rash attack was the disaster the Templars had foreseen. Within the narrow streets of the town, the intruders quickly became separated. Bitter at the massacre in their camp, the Mamluks "slashed and cut and took and bound them and dragged them into captivity. Some fled towards the river to escape death, but the Saracens were on their heels, bringing them down with Danish axes, with maces and swords, and if they reached the river, great, fast and deep, and flung themselves into it, they drowned."[20] From the Muslim perspective, a single charge against the Franks "shook their foundations, shattered their entire edifice and turned their crosses upside down. The swords and maces of the Turks set about them, inflicted on them death and wounds, and strewed them in the narrow streets of Mansurah."[21] There was great rejoicing at God's benevolence when the news reached Cairo.

There was a significance in this episode well beyond the scale of the disaster. It was the first time that Christian crusaders had experienced the tougher fighting qualities of the Turkish Mamluks. Looking back, the Arab chroniclers acknowledged a landmark moment in "the first battle in which the Turkish lions were victorious over the polytheistic dogs."[22] This encounter was destined to unleash unintended consequences for the whole future of the crusades. The victory at Mansurah had secured the survival of Ayyubid Egypt, but more broadly, it started to clarify where true power lay. Among those who chopped down the trapped crusaders was a young Mamluk called Rukn al-Din Baybars.

FOR LOUIS, THE immediate consequences were serious. Six hundred had ridden in; just a few made it back alive. Both Robert and Giles went down in the slaughter. The crusaders had lost valuable fighting men and put heart into the enemy. The king's troops had barely established themselves on the south bank before they, too, came under massive pressure from counterattacks, with armed horsemen bearing down and volleys of arrows and crossbow bolts whistling through the air. As the chroniclers recounted,

> A tremendous noise of horns, bugles and drums broke out, men shouted, horses neighed . . . they completely surrounded our forces and shot dense clouds of bolts and arrows at them; no rain or hail could have caused such darkness. . . . The king and our men had no crossbowmen with them; all who had crossed the river with the king had been killed in the vanguard, for the Saracens killed without mercy every crossbowman they took. When the king and our men saw that they and their horses were being destroyed, the spurred forward in one massed charge to escape the Turks' arrows.[23]

Joinville, finding himself in the thick of the fight, gave perhaps the most visceral eyewitness account of pitched battle of any of the crusades—though not, perhaps, without a tendency to talk up his own bravery and the deeds of the king. A mounted Muslim, he recalled, "struck me with his lance between my two shoulders, pinning me to my horse's neck and held me there so pinioned that I could not draw the sword at my belt."[24] Somehow surviving this blow, he went to rescue another knight thrown to the ground. Returning, he was attacked again by mounted warriors with lances. "My horse collapsed to its knees under the weight it was bearing. I was thrown forward over its ears. I got up as fast as I could, with my shield at my neck and my sword in my hand." As he scrambled to his feet, a second wave of horsemen "hurled me to the ground, galloped over me and sent the shield flying from my neck." Stunned and disoriented, he was led by some other knights to make a stand at a ruined house. "There the Turks attacked us from all sides; one group of them got into the ruined house and stabbed at us with their lances from above."[25] He watched as one man was wounded by three lance blows in the face, another by a lance thrust between the shoulders with a wound so large "that blood streamed from his body as if from the bunghole of a barrel."[26] Meanwhile, "my Lord Érard de Siverey was struck in the face by a sword blow, so that his nose dangled over his lip." While the apparently indestructible Joinville addressed an urgent prayer to St. James, Siverey, still able to speak (though he died later), suggested coolly that they might seek help from others nearby but only, "Sire, if you thought that neither I nor my heirs would be reproached for this."[27] The knights' honor code and fear of accusations of cowardice persisted even to the edge of death.

All day Louis struggled to maintain his foothold on the southern bank of the Tanis and to prevent his men from fleeing. It was with a measure of disbelief that the Muslims had witnessed the stupidity of Artois in being drawn into the trap at Mansurah. Now they launched wave after wave of attacks in tight formation with shouts and yells and "a great noise of trumpets, kettledrums and Saracen horns."[28] Trapped by the Tanis, Joinville watched the situation deteriorate: "We saw, as we were coming downstream, the river covered with lances and shields and with the bodies of horses and men who were drowning and dying."[29] Six horsemen had Louis's horse by the bridle but the king "singlehandedly freed himself by the great blows that he landed on them with his sword."[30] Torrents of arrows whipped through the air, and Greek fire shot from crossbows. One man "caught a pot of Greek fire on his round shield, for if any of the fire had landed on him he would have been burned to death." Joinville, now without his own shield, picked up a Muslim's padded tunic as a makeshift replacement, "which helped me greatly, since I was only wounded by their arrows in five places and my horse in fifteen."[31] Somehow, Louis managed to hold the line, encouraging the men and fighting with great bravery. By late afternoon, a fresh contingent of crossbowmen was ranged in the front line, and the Muslims withdrew. At the day's end, the Bedouins, scavengers of battlefields and cutters of throats, emerged to loot the abandoned Muslim camp, stripping it bare.

It had been, in its way, a triumph of courage and endurance, but it was only the briefest respite. The Muslims were certain they could wipe out the camp on the south bank of the Tanis. Before dawn the next day, Joinville was again roused by the call to arms. Too wounded to put on mail, he threw the padded tunic over his back and prepared to fight on. In the days that followed, Louis's men withstood repeated attacks. They managed to salvage wood from the enemy siege engines and create a stockade and trench around their encampment; a bridge of boats was built across the Tanis to link the two camps, but the death toll continued to rise.

DESPITE THE SPIRITED resistance, the situation was desperate. Louis clung on stubbornly, still blinded by the belief that the Ayyubid kingdom was on the point of collapse, that God would grant victory. Yet the evidence was otherwise. He dared not retreat over the Tanis without admitting that the crusade was lost, but the situation in the camp started to deteriorate. Nine days after the first battle, the corpses of the slain bobbed gaseously to the surface of the river and clogged the bridge joining Louis's two camps. "There was such a mass of bodies that the whole river was jammed with corpses from one bank to the other, and for as far as a small stone might be thrown."[32] Laborers were employed to dump the bodies of the circumcised Muslims on the other side of the bridge to float off downstream, while the Christians were buried in a long trench. It being Lent, the survivors ate only fish from the river, which were burbot, "and the burbot were eating the dead men, because these fish are gluttonous," Joinville recalled with his gorge rising.[33] He attributed to this the spread of "camp fever" (in all likelihood scurvy), which started to riddle the army. "There was so much dead flesh on the gums of our people that the barbers had to cut away the dead flesh to allow them to chew and swallow their food." The camp was filled with the sound of screaming as the dead flesh was cut away "because they howled like women in labour."[34] Joinville's priest collapsed in the middle of saying Mass. Joinville caught him in his arms and revived him. The priest somehow finished the service, "and he never sang again."[35] Survival now depended on supplies making it down the river from Damietta, but their plight was about to take a dramatic turn for the worse.

On February 25, the sultan's surviving son, Turanshah, arrived from Hisn Kayfa to take charge. From the start, he misread the situation. A change of sultan often meant a change of administration, but a wise ruler carried out this transition gradually. Turanshah did not. He alienated the leading emirs and army commanders. Possibly, he was unable to financially reward those who had fought at Mansurah; he appears to have failed to accord Aqtay, leader of the Mamluk regiment, the tax revenues of Alexandria that he had been promised, and he replaced the leading emirs with his own people. The new emirs were unknown to those on the ground, and they lacked support. Lurid tales were spread of Turanshah's depravity and that "when he was drunk, he gathered candles and would slash off the heads [of the candles] with his swords and would lop them off, saying, 'Thus shall I do to the Bahriyyah' and he would mention his father's Mamluks by name. The base-born were exalted and those of quality removed. He treated his father's chief Mamluks with contempt."[36] He failed to understand that the Ayyubid dynasty was now riding the tiger of its own Turkish slaves.

Despite these undercurrents, the Islamic campaign took on a new impetus, and the significance of the Mahallah canal, which the crusaders had missed on their descent of the Nile, became clear. The crusaders had ships at their camps at Mansurah and at Damietta near the coast, but Turanshah now cut the connection between the two. He had fifty galleys carried across land with the aid of camels and launched into the upper reaches of the Mahallah canal, stagnant but with enough water in its upper reaches to sail back into the Nile above the crusader camp. When the Christian supply ships came down from Damietta, they were ambushed, their supplies captured, and their crews killed or marched off into captivity. The Muslims had sprung a similar trap against the Fifth Crusade, thirty years earlier, but the ability to blockade the Nile came to Louis and his men as a complete surprise. They knew nothing about this until a small crusader ship managed to shoot past the blockade and into their encampment. "The Turks set about starving us out, to the amazement of many people," recorded Joinville.[37] They saw food prices rise to extraordinary heights. Despair gripped the camp. The sick multiplied. Everyone expected to die.

From that moment, Louis's crusade was doomed but still he hesitated, unable to relinquish the crusading dream until it was too late. Attempts to broker a reasonable truce failed. It was not until April 5, 1250, that the king finally admitted defeat and gave the order to withdraw to Damietta. Louis was insistent that the sick and wounded should be put in the boats, and that he himself would stay to the end and travel by land the forty miles back to Damietta. By this time, he was stricken with dysentery but refused to take a ship. The plan to withdraw stealthily from the south bank was botched. The man ordered to cut the ropes on the bridge panicked and failed to do so; enemy troops made it across. An orderly retreat descended into nightmare. The wounded Joinville, "struck by camp fever in my mouth and legs" and too weak to walk, was among those on a ship.[38] As night fell, he could see, by the light of fires, Muslims killing the sick who had staggered or crawled to the water's edge, hoping to be taken off. A rout took place with the Muslims pursuing and killing those traveling by land. Joinville's ship was slowed by a headwind, got lost in a backwater, and was bombarded with crossbow bolts and volleys of Greek fire from the bank. The convoy of ships was then intercepted by the sultan's vessels. Ahead, Joinville could see those on other ships being killed and their bodies thrown into the water. As they waited on their fate, anchored in the middle of the channel, Joinville threw his jewels and relics into the river. As a galley approached, a sailor begged Joinville that "unless you let me say that you are the king's cousin, they will kill you all, and us sailors too."[39] He agreed. Joinville was wrestled to the ground with a knife at his throat, waiting for the end, when a man called out, "He's the king's cousin!"[40] He instantly became a valuable commodity. Others were not. Joinville watched his priest being murdered and thrown in the river, and his clerk, who had fainted, was struck on the head with a stone bowl. "I was told that these men who were there had no value, because their illnesses had left them helpless."[41]

Louis's capture was humiliating. His dysentery was so bad that his attendants had to cut the seat out of his breeches. He was taken half-dead in a village house. It was all over. The defeat was total: "Here the *oriflamme* was torn to pieces, the *bauséant* [the black and white standard of the Templars] trampled underfoot, a sight nobody re-members having ever beheld. Over there the standards of magnates, since ancient times an object of dread to the infidel, were bespattered with the blood of men and horses . . . and were most vilely destroyed and treated with contempt."[42]

For the Muslims, there was straightforward rejoicing: "God cleansed Egypt of them."[43] One chronicler recorded that "a tally was made of the number of captives, and there were more than 20,000; those who had drowned or been killed numbered 7,000. I saw the dead, and they covered the face of the earth in their profusion. . . . It was a day of the kind the Muslims had never seen; nor had they heard of its like."[44] Damietta was surrendered. Herded into camps, the worthless were decapitated at the rate of three hundred a day. The rest were for ransom. Despite mock executions kneeling before the axe, Joinville survived. Louis retained his dignity to the last. He agreed to pay a massive sum—800,000 gold bezants—for the ransom of 12,000 men. He made a down payment of half and sailed off to Acre, with Joinville on board, to raise the remainder and thus liber-ate the army still being held.

He left for Acre on May 7, 1250, but five days earlier he was witness to a seismic shift in dynastic power within the Islamic world, one that his crusade had unwittingly provoked. Turanshah had alienated the Mamluk corps, either by lack of preferment or by his refusal to share out the spoils of war. On May 2, Aqtay, the Mamluk commander, cornered and wounded the sultan. Turanshah, stricken but not dead, promised to return to him the profits of Alexandria, but it was too late. The sultan had failed to take notice of the power shift underway. He was said to have been finished off by Rukn al-Din Baybars. Aqtay cut out Turanshah's heart and carried it with bloody hands to the exhausted Louis. He held out the gruesome trophy and said, "What will you give *me*, who has killed your enemy, who would have put you to death, had he lived."[45] Appalled, the king said nothing.

WITHIN EUROPE, NEWS of this shattering defeat hit hard. The pope wrote "words of grief, written in sorrow" to Queen Blanche, Louis's mother.[46] There was deep soul searching. How had this happened? Louis's enterprise, so pious and so well-prepared, had been annihilated. "We must take thought," pondered a sermon on the losses at Mansurah, "as to the reasons why the Lord allowed such a tragic event to befall the Christian people. . . . How, then, did He tolerate it that bought slaves . . . slaves of the Devil, full of foulness, killed such noble men, such mighty friends of God and champions of the entire Christian people?"[47] The role and social status of the slave Mamluks had been particularly troubling. The answer given was, first and foremost, sin, then a lesson to chastise, then other demonstrations of God's mysterious justice and love.

Whether Baybars actually struck the blow that killed Turanshah or this detail was a piece of retrospective hagiography is unknown. Regardless, the death of Turanshah at the hands of the Mamluks was instrumental in reshaping the Middle East. It signaled the death throes of the divided and weakened Ayyubid regime; in its place would come the Mamluks, who would bring ruthless military skill to the war with Christendom. The keys of the kingdom of Jerusalem remained in Egypt, and in due course they would be in the hands of the ambitious Baybars.

3

BETWEEN THE MAMLUKS
AND THE MONGOLS

1250–1260

WITH TURANSHAH'S BLOODY heart at Louis's feet and his body dumped in the Nile, life was draining out of the Ayyubid dynasty. It was the Mamluk regiment created by al-Salih that had massacred the Christians at Mansurah and saved Egypt. This professional military corps had become the power behind the throne, and during the 1250s, they took it. It was a convoluted process that lasted ten years and involved puppet rulers and a contest between different Mamluk factions. They were the source of discord in Cairo. Its citizens came to fear the Turkish presence in their midst. Aqtay, leader of the Bahriyyah regiment, was murdered by a rival, Qutuz, and in 1254, the Bahriyyah, with Baybars increasingly influential, were forced out of Egypt. For the rest of the decade, Baybars honed his leadership and fighting skills on behalf of different Ayyubid princelings in Syria. In Egypt, Qutuz manipulated claimants to the throne and then declared himself sultan in 1259.

LOUIS, TO HIS great credit, did not shirk the consequences of his failed crusade. Instead of returning to France, he stayed in the Holy Land for four years, ransoming prisoners from the Egyptian debacle and fortifying the remainder crusader footholds at Acre, Caesarea, Jaffa, and Sidon at considerable personal expense. He established a permanent

French regiment in Acre, a small but valuable professional force, and also set about seeking out potential allies against Islam.

For a long time, distorted echoes of the advance of the Mongols had been reaching the Christian West—and with it the hope that their kings might become, or even be, Christians. The evidence was otherwise. By the 1240s, eastern Europe was being shattered by Mongol raids. In 1249, while in Cyprus preparing to launch his crusade, Louis had received envoys from the Mongols in Persia. In reply, he dispatched two Dominican friars (one of whom, André de Longjumeau, spoke relevant languages) to encourage their adherence to the Christian faith and "to show and teach the Tartars [Mongols] what they should believe."[1] The missionaries displayed some imaginative insight into the nomadic condition of their potential converts by taking with them a portable tent chapel, embroidered with scenes from the life of Christ, along with chalices, books, and everything needed for the friars to perform mass. The trip took two years and a journey into the heart of central Asia to the Mongol court. Longjumeau returned to find Louis at Caesarea, overseeing refortification of the city after his failure on the Nile. Longjumeau's somewhat garbled report contained a brisk corrective to any blithe optimism. The friars had witnessed devastation: ruined cities, great heaps of human bones. They had been sent back with the warning that the Mongol khans put all opponents to the sword: "We point this out to warn you that you cannot have peace unless you have peace with us. So we advise you to send us enough gold and silver each year for us to keep thinking of you as friends. If you do not do this we will destroy you and your people as we did those others we mentioned before."[2] Submit or die: it was a choice that would soon confront the whole of the Middle East. Louis did not reply.

In 1253, Hülegü Khan, brother of the ruler Möngke Khan and a grandson of Genghis, was ordered to advance west with his army, "as far as the borders of Egypt."[3] The aim was to crush Islam as a step to Mongol world domination. By 1256, Hülegü was in Persia.

Two years later, the Mongols delivered a shattering blow to the Islamic world, one that echoed down the centuries. In January 1258,

Hülegü laid siege to Baghdad, seat of the Abbasid Caliphate for half a millennium, repository of scholarship and culture, intellectual center of the Islamic world. With the aid of Chinese siege engineers, Baghdad's walls were breached in early February. Surrender made no difference. The city was put to utter destruction; mosques, palaces, libraries, and hospitals destroyed. Estimates of the dead have ranged wildly between 90,000 and 800,000. The Tigris ran black with the ink of thousands of books hurled into the water, their leather covers torn off to make sandals. The last Abbasid caliph was rolled in a blanket and trampled to death by Mongol horsemen. The sack of Baghdad shook Islam to its roots.

In September 1259, Hülegü crossed the Euphrates on pontoon bridges with an enormous army, perhaps 120,000 men, his sights set on Syria. The Christian kingdoms of Outremer were in a quandary. Hethoum I, the Christian king of the principality of Cilician Armenia in southwestern Turkey, accepted the overlordship of the Mongols; it was known that Hülegü's general Kitbuqa had been converted by Nestorians to Christianity, and Hethoum naively believed that the Mongols wanted to recapture Jerusalem for the Christians. He attempted to persuade other Christian enclaves to join the Mongols; only his son-in-law, Bohemond VI, ruler of the small principality of Antioch and count of Tripoli, responded. When Aleppo fell, the Muslims were put to the sword; Armenian Christians burned the great mosque to the ground. Damascus saw what was coming and just opened its gates to the Mongols in March 1260. The city's Eastern Christians rejoiced intemperately at the discomfiture of their Muslim neighbors: they rang their bells and drank wine during Ramadan— humiliations that would not be forgotten. Soon, almost all of Syria was in Mongol hands. Most of the Ayyubid princes capitulated, and the Mongols were raiding south to the borders of Egypt. The Islamic world was facing collapse.

ACRE WAS ALSO in turmoil. During the late 1250s, it became the epicenter of the growing commercial rivalry between Genoa and Venice that culminated in a full-blown contest in the city, known as the War of St. Sabas. Ostensibly over ownership of the monastery of that saint, which lay on the boundary between the two Italian communes, the war was a reflection of a wider struggle for trading supremacy across the Mediterranean and the Black Sea. The competition sucked in almost all the city's factions and those of surrounding crusader states. The Pisans sided with the Genoese before switching allegiance to Venice; the Hospitallers were for the Genoese, the Templars and the Teutonic Knights for Venice; the powerful barons of Outremer similarly took sides. The year-long contest included sea battles, blockades, and siege warfare on an intimate scale. Within Acre, the two sides bombarded each other at close range with catapults, hurling rocks over the walls of fortified enclosures into their neighbors' quarter. The chronicles record that during 1258, "all that year there were at least sixty engines, every one of them throwing down onto the city of Acre, onto houses, towers and turrets, and they smashed and laid level with the ground every building they touched. . . . This meant that nearly all the towers and strong houses in Acre were destroyed, except for religious houses. Twenty thousand men died in this war on one side or the other . . . the city of Acre was utterly devastated by this war as if it had been destroyed in warfare between Christians and Saracens."[4] Allowing for the probably exaggerated death toll, the contest wrecked large parts of the city. Houses, warehouses, ships, and defensive towers were destroyed before the Genoese were finally expelled and their quarter flattened. They moved up the coast to Tyre. Acre required major reconstruction; its trade had been damaged, its factional divisions exacerbated, and its manpower diminished.

At the same time, the kingdom of Jerusalem was also starting to feel pressure from the Mongol advance. Hülegü's true intentions were expressed in an order to a commander in 1257 to "advance as far as the coasts of the sea, and wrest those countries from the hands of the children of France and England."[5] Acre had resisted Hethoum's urging to join the Mongol cause. That year, it received a blunt demand to submit. The determination, as expressed by the military orders, was resolute: "Let therefore these Tartars [Mongols]—these demons of Tartarus—come on, and they will find the servants of

Christ encamped and ready to do battle."[6] In February 1260, Hülegü's general Kitbuqa peremptorily ordered them to dismantle their walls. The leading council in Acre ignored him and strengthened their for-tifications, going so far as robbing outlying cemeteries of tombstones in a search for suitable building material. There was no reason to feel positive about voluntary submission or alliance. Both Armenia and Antioch had been reduced to vassal status. When the lord of Sidon launched an intemperate raid, Mongol forces sacked the city and razed it to the ground. The Mongol contempt for other groups was absolute. Calls were sent to Europe for aid, not only out of fear of the Mongols but also with the hope that with Islamic power waning and the Mongols increasingly focused on Egypt, there might actually be opportunities to expand. The claim was that

> we duly believe that Jerusalem and the whole kingdom of Jerusa-lem could, with God's aid, be obtained easily if those who are called Christians were swiftly and manfully to make ready to assist us. For the Saracens, for the most part, are now gone. And as for the Tartars, if they meet with resistance on the part of the Latins, we believe that the more [opposition] they fear they will find, the sooner they will sheathe their bloodstained swords.[7]

But no crusading ventures resulted. Acre played a distrustful and waiting game.

When the Mongol blow did fall, the crusader states were mere onlookers. In early 1260, Mongol ambassadors arrived at Cairo with a familiar message:

> From the King of Kings of the East and West, the Great Khan. To Qutuz the Mamluk, who fled to escape our swords.
>
> You should think of what happened to other countries . . . and submit to us. You have heard how we have conquered a vast empire and have purified the earth of the disorders that tainted it. We have conquered vast areas, massacring all the people. You cannot escape from the terror of our armies. Where can you flee? What road will you

use to escape us? Our horses are swift, our arrows sharp, our swords like thunderbolts, our hearts as hard as the mountains, our soldiers as numerous as the sand. Fortresses will not detain us, nor arms stop us. Your prayers to God will not avail against us. We are not moved by tears nor touched by lamentations. Only those who beg our protection will be safe.

Hasten your reply before the fire of war is kindled. . . . Resist and you will suffer the most terrible catastrophes. We will shatter your mosques and reveal the weakness of your God, and then we will kill your children and your old men together.

At present you are the only enemy against whom we have to march.[8]

Qutuz had only seized power three months earlier. His regime was fragile but his response resolute. He chopped the Mongol ambassadors in half and hung their heads from the city gates. He prepared to go out to fight rather than await a siege. The lesson of Baghdad had not been forgotten.

The army that Qutuz could potentially raise was massively outnumbered by a factor of ten to one, but luck was on his side. In August of the preceding year, Möngke, the Great Khan of the Mongols, died, exposing one of the structural flaws in the Mongol Empire. Each succession contest inevitably required a return of the leading khans to central Asia. When word reached Hülegü in Syria, he prepared to withdraw the bulk of his men, perhaps 100,000, leaving his general Kitbuqa with a holding force of 10,000 to 12,000. In a letter sent to Louis IX, Hülegü himself claimed that the withdrawal of the bulk of his army, with its tens of thousands of horses, had been a logistical necessity. The fodder of northern Syria had been used up, and it was the Mongol custom to withdraw to more temperate lands in summer. The possibility that the Mongols, once across the Euphrates, were campaigning at their operational limit was a vulnerability the Mamluks would later exploit.

The Mongol advance into Syria had displaced many Muslim refugees and Ayyubid soldiers, who now rallied to Qutuz. And these included Baybars and the Bahriyyah Mamluk contingent, battle-hardened by a decade of fighting for and against various factions in the fragmentation of Syria. Among these ventures had been raids and invasion attempts against Egypt itself. There was long-standing enmity between the Bahriyyah and Qutuz over the murder of their leading emir, Aqtay, but the differences were, for the time being, shelved. The Mongol threat created a coalition of rivals. Baybars obtained a guarantee of safe conduct from Qutuz and brought his Mamluks to Cairo to confront the gathering storm. His troops were a welcome addition.

In July 1260, the Egyptian army rode out with a force of perhaps 12,000 men, probably slightly larger than Kitbuqa's. The Egyptians consisted of a small corps of Mamluks, local Egyptian soldiers, and refugees. As Qutuz moved up the coastal plain toward Acre, he decided to ask for Christian cooperation. Within Acre, there were intense discussions on how to respond. Many were in favor. The sacking of Sidon and the intemperate Mongol threats had rattled the Christians. Qutuz was the third sultan of Egypt in six years; there was no reason to believe that he could provide a threatening stability. They could, at that moment, hardly distinguish this latest ruler from the more easy-going Ayyubids, who had been valuable trading partners. A joint campaign might ease the Mongol pressure too. However, the grand master of the Teutonic Order, Hanno von Sangershausen, argued vehemently against any cooperation and eventually talked the authorities out of it. It was unwise to risk Christian lives, and in the aftermath of a Muslim victory, Qutuz might turn on them; better to conserve their strength and watch two rivals fight it out.

The Christians may have opted for neutrality, but they hedged their bets by granting Qutuz a safe conduct. He could pass through their territory without fear of attack. For three days, the Egyptian army camped in orchards outside the city walls and were provided with provisions. There was nervousness in the town. The leading emirs entered Acre and some kind of compact was made. Among them, according to the Christian sources, was "a great emir called Bendocar, who later became sultan."[9] The Arabic sources claimed that Baybars came in disguise as a spy to gain information to store against a future opportunity. While camped outside the walls of Acre, Qutuz delivered a powerful speech to his increasingly hesitant collection of troops, now more than wary of the power of the Mongols, to whip up their courage: the future of Islam hung in the balance. Baybars was sent ahead with the vanguard to scout out the disposition of the enemy.

Qutuz and his army met the Mongols at Ayn Jalut—the appropriately named Goliath's Spring, where David was said to have slain the giant—thirty miles southeast of Acre on September 3, 1260, for a contest that has been claimed as epochal in world history. The central corps of each army, supported by allies and unreliable supporters, was similar. It was a battle between matching detachments of Turco-Mongolian horse archers from the Eurasian steppes, employing similar tactics: mounted attacks, feigned retreat, and mobile encirclement. Baybars led the vanguard charging the Mongols, alternately advancing and retreating. Twice the Mongols came close to crushing Qutuz's army. At the height of the battle, with the situation critical, Qutuz took off his helmet to show his face to his men and shouted, "O Islam, O God, help your servant Qutuz against the Mongols!"[10] With the red and yellow banners of the Mamluk detachments rallying the men, he was able to stem the rout, regroup, and shatter the enemy. Kitbuqa was killed in the heat of the battle and the Mongols were slaughtered. Those who escaped were pursued by Baybars and beaten again.

It was not the first defeat that the Mongols had incurred nor did it end their ambitions in Syria. Theirs was a relatively small army that had unwisely underestimated an adversary similar to itself. Hülegü considered it a local setback that he intended to redress. The Mamluks had not confronted the full force of Mongol military might; a further riposte was inevitable, yet it had unforeseen consequences. Qutuz's rallying cry was prophetic of the ability of Turkish-speaking peoples, nomads from the Asian steppes, to unify Islam. The battle of Ayn Jalut conferred prestige and legitimacy on these outsiders.

QUTUZ WAS NOT destined to enjoy the fruits of victory. Maybe he had made overgenerous promises to his leading emirs—including the offer of the governorship of Aleppo to Baybars—which he failed to keep. In the aftermath of Ayn Jalut, the distrust between the Mamluks of Qutuz and those of the Bahriyyah bubbled to the surface again, and so it was probably just a question of which side struck first. The Bahriyyah had never forgiven Qutuz for the murder of Aqtay. On the way back across the desert to Cairo, Qutuz expressed a desire to stop and engage in his favorite sport of hare coursing. He turned off the road, accompanied by his emirs. When the hare had been caught, it signaled the Bahriyyah contingent to make their move. The most likely version of events is something to the effect that Baybars—or perhaps another emir—approached the sultan to ask a favor. Baybars moved to kiss his hand. This was the signal. Baybars firmly gripped Qutuz to prevent him drawing a weapon. A second emir stabbed him with a sword. Qutuz was finished off with arrows. Baybars did not act alone nor was he most likely the one who struck first; as with the murder of Turanshah, history was possibly rewritten to favor him. In the process of election that followed, Baybars claimed primacy on the basis that he was the one who had struck Qutuz down. Although the position of Mamluk sultan came to depend on a supporting confederacy of leading emirs, Baybars was to set about establishing unfettered personal rule.

FROM ACRE, THE murder of Qutuz must have looked like just another sign of the welcome dysfunctionality of the Islamic world—one ruler following another in a bloodbath of fragmenting petty kingdoms. The Christians breathed a sigh of relief. The Mongols were defeated, Egypt and Syria remained divided. What they did not know was that with Baybars, a new Turkish dynasty would unify the Islamic Middle East with an uncompromising commitment to jihad not seen since the days of Saladin, nor that the Mongols, despite sorties, would never return with sufficient desire to provide a counterbalance to Baybars or create the space to play off two more powerful opponents.

For Acre particularly, the dislocation caused by the Mongols and the rise of the Mamluks had severe economic consequences. With Baghdad ruined, the long-range trade routes that had ended at Acre and Tripoli moved north. The great days of economic prosperity were over, and the lords of Outremer were no longer so rich. Increasingly, they leased or sold their castles and lordships to the military orders, which would become the only viable defense of the Christian Holy Land. It was Baybars who would slowly squeeze their room to breathe. His stealthy reconnoiter of Acre was to be put to good use.

Baybars himself never forgot the allegiances made by some Christians with the Mongol foes, nor the burned mosques. The remaining crusader states were to confront a stable, unified Islamic dynasty and an unrelenting foe in Baybars, who would rule for seventeen years. The new sultan was said to be short of stature, broad chested, with a powerful voice. In one of his blue eyes there was an unusual white fleck. When he was first sold as a slave, he had fetched a cheap price—one purchaser promptly returned him to the auctioneer as spoiled goods. It was said that there was something evil in his eye. He rarely blinked.

4

THE LION OF EGYPT

1260–1269

FOR 150 YEARS, with the rare exception of Saladin's reign, the Islamic Middle East had been too divided to unite in common cause in the face of the inexplicable irruption of the Franks onto the shores of Palestine. The Ayyubids may have talked of jihad, but it was theoretical rather than practical, and the material benefits of long-distance trade with Europe had overridden any unified call to holy war. Rather, the crusader kingdoms had been largely absorbed into the pattern of alliances and conciliations that operated throughout Palestine and Syria. With Baybars and the ascendancy of Turkish peoples from the Asian steppes, everything changed.

Baybars was a first-generation convert to Islam. He had fought at Mansurah to protect Egypt from catastrophe, and on his return in October 1260 he brought back a harder ideology: a commitment to an orthodox Sunni caliphate and the unification of Egypt and Syria under the banner of war. With the threat of the Mongols, the Islamic world had been on the edge of collapse. He now set about unifying the people against their enemies east and west: the Mongols and the Franks. He was single-minded, tyrannical, and puritanical in forging a new Islamic empire.

His arrival in Cairo was met with consternation. The city's people were expecting to see Qutuz enter in triumphant procession. Instead, they were confronted with yet another cycle of bloody turmoil, a further quick change of sultan within the space of a year. The Turks were outsiders to the orthodox world—potentially usurpers—and Baybars had come to power through murder and a fixed election. The people were horrified and frightened by the prospect of a return to the 1250s, when the Mamluks had brought disorder, violence, and fear to Cairo's streets. Baybars worked swiftly to alleviate their apprehension. He lowered taxes and set about creating for himself the image of a legitimate Sunni ruler, heir to Saladin and the Ayyubids. Pious works were undertaken—the construction of mosques, the provision of work, and charitable food supplies in time of famine. He repaired the Dome of the Rock and the al-Aqsa mosque in Jerusalem, as well as Cairo's dilapidated great al-Azhar mosque, and assiduously cultivated the religious class. He was both farsighted and ruthless. He sidelined his fellow conspirators in the assassination of Qutuz and demolished the grave to prevent it becoming a pilgrimage site. The cult of his personality was projected through both word and image. His heraldic symbol, that of a lion, appeared on coins and the facades of public buildings—gates, fortresses, and bridges. The lion held its right paw raised mid-pounce and ready to strike or in the act of crushing in its claws a trapped rat: the enemies of Islam.

Baybars, in the role of a pious Muslim, revived the office of the Sunni caliphate; a descendant of the last caliph murdered at Baghdad was conveniently discovered, to whom Baybars swore allegiance. The caliph, in turn, invested Baybars as universal sultan in a solemn ceremony. Wearing the black turban of the Abbasid caliphate and a violet robe, and presented with banners, swords, and a shield, he pledged to levy just taxes, restore the caliphate to its ancient glory, and wage holy war. Legitimacy was conferred on what Arab historians of the time called the State of the Turks. Shortly after, the caliph was encouraged to embark on a suicide mission to retake Baghdad with a small force, which was swiftly and conveniently annihilated by the Mongols. A second caliph was effectively a puppet, and the office of caliphate would gradually become merged with that of the Mamluk sultans.

Building a military state was Baybars's first priority, which he undertook with rigor and efficiency. First, the defense of Egypt.

Remembering Louis's crusade, coastal fortifications, watch towers, and dredging schemes were undertaken to ensure adequate defense of the Nile; then, the rebuilding of the walls of Damascus and other cities that had been razed by the Mongols. The supply of military slaves to bolster the Mamluk regiments required regular shipments from the Black Sea; from the 1260s, it would be the Christian Genoese who would provide the manpower that was destined to confront their co-religionists in the years ahead.

At the same time, Baybars made structural reforms to the army. The enslaved Mamluks were native Turkish speakers and mainly operated under their officers in their own language. Baybars built a core group of about 4,000 Mamluks. Some were his own elite troops, others were owned by his emirs. There was also a corps of freeborn cavalry. Alongside these were infantry, mainly from Syria, and less-trained volunteers. Although his enemies routinely overestimated the total size of Mamluk armies, Baybars could muster perhaps as many as 40,000 men for particular campaigns.

In addition, he fostered military training regimes. He built two new *maydans*, hippodrome training grounds for the practice and development of military skills and physical fitness. Here the Mamluks would practice the disciplines of archery and fencing, and the use of the mace and the cavalry spear. There would be wrestling and mock combat—particularly the use of the short, whippy composite bow—on foot and on horseback. A skilled archer should be able to loose three arrows in one and a half seconds, and hit a target one yard wide at eighty yards. The Mamluks also employed a wide variety of incendiary weapons and trained their cavalry in fire games. Horseback maneuvers involving these weapons were performed to develop the skill of their riders and the temperament of their mounts against startling at the noise and flames.

To unify Egypt and Syria, Baybars set about systematically undermining or destroying autonomous Ayyubid princelings and linked the furthest reaches with a remarkable communications network. He established an efficient postal system of swift riders, relay stations, pigeon messenger services, and fire signal towers, and built bridges

Mamluk cavalry training. One man wields a mace. The other aims at a target from a galloping horse. (Oliver Poole, redrawn from *Kitab al-makhzun*, Oriental Institute Library, Academy of Sciences, St. Petersburg)

to speed troop movements and couriers. Intelligence gathering lay at the heart of his state building; he consistently surprised opponents with his ability to respond rapidly. His postal riders, who reported directly to him, were well rewarded. They could bring a message the six hundred miles from Damascus to Cairo in four days. He alone could open and read the correspondence, which he responded to immediately by day and night. On one occasion it was observed that "while he was taking a bath in his tent, the post arrived from Damascus. Without waiting an instant, without giving himself time to cover his nakedness, the prince had the letter read."[1] The reply was back in Damascus four days later.

Baybars was the sultan commander who slept little and never relaxed. Over the seventeen years of his reign, he ruled from the saddle, rode 70,000 miles, and fought thirty-eight campaigns, twenty-one of these against the Franks. He waged war even in harsh winter weather. He acted secretly, unnerved even his most loyal emirs by his unpredictable appearances, walked the streets of his city incognito, never divulged in advance the objective of a military expedition. Surprise and deception were weapons of war. If, as usurper of Turkish origin, he kept himself aloof from the indigenous population, his emirs also felt themselves continuously watched, and his enemies were kept guessing. A truce was only ever provisional, to be abrogated as the situation demanded. This restlessly energetic, controlling figure both rewarded the loyal, the brave, and the pious and carried out exemplary acts of cruelty—blindings, crucifixions, and bisections—to terrify and command obedience.

External threats were the justification for tyranny; Baybars's policies were all framed with the eventuality of warfare with the Mongols and the Franks. The help given to the Mongols by Antioch and Armenia led him to consider the activities of the two as linked. Both were enemies and he was wary of the possibility of fresh crusades from the West. The threat of Mongol incursions loomed large after 1260, but a major invasion by Hülegü never happened. The Mongol Empire, stretched to its geographical limits, was starting to fragment. Hülegü, as khan of Mesopotamia, was at loggerheads with Berke, ruler of the neighboring Mongol khanate of the Golden Horde. Berke, a convert to Islam, was outraged by the Mongol destruction of Baghdad. By 1263, the two were at open war. Baybars was able to establish cordial diplomatic relations with Berke, thus neutralizing a larger threat to the Islamic Middle East. Looking west and aware that the papacy was making diplomatic overtures to the Mongols, Baybars also established cordial relations with its rivals, the Hohenstaufens, rulers of Sicily, and then with the Hohenstaufens' own enemies, the Byzantine emperors, through whose waters the cargoes of military slaves from the Black Sea had to pass.

By 1263, Baybars had stabilized his position as the sultan of Egypt and Syria and was readying his army to move against the Franks.

Training, morale, and discipline were critical. He commanded the men to ensure that they were properly equipped: each was personally responsible for providing his own armor. The arms market in Damascus boomed. To ensure compliance, Baybars staged reviews in which the sections of his army filed past one at a time to prevent the men from exchanging equipment. The spirit of jihad was prominent in these mobilizations and the language uncompromising: the troops were enjoined "to remove all excuse for abstaining from the Holy War."[2] He forbade the brewing and drinking of beer and threatened to hang miscreants for drinking wine.

Baybars then embarked on a series of stop-start campaigns to intimidate and undermine the crusaders' fragmentary possessions that had survived Saladin's reign—Jaffa, Caesarea, Acre, and Tripoli—but his particular anger was directed against Bohemond VI, ruler of Antioch and Tripoli, and the Armenian king Hethoum I for their support of the Mongols. Baybars waged asymmetrical warfare—a bewildering combination of sieges and raids. His armies would appear quite suddenly, ravage the countryside, show their flags outside the walls of castles, and vanish again. These tactics were used to apply political pressure, to intimidate into favorable treaties and concessions, and to inflict economic damage. Objectives were always hidden, motives undeclared. The Mongols provided a convenient justification. Almost every year there would be scares of their incursions from across the Euphrates; few materialized, but for additional security the pastureland of northern Syria was routinely burned to deny grazing to Mongol horsemen. The Mongols were to be given nothing. Their threat both justified and required attacks on the crusader states.

Baybars had little regard for the advantages of Levantine trade that had seduced the Ayyubids to cooperate with the Franks. He worked to encourage the rerouting of commerce to Egypt. In the interim, though the Muslims held no harbors on the coast north of Gaza, he found ways to turn some of the Frankish ports to his advantage. When Jaffa, the most southern of the Frankish coastal cities, submitted, he used it to import grain for famine relief. When it was no longer useful, Jaffa was destroyed. Where the Ayyubids had recognized local Christians as a clearly protected minority, a greater intolerance now prevailed. Baybars had not forgotten their celebrations at the fall of Damascus to the Mongols. His actions were punitive, barring pilgrimage to Jerusalem and ordering his troops to raze to the ground the hugely significant church of St. Mary in Nazareth, the supposed site of the Annunciation.

The pressure he brought to bear on the crusader states became increasingly alarming. Acre, which he had secretly reconnoitered on his way to Ayn Jalut, was subjected to continuous visitations. In April 1263, his army suddenly appeared outside the city and attacked some of its outer defenses. There was fierce fighting that forced the defenders back. An Arabic chronicler left a vivid, if partisan, account:

> The Franks retired, routed, to Acre, while the Muslims burned the surrounding towers and walls, cut down trees and burned the fruits. There was nothing to be seen but smoke, clouds of dust, flashing swords and cutting, gleaming spear points. The Muslim army rode up to the gates of Acre, killing and taking prisoners . . . the remaining Franks then rushed to the gates of the city walls and came down to defend them. They were all shouting together: "The Gate! The Gate!," in fear that an attack was going to be made on them. Meanwhile the sultan was standing on the Acre side of the summit of the Tell [a nearby hill], making gifts and promises.[3]

Then, just as suddenly, Baybars withdrew. It was not a concerted attempt to take the city, rather a policy of softening up, disrupting agriculture, keeping opponents on edge. Every time his army moved, anxiety rippled throughout Outremer. Acre was raided in this way on an almost annual basis, its orchards uprooted and its crops burned. Baybars was back in 1265, again in the vicinity in 1266. In May 1267, he got up to the city gates by deception, flying the banners of the Templars and Hospitallers. He surprised the peasants working in the fields and captured and killed five hundred of them. He came again in 1269.

Often these attacks were diversionary episodes designed to distract from more major operations against crusader castles. The 1266 raid on Acre was only one of a number that year. Baybars had the military resources to send simultaneous raiding parties against Tyre, Sidon, and the Teutonic Knights' castle at Montfort, throwing dust in the eyes of Christian defenders, while his main army besieged the Templar castle at Safad. Tripoli and Antioch each experienced three such assaults during the 1260s. In 1270, the Hospitallers' stronghold of Krak des Chevaliers, the most formidable fortress ever constructed in the crusader era, was softened up with a devastation of its hinterland. He was scorching away the economic foundations of the last crusader states. The damage to Acre's agricultural lands was so severe that Muslim writers felt compelled to find religious justifications for malicious destruction. In the area around Tripoli, he destroyed irrigation channels and aqueducts dating back to the Roman Empire. This devastation of fertile land to inhibit, demoralize, and economically weaken was to scar the coastal strip of Palestine and Lebanon for hundreds of years.

The Franks did not help themselves. Unable to put out enough men to risk open battle, they resorted to tit-for-tat counterattacks that lacked strategic forethought or coherent effort. After the raids of 1263, the two sides patched up a truce. This did not prevent the Templars and Hospitallers, acting as autonomous bodies, from mounting further sorties two months later. This was followed shortly after by the arrival in Acre of a small contingent of French troops, eager for action. They promptly attacked nearby Muslim villages, snatched people and animals, and set fire to houses. Whereas Baybars engaged in such tactics with strategic intent, these uncoordinated Christian initiatives, with no clear purpose beyond releasing pent-up frustration, served only to alienate local Muslim people and to infuriate Baybars.

At no point were the crusader states capable of combined action. Each made its own piecemeal truces with the Mamluks in the hope of temporary respite and usually on disadvantageous terms. When Acre tried to arrange a prisoner exchange with Baybars, both the Hospitallers and the Templars refused to participate because the Muslims they were holding were skilled craftsmen and too expensive to replace. Such actions earned them growing criticism from fellow Christians for selfishness and self-interest: "They ought to have made the exchange, for the sake of God and the deliverance of the poor Christian slaves," was one critical verdict.[4] They not infrequently made their own agreements with Baybars regarding territory they controlled around their inland castles, while the Frankish barons were capable of reckless bouts of destruction. All this served to broaden support for the State of the Turks, and further legitimize Baybars's claim as Sunni sultan and liberator.

But the language of power spoke louder than the language of diplomacy. Baybars could pick and choose his terms. In 1267, he refused a truce with Acre while the grand master of the Hospitallers signed a humiliating ten-year agreement in return for nonaggression against their castles in Lebanon, with the sultan's right to abrogate it whenever he wished. Truces with the Frankish states were frequently canceled by Baybars on grounds of minor technical infringements or simply uncorroborated assertions.

For Baybars, the Frankish settlements along the coasts of Palestine, Lebanon, and northern Syria were strategically significant. They threatened the direct route from Cairo to Damascus, and they occupied the best agricultural land. Dominance over the landscape was maintained by a chain of castles commanding the hills of Palestine, Lebanon, and northern Syria. From there, they controlled territory, though at no point did they constitute a coherent defensive system; rather, the territory was a patchwork of independent local fiefdoms owned by the military orders and Frankish barons. As crusader control of territory shrank with the campaigns of Saladin, so the importance of these castles grew. The disaster at Hattin had quenched any Frankish enthusiasm to take on the armies of Islam in extensive, open-field warfare. The thirteenth century saw the military orders, increasingly the only bodies with the resources, construct or remodel castles on a massive scale. They spent money and energy on sophisticated concentric fortifications and defensive features that exposed attackers to heavy counter-bombardment and slowed down the operations of their miners and siege engines. South of Acre, the Templars erected the near-impregnable redoubt of Chateau Pèlerin on a headland above the sea; the Teutonic Knights built their head-quarters castle of Montfort, six hundred feet above a valley on an inaccessible bluff; in northern Syria, the Hospitallers remodeled Krak des Chevaliers after an earthquake into the most formidable bastion in all of Outremer. Such fortresses compensated for lack of manpower and allowed small garrisons to dominate landscapes and intimidate local populations and would-be attackers.

The castles' weakness was that Baybars's campaigns of attrition were rendering them increasingly isolated. Now, with the reunification of Egypt and Syria and Baybars's army in a high state of readiness, the sultan felt himself in a position to take on these discrete fiefdoms and their castles in earnest. The Mamluks' traditional fighting skills were as mounted cavalry, but 1265 saw them deploy the techniques of siege warfare that were ultimately to drive the Franks out of the Holy Land. They had inherited siege craft from earlier Islamic dynasties, but under Baybars they established a competency in the complex technical and logistical requirements of besieging and taking fortified places that surpassed those of their forebears. The siege campaigns begun in the spring of 1265 would last until 1271 and destroy much of the military strength of the crusader states.

THE PRETEXT WAS a threatened Mongol attack of northern Syria. As Baybars scrambled forces to intercept and harry the Mongol invaders—a process hastened by his network of fast couriers—he believed that the Franks had now shifted from the position of neutrality that had marked the march to Ayn Jalut and had tipped the Mongols off that Mamluk cavalry had scattered for the season. Rapid mobilization dissuaded the Mongols from a major assault, but it alerted the ever-watching Baybars to the dangers of the alliance. He wrote to the constable of Jaffa complaining that the Frankish leaders "have committed many wrongs against me, such as their writing to the Mongols to attack my territories."[5]

Baybars's first targets were two cities on the coast of southern Palestine, Caesarea and Arsuf, and demonstrated the techniques and resources that the Mamluks brought to the crusader wars: deception, disregard for treaties, technical expertise, deep planning, propaganda for holy war, and overwhelming resources of manpower. Under cover of conducting a lion hunt in the area, Baybars reconnoitered the fortifications of the two cities. At the same time, he began cutting wood for siege machines on site, ordering up a skilled work force of stonemasons, tunnelers, and engineers. Stone balls were prepared, and the troops already gathered were put to work constructing ladders. Prefabricated siege engines that could be disassembled and transported by camels or carried by men were being constructed in Damascus.

On February 27, Baybars showed up without warning at the gates of Caesarea, encircled it, and attacked. Laudatory accounts depicted Baybars himself participating in the fighting: the morale of the men demanded that the sultan should be seen. Taken completely by surprise, the outer walls were apparently overcome by ingenious improvisation without the use of ladders. Like climbers hammering pitons into a rock face, "using iron horse pegs, tethers and halters onto which they clung, they climbed up from all sides and set their banners there. The city gates were burnt and its defences torn away."[6] Caesarea surrendered in a week, and the survivors sailed off to Acre. In the immediate aftermath, Baybars embarked on the complete destruction of the city. Meanwhile, he sent raiding parties off to harry Acre (and various other locations) to distract and pin down potential relief. A Christian delegation that arrived to question the reasons for this attack was warmly and disarmingly received while the sultan quietly prepared his next move.

On March 19, Baybars left Caesarea. Two days later, his army appeared, equally unexpectedly, at the fortified stronghold of Arsuf on the coast twenty-five miles south. For Baybars, a treaty was only a treaty as long as he wanted it to be. In 1263, he had complained to the Hospitallers that they had reinforced the fortifications of Arsuf in breach of an agreement. At the time, gifts had been sent to mollify his anger, and the ambassadors were assured that the city would not come under attack. Now it did.

Arsuf was well fortified and stoutly defended, but the ensuing siege reflected both the asymmetry of numbers and the increasingly sophisticated techniques, and the resources that the Mamluks were able to employ. Substantial tunneling and trench-digging work was undertaken by skilled men, and despite equally professional counter-measures by the Hospitallers who used barrels of grease and fat, ignited and fanned by bellows, to destroy the tunnels, the scale of the siege works allowed the attackers eventually to undermine the outer walls. The Mamluks had brought a range of projectile-throwing artillery to Arsuf, and the catapult bombardment was considerable. Baybars himself was said to have participated in hauling the ropes that launched the stone missiles. Religious enthusiasm was another ingredient that was to become a hallmark of Mamluk mobilization and commitment. Prayers were said in the open, while Baybars himself traveled with a personal tent mosque. A visible religious contingent—"pious people, ascetics, legal scholars and indigent Sufis"[7]—came at Baybars's behest to inspire the men to fight and die for jihad. Baybars himself was con-tinuously present, close to the fighting: "Now . . . in the ditch, now at the openings which were being made, and now by the sea shore shooting at the Frankish ships and pulling on the mangonels . . . he would climb to the top of palisades so as to shoot from there, showing everyone his part to play, ordering them to exert themselves, thank-ing those who deserved it and giving robes of honour to those who had distinguished themselves by some act of merit."[8] The presence of the sultan at Arsuf, his energy and his personal bravery, provided inspiration and motivation during the campaigns that followed.

It took five weeks to ready a final attack: rushing the walls, taking the outer city, then subjecting the inner citadel to furious assault with catapults and arrows. On April 29, the outer barbican of the citadel collapsed from mining and bombardment. Baybars offered surrender with a guarantee that lives would be spared. The defenders accepted. They were unable to escape by sea: the harbor was too small and was within range of Baybars's artillery. As with Caesarea, Arsuf, a city since ancient times, was demolished and never inhabited again.

On May 29, Baybars made a ceremonial entry into Cairo. In his train walked the captured Franks from Arsuf with broken crosses round their necks and their banners reversed. In the aftermath, Baybars lost no time exploiting the propaganda value of the conquest. To Jean d'Ibelin, lord of Jaffa, the bombastic threats would soon become familiar to crusader lords:

> We brook no oppression: if anyone takes a field [of ours], in its place we capture a lofty citadel, and for any peasant of ours captured we seize a thousand armed warriors. If they destroy a house wall, we destroy the walls of cities. The sword is in the hand of one who strikes and the horse's reins are in the grasp of the rider. We have a hand which cuts necks and another which reaches the porticos [of palaces]. Whoever wishes to pick a quarrel [with us] must know what he is about; and whoever wishes [to take] something [from us] will find [disasters such as] those ordained for him.[9]

The numbers on each side at Arsuf had been mismatched. Whereas the defenders could muster just 270 skilled Hospitaller knights, a few auxiliaries, and the efforts of the townspeople, Baybars could draw on thousands of troops. As well as those with specialist skills in the construction and operation of catapults, there were engineers, masons, tunnelers, carpenters, and all the logistical support. Yet Arsuf was a stoutly fortified stronghold, access to which was limited by its position on the sea, and defended by men who also knew what they were doing. The Franks had compensated for a shortage of manpower by placing their faith in their highly sophisticated fortified defenses. These had proved insufficient.

What Arsuf demonstrated was that the Mamluks had rapidly grasped and refined the elements of siege craft. This siege was the prototype of successive blows about to fall on Outremer. Its strategies would be repeated again and again: dissimulation, careful planning and logistical arrangements, religious motivation, inspirational—and intimidating—leadership, large numbers of troops, the combined skills of mining and artillery bombardment, and a frenetic pace to deliver quick knock-out blows. Sieges usually ended in surrender in the face of the inevitable, less frequently with a full-front assault and a massacre. It became standard practice to demolish coastal installations that might provide beachheads for counter-crusades. Disorienting raiding and economic warfare were one arm of Baybars's campaigns. Isolating and picking off stoutly fortified castles one after another was the other. In the next few years, Baybars would come close to decapitating the Frankish states, and these twin techniques would be in play right up to the walls of Acre in 1291.

AT ABOUT THIS time, Baybars added to his list of honorific titles that of "annihilator of Mongols and Franks."[10] Inscriptions praised him as the Alexander of the Age, "the victorious prince, the pillar of the world and religion, the sultan of Islam and the Muslims, the killer of infidels and polytheists, the tamer of rebels and heretics, the reviver of justice in the two worlds."[11]

The following spring, in 1266, Baybars opened his campaign by ravaging the area around Tripoli and showing up outside the walls of Acre, Tyre, and Sidon, but these were just sideshows to intimidate and confuse. His real target was the Templar castle of Safad. It was the last Christian fort in inland Palestine, strategically placed to threaten traffic to Damascus. In a trope often applied to Christian fortifications and cities, it was "an obstruction in the throat of Syria and a blockage in the chest of Islam."[12] At the same time, Baybars was busy improving communications within the kingdom with bridges across the Jordan river. While the pattern of raids distracted and alarmed—and even his commanders, equipped with sealed orders, were kept in ignorance of his objectives until the last moment—siege equipment was being prepared in Damascus. When he arrived suddenly outside the walls of Safad, a host of embassies from other pillaged places quickly showed up and sought treaties and offered gifts. They were all dismissed. The ruler of Tyre's representative was reproached for alleged treaty breaking: "If you want me to grant you security, then drive out my Frankish enemies from your midst. For it was part of our oath that my enemies should be yours."[13]

The siege was timed to open on the feast day that ended the Ramadan fast. Pious religious practice was rigorously enforced on his troops: any who celebrated by drinking wine would be hanged. Full-hearted zeal was nonnegotiable; when a first direct assault failed in the face of resolute resistance, Baybars temporarily imprisoned forty of his emirs for insufficient effort. The siege skills that had reduced Arsuf gradually prevailed and when his army had broken through the outer wall, the defenders withdrew to their inner citadel and attempted to negotiate surrender. The end was played out in disputed versions—either Baybars was again using his dominant position to break an agreement or the Christians had breached the sworn terms.

The defenders thought they had brokered a safe conduct. Instead they were detained: Baybars declared they had breached the agreement by trying to depart with concealed weapons. It was clear,

The intimidating Baybars receives an audience in his tent. The spears of his army and his standards in the background. (Oliver Poole, redrawn from the *Cantigas de Santa Maria*)

though, that throughout the crusader period Islam particularly detested the military orders. The Templars were marched to the top of a nearby hill where they had executed their own Muslim prisoners, and all 1,500 were beheaded. According to the Christian chroniclers, the remnants were left there as a grim warning: "He had a circular wall erected around them, and their bones and heads may still be seen."[14] Only two survived: an Arabic-speaking Armenian who had negotiated the deal (and who may have been complicit in the Templars' fate), and one other who was sent back to Acre to bear witness to what had happened and what would come. Baybars was waging war to the knife. There would be no quarter without unconditional surrender. Unlike the coastal fortifications, which were all demolished, Safad was occupied and rebuilt to guard the way into Syria.

In 1268, Baybars was on campaign again: the same tactics and mobilizations. In March, he attacked Jaffa, vulnerable after its lord's death in 1266, and reduced the city to ashes. In April, it was the turn of the Templars' castle at Beaufort, which surmounted a crag in southern Lebanon. In between, there were raids to Tripoli and Acre. Each of these campaigns not only removed substantial defensive structures; they also induced the voluntary surrender of other small forts, along with concessions, placatory gifts, and new treaties on terms increasingly disadvantageous to their residents or defenders.

But it was Antioch on which Baybars's fiercest anger was turned. The alliance of its ruler, Bohemond VI, with the Mongols still rankled. The sultan surrounded this large and populous city, whose extensive perimeter was stoutly walled. He demanded an annual tribute of a dinar a head of the whole population—a large sum, but no more than they had been paying the Mongols. Antioch's refusal was unwise, given its expanse and an insufficient number of defenders. Baybars issued a final ultimatum. No response. On May 15, 1268, his army stormed it, breaching the walls. The sultan ordered the city gates closed so that no one could escape, then gave it over to slaughter and sack. Tens of thousands were trapped inside. Those who were not killed were enslaved, and the city's wealth produced huge booty. Each soldier in the army was granted a slave; so many slaves were taken that there was a glut on the market and a huge drop in prices. Then much of the city was torched.

ANTIOCH, A CITY of Biblical significance, was iconic in crusader memory. It had been the gateway to the Holy Land for the First Crusade. Its almost miraculous capture after eight months of perilous endeavor and retention against overwhelming odds had paved the way for the taking of Jerusalem. It fell to Baybars in a single day.

After this sack, Antioch never recovered its former prominence. With its loss, the last Templar outposts were abandoned and only the tiny coastal port at Latakia remained. Frankish Syria had collapsed.

Bohemond, absent from his capital at the time, received a taunting letter from Baybars congratulating him on his survival. Written with threat and flourish, it conjured images of apocalypse and hell to be visited on the infidel:

> We took the city by the sword on the fourth hour of Saturday, the 4th of the month of Ramadan (19 May). We killed all those whom you had chosen to guard and protect it. . . . You could have seen your horsemen thrown down between the legs of the horses, houses in the power of the plunderers . . . your goods being weighed by the qintar, your ladies being sold in fours and being bought with a dinar of your own money.
>
> If you had seen your churches with their crosses broken and rent, the pages of the false Testaments scattered, the graves of the patriarchs rifled, your Muslim enemy trampling down the sanctuary; had you seen the altar on which had been sacrificed the monk, the priest and the deacon . . . if you had seen the fires burning in your castles and the slain being consumed in the fire of this world, the state of your palaces altered, . . . the churches . . . tottering to their final ruin—had you seen these things, you would have said: "Would that I were dust" . . .
>
> This letter then gives you good news of the safety and prolongation of life that God has granted to you because you were not staying at Antioch at this time. . . . The living rejoice in the preservation of

their own lives when they see the dead. Perhaps God has granted a delay only that you may make up for your past lack of obedience and service. . . . Since no one escaped to tell you what has happened, we have told you ourselves.[15]

BY THE END of the 1260s, Baybars could draw a pause to his campaigns. The yellow flag of the Mamluks had been hoisted on one captured citadel after another, but they had been hard-won victories. The sultan had pushed forward campaigns through rain and cold, and in the height of summer. Crossing the mountains of Lebanon in the spring snow in 1268, it was recorded that his army "could find nothing [to eat] except snow, which they ate themselves and fed to their horses."[16] Baybars later boasted to the hated Bohemond that there was no crusader fastness to which he could not haul his siege artillery and no season in which he would not campaign. He described how, in order to attack the crusader-held fort of Akkar in northern Lebanon in 1271,

we transported the mangonels there through mountains where the birds think it too difficult to nest; how patiently we hauled them, troubled by mud and struggling against rain; how we erected them in places where ants would slip were they to walk there; how we went down into valleys so deep that were the sun to shine through the clouds there it would show no way out except the precipitous mountains.[17]

Despite the exaggerations, siege warfare was a terrible slog. And the Lion of Egypt had been cautious; he had never yet attempted to drag a siege train to the walls of Acre. After the near collapse of Islam, his campaigns were, in large measure, defensive. It was necessary to pick off enemies one at a time, above all to avoid provoking a working alliance between the Mongols and the Christians or inciting a major new crusade from Europe.

IN JULY 1269, he made the pilgrimage to Mecca in strictest secrecy to ensure no insurrection among dissident emirs. Elaborate arrangements concealed his departure. It was given out that he had gone hunting. His confidential messengers continued to bring him the mail; replies were dispatched as if he had never gone. When he returned from Mecca at the end of August, he arrived without warning in Damascus, and then in Aleppo. His aim was to keep his provincial governors in uneasy obedience, aware that he was always watching and could unexpectedly call them to account at any moment.

5

A Puppy Yelping at a Mastiff

1270–1288

B Y THE TIME Baybars had departed for the *hajj* in 1269, he had inflicted serious damage on the crusader states, prizing away their castles one by one, depriving them of revenues and tribute, and destroying their agricultural hinterland. They were increasingly dependent on resources from the west. The quarrels between factions of the noble families of Outremer and among the Italian merchants continued unabated. All seemed blind to the possibility of a final collapse, but to those alive to the political and military realities, there was a sense of impending doom. An increasing burden was falling on the wealthy military orders for the defense of the Christian footholds, and they were realistic about the prospects. As early as 1261, "If the kingdom is lost" had begun to appear as an ominous qualifier to their contracts on property and land.[1]

The Genoese departure from Acre after the war of St. Sabras further weakened the city's position as an emporium for trade, and the irruptions of the Mongols had diverted caravan routes further north. Its great days as the richest city in the Mediterranean world seemed to be coming to an end. The disintegration of authority in Acre and the disputes between factions in the kingdom of Jerusalem hampered any coordinated effort. By the mid-1260s, the only real leadership in Acre was the patriarch of Jerusalem, who was also the bishop of Acre. He was not just the spiritual leader, but effectively the city's temporal lord. The patriarch was given unlimited powers by the papacy to manage the kingdom's affairs—in so far as the citizens and factions would obey the pope. As de facto head of state, he was authorized to act against disputatious military orders, and at times given money for troops and funds to repair fortifications, build war machines, and redeem prisoners. It was the patriarch who was destined to be the commanding figure in Acre's final crisis.

An awareness of Baybars's devastations was seeping back into Europe too. Despite the continuing struggles between the papacy and the Hohenstaufens, the growing crisis in the Holy Land was unavoidable, but the only states stable enough to respond to a fresh crusading call were England and France. Papal initiatives were stop-start, but the possibility of complete loss stirred Clement IV to raise funds and issue a call for a new crusade. The intertwined rivalry between the kings of France and their French-speaking neighbors, the kings of England (who also held land in France), formed a running backstory to crusader ventures. Both were deeply steeped in a crusading tradition whose origin was French, but the mutual suspicion between Richard the Lionheart and Philippe Augustus of France had soured the siege of Acre in 1191. When Louis IX had launched his ill-fated crusade to the Nile in 1249, the English king Henry III had sworn to go—and failed to do so, with considerable loss of face and, more seriously, breach of a sacred vow. Now Louis, himself haunted by Mansurah and obsessed with the golden dream of Jerusalem, again responded. The embarrassment of the English crown if it failed to commit a second time would be doubled.

It was Henry's oldest son, Edward, who answered the call. The English prince was in his late twenties, blond and dashing. He was nicknamed "Longshanks": at six foot two, he cut an imposing figure at a time when most men were barely five foot six. And he was a fighter well-versed in the knight's code of chivalry, with combat skills honed in tournaments and mock battles. The desire to do heroic deeds in the Holy Land ran in his bloodline. He had been fed crusader stories since his childhood. Richard the Lionheart was his great uncle; another crusader, Richard of Cornwall, his uncle, and he had in his entourage older French knights who had fought with Louis at Mansurah.

Edward also had early firsthand experience of war. He had led his father's armies against the rebel Simon de Montfort at the battle of Evesham in 1265, at which both sides had worn crosses on their surcoats. Edward won, but rather than ransom the rebel nobles who attempted to surrender, they were slaughtered on the battlefield. Men seeking sanctuary in the abbey church were cut down at the altar. It was dubbed "the murder of Evesham"—an unprecedented breach of chivalric protocol.[2] Edward and his knights may have felt they had blood on their hands. Crusading was not only an opportunity to perform heroic deeds. It was also an expiation of sins.

In a carefully choreographed ceremony in June 1268, the pope's cardinal preached the call to crusade in the church of the Holy Sepulchre in Northampton, England. The venue had special resonance. It had been built by a knight from the First Crusade in imitation of the church of the Holy Sepulchre in Jerusalem. That day, Edward and his younger brother Edmund both took crusading vows, along with hundreds of other nobles and their followers. Among this band were two knights destined to play a leading part in Acre's fate. Othon de Grandson was thirty, just a year older than Edward and his closest friend. Grandson came from an old noble family from Swiss Savoy, and he, too, came from crusading stock: his grandfather had died in the Holy Land. He was reliable, brave, and versatile, both a fighter and a skilled diplomat destined to give years of service to the English crown. He had fought in Edward's civil war battles and been rewarded with a knighthood and land. Another knight from Savoy, Jean de Grailly, somewhat older, was one of Edward's counselors; he had also been rewarded by the prince for reliable service.

Louis's financing and organization of his second crusade was as efficient as the first—he again demonstrated the bureaucratic, emotional, and financial skills necessary for a well-organized crusade. Crusading was expensive. When Edward found it difficult to raise the funds for an English contingent, Louis lent him £17,000. Tellingly, the loyal Joinville had declined the invitation to a second brush with death.

If the preparations were again impeccable, the results were no better. For political and misconceived strategic reasons, Louis set out not to the Holy Land, or even back to the graveyards of the Nile, but to Tunis, which he believed, once captured, would be the gateway to Egypt. Instead, the king and his army were struck down by dysentery and the crusade petered out in stalemate and a peace treaty.

Louis died near Carthage in August 1270; his whispered last words were reported to be "Jerusalem! Jerusalem!"[3] While many returned to France, part of his expedition followed this injunction and sailed on to the east, but most of the fleet was wrecked in a storm at Sicily. Only the detachment of Prince Edward of England made it to the Holy Land.

Longshanks arrived in Acre in May 1271 with a small force, probably a thousand in total, of whom 250 were knights. His party included the churchman Teobaldo Visconti, who received word while in Acre that he had been elected to the papacy. If any pope understood the critical situation of the Frankish states, it was Visconti; his final sermon before he sailed was on the text "If I forget you, O Jerusalem, let my right hand forget its skill! Let my tongue stick to the roof of my mouth if I do not remember you."[4] No pope could have had a deeper commitment to the plight of Outremer.

Edward was appalled by the political and commercial realities of the crusader states. He could see with his own eyes ships of the Italian merchant republics in Acre harbor en route to Alexandria with weapons, food supplies, and enslaved manpower for the Mamluk army. Successive popes repeatedly outlawed these trades with dire threats of excommunication; in 1202, so suspicious was Innocent III that he was issuing categoric threats to the Venetians on this subject even as they were preparing to participate in the Fourth Crusade: "[We] prohibit you, under strict threat of anathema to supply the Saracens by selling, giving or bartering, iron, hemp, sharp implements, inflammable materials, arms, galleys, sailing ships, or timbers."[5] Versions of these carefully framed interdictions were repeated regularly during the thirteenth century—to little purpose. Even when the republics' state authorities were forced to repeat the ban, illegal trades—smuggling or consignments on foreign ships—continued.

Acre's role as a great trans-Mediterranean trade hub may have been diminishing, but it remained an important regional hub for transshipment and transit, a link in the chain that connected the slaves of the Black Sea, the iron and wood of Turkey, and the wheat and weapons of Europe to Alexandria and the state arsenal in Cairo. Acre had its own slave market. The timber went to make war machines, crossbows, ships, and spear shafts; the pitch for Greek fire; the wheat to offset shortages in Egypt and pacify dissent in Cairo; the metal for blades, and sometimes as finished weapons; the slaves to wield or operate these weapons against Acre's own walls.

Seen from Edward's perspective, Acre was complicit in eating itself, yet within the city these trades induced a degree of complacency. It was believed that it was simply too valuable to be destroyed. The feuding barons of the crusader states, so intent on their own privileges and prerogatives, were unable to see the route to disaster.

Nor had Edward come in time or been in any position to prevent what was to prove Baybars's most spectacular siege campaign. Released from the Mongol threat, Baybars could turn his attention back to picking off crusader forts. In March 1271, he moved against the Hospitallers' spectacular castle of Krak des Chevaliers. Situated in northern Syria, the castle was of considerable strategic value. It overlooked the Homs Gap, an important thoroughfare through the mountains, and from here it dominated territory and extracted tribute from the surrounding area. King Andrew II of Hungary, who came in 1218, called it the key to the Christian lands. At its peak, it housed a garrison of 2,000 men and provided a base for offensive operations; but by the second half of the thirteenth century, the Hospitallers' finances and manpower were both in decline. The English-born grand master Hugh Revel complained in 1268 that there were only three hundred Hospitaller knights in all Outremer. Baybars's campaigns of economic attrition had stripped away valuable revenue and devastated the hinterland. By 1271, the castle was isolated and poorly garrisoned.

The Mountain: a reconstruction of Krak des Chevaliers. (*Étude sur la topographie de la ville d'Acre au XIII siècle*, Paris, 1879)

Nevertheless, Krak des Chevaliers was exceptional—the most formidable fortification the crusaders ever built. Positioned on a steep-sided bluff, 2000 feet above sea level, that could only be accessed along a level approach from the south side, it was a work of extraordinary skill. Erected on a bedrock of hard basalt out of high-quality limestone blocks so perfectly fitted that there was barely need for mortar, the inner keep rose 160 feet, its outer walls 30 feet. It was nicknamed "the mountain." As well as a moat, fed from a spring between the two walls on the southern side, it comprised sophisticated defensive features: overhanging box machicolations of stone allowed well-protected defenders to drop projectiles onto the heads of attackers at the base of sheer walls, arrow slits were staggered to limit the area of dead ground, and a twisting 150-yard passage with blind turns would force any attackers to launch their final assault under fire from above. Its capture by storm was almost an impossibility against a determined defense.

Baybars, at the head of an army of 12,000 men, hauled the siege equipment up the rocky outcrop in the spring rain. The wooden components of the trebuchets swelled in the wet and could not be set up. The archers' bow strings were unusable. The army waited eighteen days for the weather to ease. When it did, Baybars brought into play all the skills he had honed over the past decade. On the south side, his troops quickly overcame the outer works, probably wooden stockades. He then erected his catapults and set the miners to work. While the catapults hurled stones weighing up to 220 pounds against the parapets, keeping the defenders' archers at bay, it was the miners who eventually brought down a tower on the southwest corner of the outer wall. At this point Baybars was still confronted with the moat, which could not be mined, and the mountain itself, rearing up above. And, against his usual practice of demolishing castles, he wanted to take this one intact, without a fight.

Deception always formed a key ingredient of Baybars's armory. In 1268, he had succeeded in intercepting a letter to the besieged garrison at Beaufort and replacing it with a forgery designed to undermine the defenders' morale. Now at Krak des Chevaliers, it's probable that he again fabricated a letter from the Hospitallers' grand master in Tripoli to state that no relief was on the way and giving them permission to surrender. The castellan of the fort sought terms, and on April 7, the garrison capitulated. Baybars was handed the great fortress largely undamaged. Whether the forgery actually occurred or just provided the castellan with a convenient explanation, it is clear that the isolation of crusader forts and their lack of manpower rendered even the most impregnable stronghold obsolete against the Mamluk tactics of total war.

Baybars honored the safe conduct and addressed a taunt to the Master of the Hospitallers in his now familiar style:

> To frère Hugues—may God make him one of those who do not oppose destiny or rebel against Him who has reserved victory and triumph for His army . . . to inform him of the conquest, by God's grace of [Krak de Chevaliers], which you fortified and built out and furbished . . . and whose defence you entrusted to your Brethren. They have failed you; by making them live there you destroyed them, for

they have lost both the fort and you. These troops of mine are incapable of besieging any fort and leaving it able to resist them.[6]

It was a boast, but no more than the truth. Krak des Chevaliers had been the ultimate test for Baybars, and the castle's capture called into question the ability of any fortress to resist Mamluk siege craft. On a column of its elegant gallery, the Hospitallers had once carved a short poem in Latin that served perhaps as a warning: "Have richness, have wisdom, have beauty but beware of pride which spoils all it comes into contact with."[7] Baybars was remorselessly puncturing any remaining crusader pride. He moved on to the castle at Akkar, at the northern end of the Homs Gap, transporting his siege engines on carts, on which he was said to have ridden. A breach in the outer wall led its garrison quickly to seek terms.

From there, Baybars resolved to wipe Tripoli off the map. Bohemond VI had escaped the fires of hell that had engulfed Antioch, but Baybars still had a score to settle with the counts of Tripoli for allying with the Mongols. Bohemond received another letter warning him of what was coming and advising him to flee by sea: the prison fetters awaited. Yet news of Prince Edward's arrival at Acre caused the sultan to pause. Wary of new crusader armies led by royal commanders and unable to ascertain the level of the threat posed by the English prince, he agreed a ten-year truce with Tripoli.

Edward's presence raised morale, but he had far too few men to make any substantial difference to Acre's strategic situation. Baybars moved immediately to threaten the English prince, appearing in the vicinity of Acre, then turning north to tackle the redoubtable fort of the Teutonic Knights, Montfort, perched on the edge of a ravine twelve miles to the east. Despite the operational difficulties of the terrain both for his trebuchets and his miners, within a month he had compelled the garrison's surrender with a guarantee of safe conduct. Edward was treated to the dispiriting sight of these men being released in front of the city walls and the sheer size of a Mamluk army. It was a rude awakening to the realities of the Holy Land.

But Edward had seen other possibilities. Upon arrival, he immediately dispatched ambassadors to Abaqa, the Mongol ruler in Iran, to propose a combined operation against the Mamluks. While awaiting a reply, he embarked enthusiastically on raiding the hinterland and carried out an attack with the Hospitallers and Templars on a nearby Mamluk stronghold. It inflicted damage but also provided the English knights with a sobering lesson in the risks of military operations in the height of summer; in their heavy chain mail, numbers of his men died of thirst and heat stroke. This kind of military tourism had become a repeated and, at times, aggravating problem for the kingdom of Jerusalem. Newly arrived crusaders, hungry for action but often never staying long enough to make a substantial difference, stirred up trouble without any comprehension of the delicate compromises that now allowed Outremer to survive. It was a tendency that would precipitate Acre's final crisis.

The Mongols' reply to Edward, which took months to arrive, was encouraging. They undertook a new campaign, drove the Mamluks out of Aleppo, and compelled Baybars to move north. In the interim, Edward launched a second front, attempting to capture the Mamluk castle of Qaqun, forty miles to the south, which guarded the road to Jerusalem. His small force again ravaged the land around, but the castle held out, being "very strong, surrounded by ditches full of water."[8] Any hopes of real progress were further dented by the news that the Mongols had withdrawn from Aleppo in the face of Baybars's advance. As to Qaqun, the sultan scornfully remarked that "if so many men cannot take a house, it seems unlikely that they will conquer the kingdom of Jerusalem."[9] A further perplexity for new arrivals in the Holy Land who came with preconceptions of the implacable confrontation with Islam was that the people of Qaqun were routinely accustomed to selling their agricultural surpluses in the markets of Acre.

OVER THE WINTER of 1271–1272, Edward borrowed money to strengthen Acre's defenses by constructing a new tower on the critical section of the outer wall, fronting it with a further low wall to protect its base. He additionally founded a small military order, the Confraternity of St. Edward the Confessor, expressly dedicated to the defense of this English Tower. Meanwhile, Baybars pondered the continued threat represented by Edward's presence. In December 1271, he feinted a further attack on the city, a calculated attempt to unsettle and undermine.

But Baybars had in his repertoire a second strategy for dealing with the heir to the English throne. It required cunning and patience. Versions differ as to the exact details, but most probably his plan involved the dispatch of a loyal emir with an entourage to the gates of Acre. He came bearing gifts and with a tale to tell: that he had come to betray the sultan. They were cautiously welcomed, and Edward, not above deception himself but probably encouraged by the possibilities, was taken in. Some time passed. Suspicions were lulled. On June 17, one of the party secured a private audience with the prince and his interpreter with the promise of important news. Coming near, he drew a dagger and struck. Edward fought back and killed the assassin, but not before he had been badly wounded with a weapon believed to be poisoned. In legend, either his wife, Eleanor of Castile, sucked the venom from the wound and saved his life or his friend Othon de Grandson did, but the following day the spread of infection caused Edward to write his will and prepare for the worst. He was saved by radical and painful surgery, the doctor cutting away the infected flesh.

With this act, Edward's crusade was over. He departed shortly after, thwarted but resolved to return. He never did, but his two close companions, Othon de Grandson and Jean de Grailly, would. Twenty years later, these men, along with the Templar commander at nearby Tripoli in the early 1270s, Guillaume de Beaujeu, would be forming a council of war to defend Acre for the last time.

Edward's brief intervention had at least bought the city some time. By the early 1270s, Baybars must have felt himself poised for a final attempt on Tripoli and Acre, but the fear of Mongol attacks, encouraged by Edward's initiative, had led the sultan to seek other means to defuse crusader pressure and free his hands to deal with the larger problem. In

April 1272, shortly before the assassination attempt, he had signed a truce with the city of Acre of ten years, ten months, ten days, and ten hours, in the Islamic formulation. Edward had again been dismayed by the realpolitik of the Levant and had refused to participate in signing, but it had cut the ground from under his feet. When Guillaume de Beaujeu returned to Acre in 1275 as grand master of the Templars, he wrote to Edward, now king of England, to describe the state of affairs in Outremer. His account was gloomy. He feared further attacks from Baybars, who had stripped the land of its resources. Revenues from the land that they had once held were no longer coming in; the kingdom of Jerusalem was impoverished, and the Templars were faced with the increasing costs of maintaining their castles.

It seemed that only the counterpressure of the Mongols was keeping the crusader states alive. The specter of encircling alliances haunted Baybars. If it increased his desire to eradicate the Franks, it was always a secondary consideration. In the years after 1272, the sultan moved to confront the Mongols on their own territory. In 1277, he took an army through Syria into Anatolia—southern Turkey—where he inflicted a shattering defeat on a Mongol army; but with a second Mongol force on its way, he deemed it wise to retreat.

WITHIN EUROPE, THE enthusiasm for crusading ventures was dying. Teobaldo Visconti, the former patriarch in Acre, now Pope Gregory X, set about energetically trying to rally support. In 1274, he called a council to discuss the organization of a new crusade. Only a single crowned monarch came, and the lack of enthusiasm was resounding. One veteran of both of Louis IX's crusades, Érard de Valéry, who did attend and was wise to the realities of confronting the Mamluks, commented that the puny resources that could now be mustered against the infidel were like a small puppy yelping at a mastiff.

It was a blunt assessment of the difficulties facing any crusading venture. The initiative collapsed with Gregory's death in 1276. Baybars himself died in Damascus the following year after drinking fermented mare's milk while watching a polo game. Poison was suggested, but rumors of foul play routinely circulated around a sultan's death.

Although the Mamluk succession was traditionally a tribal election process among the leading emirs with no hereditary prerogatives,
Baybars attempted to make his son sultan. He failed. The sultanate
required the building of a confederacy of support and was frequently
a bloody process. After some years of confusion, it was one of Baybars's most trusted and successful generals, al-Mansur Qalawun, who
emerged as sultan in 1280. Qalawun was about sixty, and he had been
a leading commander in several of Baybars's campaigns. He belonged
to the same Kipchak tribe as Baybars and had been enslaved quite
late so never became fluent in Arabic. Like Baybars, he was not initially popular in Cairo. For several months he feared to go about the
streets, and when he did, the people provided the traditional show of
contempt by pelting him with offal. But he wisely followed Baybars's
example, carrying out public works and showing piety toward orthodox Sunni Islam, even if he never quite shook off his Turkish roots.
He was said to have retained some of the shamanistic practices of his
steppe origins, such as predicting the future from the shoulder bones
of sheep.

Qalawun, however, was an astute and successful general, fully
aware of the greater threat of the Mongols and equally wary of possible alliances with the Christians. Between 1276 and 1291 the
Mongols sent six embassies to the courts of the west. They achieved
nothing. The distances and the communication times, and growing
disenchantment with large crusading ventures, ensured that such coordinated plans remained in the realms of fantasy. The death of Baybars had (however temporarily) eased the pressure on Acre.

Within the enclaves on the coast of the Levant, feuding continued unabated. Bohemond VII, count of Tripoli, was at war with the
Templars; a contest between Charles of Anjou and the kings of Cyprus for the title of king of Jerusalem rumbled on between 1277 and
1285, while the friction between Genoa and its rivals ensured continuous disruption. These schisms were reflected on the streets of Acre.
Hugh III, king of Cyprus and nominally of Jerusalem, left the city in
1276 and returned to Cyprus, regarding the place as ungovernable. In
1286, the French contingent at Acre refused to accept the claim of

his son Henry II to be king in Acre and temporarily barricaded themselves in the royal castle, denying him access. The following year, as the storm clouds were gathering once more, the Genoese were blockading the port and fighting with the Pisans in the city streets.

Qalawun's preoccupation with the menace of the Mongols made him keen to neutralize the Franks at his rear. He signed truces with the Hospitallers' stronghold at Margat in the Lebanon and with Bohemond VII as Count of Tripoli in 1281 in order to have his hands free to confront the Mongol threat. That year, he put the Mongols to flight at the battle of Homs in Syria—a nominal victory that cost him as many men as his opponents. Securing his position against internal revolts from the Bedouins and dissident factions prevented any sense of threat to Outremer.

In 1283, Qalawun signed another ten-year truce with Acre by the terms of which he specifically also bound the Hospitallers and the Templars. As independent entities not answerable to the commune of Acre and as the most effective military forces, they had a history of wriggling free of agreements that they had not personally signed. One signatory to this agreement was Guillaume de Beaujeu, now grand master of the Templars, who would have cause to reexamine the document's exact wording just a few years later.

Critical to Qalawun's bid to counter multiple threats was the desire to build up the core group of Mamluks, a reliable military cadre loyal to the sultan and his group of emirs. The slave trade gathered pace in the second half of the thirteenth century, consisting of kidnapped or displaced tribal peoples from the shores of the Black Sea, traded through Constantinople on Genoese ships, or from ports in southern Turkey. He had agents in the Black Sea to facilitate this trade, critical to his mission. He obtained many more Mamluks than Baybars ever had, a figure of somewhere between 6,000 and 12,000, from further-flung places. Some of the captured who entered his service were even of Greek or Prussian origin.

The victory over the Mongols may have been pyrrhic, but it quieted the frontiers of Syria and, in time, Qalawun turned his attention back to the Franks. Despite the spirit of jihad, the desire to rid the

Islamic world of the Europeans was in large measure defensive. The prospect of fresh incursions from the west never died, nor did the fear of a pincer movement—that the Islamic world could be caught in an alliance between Christians and Mongols. In 1285, Qalawun besieged and took the powerful Hospitaller fort of Margat, a loss that further shook Christian morale. In 1287, he occupied the coastal port of Latakia. Now all that was left in Christian hands was Tripoli, Acre, and a few other fortified coastal enclaves, such as Tyre and Sidon.

THE MAMLUK THREAT was drawing ever closer, but Acre was living out its last few years with an attenuated splendor. With the death of Charles of Anjou in January 1285, the long-running contest for the crown of the shrinking kingdom of Jerusalem was over. In August 1286, the coronation of his rival, the sixteen-year-old Henry II of Cyprus, took place in Tyre. Henry then came to Acre for festivities that lasted a fortnight in the grand hall of the Hospitallers' compound. "It was," according to the chronicles, "the loveliest festival anyone had seen for a hundred years, with amusements and jousts with blunted lances. They re-enacted stories of the round table . . . with knights dressed up like women jousting together. Then they had nuns who were dressed as monks and who jousted together, and they role-played Lancelot and Tristan and Pilamedes and many other fair and delightful and pleasant scenes."[10] It was a decadent fantasy in the face of known facts, but beneath the brawling, the fighting, the feuds, and the bombardments, Acre sustained a late flowering of medieval culture.

The time that Louis IX spent here after his disastrous crusade had stimulated Acre. Although never a major center of learning—it was more an administrative hub, a launch pad for crusader armies and a warehouse for merchants—the city was energetic and vibrant. With its come-and-go of peoples, it attracted cultured visitors, leading churchmen, and kings. Francis of Assisi had preached here, and its last half century saw the development of a school of book production, painting, and manuscript illumination, ranging from copies of the Bible to editions of the classics and histories of the crusades. In the margins of these volumes, the illustrators portrayed the world they knew: mailed crusaders, weapons, ships and castles, silk pavilions, coronations and kings. An element of oriental sophistication softened this crusader world. The common use of glass in the windows of houses, fine carpets and textiles, new tastes and cuisines—olive oil, citrus fruits, sugar and spices—all contributed to a sense of the exotic.

Nearly half a century after its fall, the German traveler Ludolf von Suchem conjured a wistful and romantic portrait of Acre's splendor, though there was perhaps some measure of truth. He described the city, of which he could see only the ruins standing, as

> on the sea-shore, built of square hewn stones of more than usual size, with lofty and exceeding strong towers, not a stone's throw distant from one another all round the walls. Each gate of the city stood between two towers and the walls were so great that two carts driving along the top of them could easily pass one another, even as they are at the present day. On the other side also, toward the land, the city was fenced with notable walls and exceeding deep ditches, and variously equipped with divers outer works and defences, and conveniences for watchmen.[11]

He imagined the palaces "adorned with glass windows and paintings" and houses "not built merely to meet the needs of those who dwelt therein, but to minister to human luxury and pleasure . . . the streets of the city were covered with silken cloths, or other fair awnings, to keep off the sun's rays. At every street corner there stood an exceeding strong tower, fenced with an iron door and chains." He painted a world of court ceremonial in which "princes, dukes, counts, nobles, and barons walked about the streets in royal state, with golden coronets on their heads, each of them like a king, with his knights, his followers, his mercenaries, and his retainers, his clothing and his war horse wondrously bedecked with gold and silver," the military orders with their headquarters and their garrisons, the many churches, and also "the richest merchants under heaven, who were gathered together therein out of all nations" and where "everything that can be found in the world that is wondrous or strange used to be bought thither."[12] Evidently, there were such shows of extravagant splendor. When the sultan of Homs came to Acre in 1252, the city "greeted him with such honour in Acre that cloth of gold and silk was laid on the ground everywhere he went."[13]

Generations of stone masons, many of them Muslim slaves, had constructed this city of splendor and filth, with its Romanesque and Gothic churches, its monasteries and chapels, its double walls and its foul-smelling harbor and spice bazaars. Beauty there certainly was. A Muslim writer described the portal of one of these churches as "one of the most marvellous things made by man, for it is of white marble and of wonderful shape and of the highest quality of workmanship . . . the bases, capitals and shafts being all of one piece."[14] The impressive castle of the Templars stood perched on the edge of the sea, a landmark for arriving ships. Out toward the city walls was the equally imposing compound of the Knights Hospitallers, with its extensive series of pillared halls, undercrofts, courtyards, and towers that combined the functions of palace, fortress, infirmary, and church. Acre in its heyday rivalled Alexandria and Constantinople as a great emporium. To live here was to sense the possibility of larger worlds. After André de Longjumeau's journey to central Asia, King Louis dispatched another ambassador. The Flemish Franciscan missionary Willem van Ruysbroeck (William of Rubruck), a Marco Polo before Marco Polo, spent two years from 1253 to 1255 traveling to the court of the great Mongol khan at Karakorum and came back to Acre with his written account. Niccolo and Maffeo Polo, Marco's father and uncle, who traded in the city, followed in his footsteps. They returned here in 1269 after their first expedition east, a nine-year journey to China. In 1271, they set out from Acre again, this time taking Marco with them.

WHILE THE NOBILITY were play-fighting with blunted lances, they were also doing what they could to shore up the city's defenses. The last half of the thirteenth century saw concerted reinforcement of the walls and the addition of new towers at individual initiative and expense. The work intensified as the Mamluks drew closer. Louis IX, after the debacle on the Nile, had completed the fortification of the new suburb of Montmusard in 1250; Edward's English Tower of 1271–1272 was accompanied by the construction nearby of a barbican—an external defensive structure connected to the main wall by a walkway—by King Hugh III of Cyprus. In 1286, his son Henry II built a stout, round tower at the very northeastern tip of the outer walls. This, known informally as the King's Tower, was designed to buttress defense of the critical Accursed Tower. It was fronted with a further defensive curtain wall. The following year, Alice, Countess of Blois, also funded an adjacent tower that bore her name and gave money for strengthening the wall that protected Montmusard. One year after that, the pope advanced a loan to the patriarch and papal legate Nicolas de Hanapes to carry out repairs to the moat and walls and to rebuild a further tower gate, that of the Patriarch, to watch over the seaward end of the east wall. One witness to this late spurt of defensive building was the Venetian statesman and geographer Marino Sanudo Torsello. Sanudo was a widely traveled observer of the Mediterranean world and the front lines between Islam and Christendom. Toward the end of 1286, he spent several months in Acre and produced an invaluable contemporary plan of its walls, towers, and the internal layout of the city.

Barring two years when Saladin had occupied it and turned the cathedral church of the Holy Cross into a mosque, Acre had been a Christian city for nearly two hundred years. The city held a population of about 40,000, many of whose families were deeply settled in the Holy Land and had lived there for generations. Baybars, for all his raids and devastations of Acre's hinterland, had never brought siege engines and mining teams to seriously threaten its defenses. Its resolve and its walls awaited a final test.

6

WAR TO THE ENEMY

Winter 1288–Autumn 1290

DURING THE WINTER of 1288, two men arrived in Alexandria to speak to Qalawun. They had come from the County of Tripoli. By now this crusader kingdom had been reduced to a tiny enclave on the coast of Lebanon, consisting of nothing more than the city itself, but still a valuable port used by the Venetians and the Genoese. It was hamstrung by factional disputes over its governance after the death of the ruler Bohemond VI and had almost descended into anarchy. In this situation, it seemed likely that the Genoese would get the upper hand. This would potentially give Genoa control of both the lucrative Black Sea slave trade and commerce with northern Syria.

The visitors had a tale to tell: a Genoese coup in Tripoli would allow them to dominate regional trade, and this would be detrimental to the sultan's interests. Without the Genoese, Tripoli could arm ten to fifteen galleys:

> But now that the Genoese have it within their grasp, they will be able to arm thirty of them, for they will flock to Tripoli from everywhere; and if they have Tripoli, they will be lords of the seas, and it will turn out that those who will come to Alexandria will be at their mercy, both going and coming and within the port itself, and this thing bodes very ill for merchants who do business in your kingdom.[1]

These words were reported by an exceedingly well-informed resident of Acre whose identity has never been satisfactorily established.
He may or may not have been a knight called Gérard de Montréal,
but he is generally known to history more anonymously as the Templar of Tyre. He seems to have been a minor noble of the leading
families of the kingdom of Jerusalem, and while in the service of the
Order, was not himself a Templar. As an Arabic speaker, he acted
as translator, adviser, and probably intelligence officer to Guillaume
de Beaujeu, grand master of the Templars. The Templar chronicler
was about thirty-five years old, continuously close to events in the
kingdom of Jerusalem—and he would leave the most vivid Christian eyewitness account of the siege of Acre in the spring of 1291,
even if his judgments were probably slanted in favor of the order that
he served.

He evidently knew the nationality of Qalawun's visitors—"I could
tell you who they were if I were so inclined"—but he was not saying.[2]
In all likelihood, they were Venetians, and the merchants who would
be particularly disadvantaged by a Genoese coup in Tripoli would
be their own. The hostility between the three Italian city-states had
continued unabated since the War of St. Sabas, with the Venetians
and the Pisans generally siding together and the Genoese striving
to reestablish their lost position on the coast. The two Venetians
were probably there to finalize negotiations for Venice's own trade
privileges with the Mamluks, which were accorded in November of
that year, and the opportunity to discredit the Genoese was one not
to be missed. Their report provided Qalawun with the incentive and
opportunity to proceed against Tripoli, since his truce with the city
had been agreed to personally with its ruler Bohemond VII. With his
recent death, it was now void. Continuous factional disputes were
helping to shake the remnants of Outremer apart.

IN JANUARY 1289, the Mamluk army began to assemble near Cairo,
and logistical preparations were made for a campaign. Following the
practice of Baybars, no objective was stated; but in Acre, Guillaume
de Beaujeu was soon aware that Tripoli was to be the target. The

source of all the information leaking out of the Mamluk court was one of Qalawun's own emirs, Badr al-Din Bektash al-Fakhri. The Arabic-speaking Templar of Tyre was quite frank about Beaujeu's arrangements with this man. "This emir was the Emir *Silah* [in charge of the weapons], and he was used to warning the master of the Temple of matters profitable to Christendom, when the sultan wished to harm Christianity in any way, and this service cost the master valuable presents, which he sent him each year."[3] The game of spies was played by both sides. Qalawun had his own informants within Acre, including a man called Jawan Khandaq, who reported back on crusader maneuvers.

When the grand master of the Templars, Guillaume de Beaujeu, warned Tripoli, he was not believed. The grand master was notorious for his political machinations. It was thought to be a ruse. Meanwhile, the Mamluks advanced with their usual thoroughness; supply dumps were established along the way, wood cut for siege engines and protective screens, volunteers rallied to the cause. Beaujeu sent a second messenger, but the factional intrigues continued unabated until the sultan's army was almost in view of the city in late March 1289.

Last-minute reinforcements marched up the coast from Acre. The Templars and the Hospitallers each sent detachments under the command of their marshals, Geoffroi de Vendac and Matthieu de Clermont. A French detachment went under Jean de Grailly, and Henry II, king of Jerusalem and Cyprus, sent his younger brother Amalric, only about seventeen years old at the time, with knights and four galleys.

Tripoli was not an easy place to besiege without a fleet, and Qalawun did not have one. In the description by the Syrian nobleman Abu al-Fida, who was present at the siege, "The sea surrounds most of this city and no land engagement is possible except on the east side, where there is little space."[4] However, the Mamluks' practiced siege craft was formidable, and the sultan had assembled a sizeable army. According to the Templar, "The sultan set up his siege engines, both great and small, and erected his *buches* [wooden protective screens] in front of the town and his *carabohas* [smaller siege engines] and devastated the surrounding countryside and tunnelled his mines underneath the ground and got inside the first defensive ditches."[5]

Despite Tripoli's spirited resistance, the skills and resources of the Mamluks were impossible to match. They quickly identified the weakest spot—the aging Bishop's Tower. "The siege engines battered it so fiercely that it was completely shattered," reported the Templar. "Similarly, the Hospitallers' tower, which was very strong and newly constructed, was so badly split apart that a horse could pass through the middle. The sultan had so many men that at each position twenty Saracen archers were deployed to shoot, so that none of our crossbowmen dared expose themselves to fire either bows or crossbows. If they tried to, they were immediately hit."[6]

With the city's situation deteriorating, the Venetians, largely responsible for the debacle, were the first to leave. They loaded their ships and sailed off, quickly followed by their rivals the Genoese. Morale drained away. On April 26, Qalawun ordered a general assault and overwhelmed Tripoli's resistance, "because it lacked sufficient defenders, who one by one had abandoned the defence."[7] There was a rout and a rush for the port. The nobility got away—the Templar and Hospitaller lords; the nominal ruler of Tripoli, Countess Lucia; Jean de Grailly; and Prince Amalric. It was the poor who bore the brunt. Most of the men were slaughtered, the women and children taken captive. As a last-ditch refuge, many took rowing boats or swam to the small offshore island of St. Thomas and sheltered in its church, but there was no escape. "I was a witness of the siege," wrote Abu al-Fida. "When Tripoli was taken, a vast number of Franks and women fled to the island and its church. The Muslim army plunged into the sea and swam across to the island on horseback. They killed all the men and took the women and children as booty. After the people had made an end of plundering, I crossed to this island in a ship and found it full of the slain, so that one could not stay there because of the stench of the slain."[8]

Qalawun demolished Tripoli and founded a new city a few miles inland. The intention was clear: to extirpate the infidels from the shores of Palestine and to make any return impossible, and the plunder had whetted the popular appetite for new conquests. Abu al-Fida piously recorded precisely, if somewhat inaccurately, the occupiers' tenure of Tripoli. "The Franks had captured Tripoli on 11 Dhu'l-Hijjah [July 1, 1110] and it remained in their hands until the early part of this year 688 [1289]. So, the space of time it remained with the Franks was about 185 years and some months."[9] Twelve hundred men were retained for forced labor and marched off to Alexandria to work on building the sultan's new arsenal.

BOTH CHRISTIANS AND Muslims recognized the significance of Tripoli's fall. It had been the Franks' longest continuous possession in Palestine. Its loss seemed like the harbinger of an end game, and the news reverberated around Europe. Now only the coastal strip of the kingdom of Jerusalem remained, with Acre as its one stronghold. In 1283, Qalawun had signed a truce with the kingdom, its duration being "ten complete years, ten months, ten days and ten hours, beginning on Thursday, 3 Haziran 1594 of the era of Alexander, the son of Philip the Greek."[10] The Muslims generally abided devoutly by such legal agreements, sworn in the name of God, but these were always of limited duration—and there were always loopholes. There could be a truce but never permanent peace. With theological belief in the eventual universal spread of Islam, an underlying state of war with infidel peoples was a basic tenet of its jurists.

However, during the negotiations of 1283, Qalawun had privately acknowledged the ongoing economic advantages of peaceful relations with the Latin Kingdom, "for Acre is a caravanserai to which our merchants resort, a place from which comes a wider range of choice for us," and this line of thinking prevailed in Acre.[11] It had become complacently accepted that the Frankish presence there would remain tolerated because the commercial benefits that it provided to the Islamic world rendered it too valuable to annihilate. The fate of Tripoli now suggested otherwise. Within the Mamluk army, there was considerable enthusiasm for an attack on Acre. Both the spirit of jihad and the lure of booty had given the notion considerable momentum, and the survivors' tales shocked the complacent merchants of Jacques de Vitry's corrupted and luxury-loving city. For those who could see, the writing was on the wall.

Three days after the fall, King Henry himself came to Acre from Cyprus to find an envoy of Qalawun already there, complaining that the aid sent to Tripoli had been a breach of the 1283 truce. He was outflanked on a technicality: the truce had only applied to the kingdom of Jerusalem. If it had applied also to Tripoli, Qalawun had broken the truce first. The logic of Henry's case was unimpeachable. He sent an embassy back to Qalawun in Damascus requesting a further ten-year extension to the truce, to which the sultan agreed, lulling suspicion while he dealt with trouble in Nubia. A better justification would be required for Qalawun to mount a final assault. Within the year, his secretariat would be given a more favorable opportunity to scrutinize the terms of the truce, in which the commercial interests of Muslim merchants would again be at stake.

Henry sailed back to Cyprus in September, leaving his young brother Amalric, lord of Tyre, as constable of Jerusalem and regent of Acre. At the same time, he dispatched Jean de Grailly to Europe to warn Western potentates about the severity of the situation. Grailly arrived in Rome to meet the recently elected pope, Nicholas IV. Nicholas was intensely keen on a major new crusade involving the titled monarchs of Europe, but the difficulties were immense. Europe was completely preoccupied by the contest between King James II of Aragon and the Angevin kingdom in southern Italy, supported by the papacy, for the lordship of Sicily. The so-called Wars of the Sicilian Vespers split Europe down the middle. Great hope was invested in Edward I, now king of England and the only monarch with crusading experience, who expressed continuous commitment to the Holy Land. He had taken the cross again in 1287 with the intention of proceeding east but was preoccupied with attempts to conquer Scotland. Others were pursuing their own interests. Just as Nicholas was trying to rally a crusade, emissaries from Aragon were in Cairo, signing a treaty with Qalawun. As far as any support for Acre was concerned, a critical clause read,

if one of the Franks of Acre, Tyre, the Coastlands or elsewhere, being in truce with our lord the Sultan, break the conditions of the
truce established between himself and them, thereby annulling the
truce, the king of Aragon and his brothers, horsemen, knights and
the people of his territory shall not assist them with horses, horsemen, weapons, treasure, aid, supplies, vessels, galleys or otherwise.[12]

At the same time, the Genoese, having launched a bad-tempered
raid on Alexandria, had patched up their relationship and also signed
a new commercial arrangement with Qalawun. The trade advantages
to both sides, including the supply of war materials, were considerable.

The Genoese, who had been largely excluded from Acre since the
War of St. Sabas, had few commercial interests in the city. The Venetians, however, had many. They were quite happy to see the Genoese lose their base in Tripoli, a loss in which they were implicated.
Acre was a different matter. The pope's attempts to coax the crowned
heads of Europe and the supporting sea power of the Italian maritime
republics into a major crusade was doomed to fail in the short run, but
the urgency of the situation called for some response, even if more
limited in scope. Four months after the fall of Tripoli, the call to crusade was being preached in Venice, throughout northern Italy, and
along the Adriatic coast. Nicolas de Hanapes, the newly appointed
bishop of Acre, was invested with powers to oversee the whole venture. These included the right to excommunicate those in Acre who
proved intransigent. The funds that the pope had entrusted to Nicolas de Hanapes were put to use repairing and strengthening walls and
outworks, gathering munitions and armaments, and for the construction of powerful trebuchets. Further finance was raised from church
taxation and bankers. Emissaries from the Mongols had also visited
Rome, increasing the pope's hopes of a vast anti-Mamluk campaign,
but none of these grander plans came to fruition. In January 1290, the
pope issued a general encyclical exhorting people to take the crusade.

This call had little effect. It had become impossible to unify the
leaders of Christendom around crusader projects. The Venetians

provided twenty galleys under the command of Niccolò Tiepolo, a son of the doge. Edward I, who still hoped to come on crusade, ended up sending his trusted lieutenant, Othon de Grandson, both a capable organizer and a good fighter, with just sixty knights, with the intention that he would take charge of the English knights of the Order of St. Thomas in Acre. The Aragonese king of Sicily, James II, had offered to provide 30 galleys and 10,000 infantry, but political wrangling with the papacy cut this number ultimately to just five galleys and a small Spanish force—and without James himself.

The popular response to a crusade was similarly unpromising. Northern Italy was the only region to participate, and none of the great barons, who could contribute professional soldiers and inspiration, signed up. Instead, the main recruits were most likely from Tuscany and Lombardy, a mix of urban militias, mercenaries, and citizens, together with a less-disciplined contingent of peasants and the unemployed. Religious piety was mingled with the idea of adventure and the possibility of booty. This contingent did not inspire confidence.

The pope sought information on the preparation of the fleet for which he had laid out money, and he was not impressed by what he learned. The fitting out had been inadequate, and the supply of weapons (particularly crossbows) left a lot to be desired. Unsatisfactory as these resources might be, they were all that were available. In January 1290, the fleet was considered ready to sail, with at best 3,000 men. Tiepolo was its captain, while the command of the crusaders was shared among Nicolas de Hanapes, Jean de Grailly, and Bernard, bishop of Tripoli, who had escaped the city's final collapse. Hanapes was the central figure of the expedition and would prove to be the sole unifying force within Acre itself. His triple offices of bishop, patriarch, and papal legate—the latter title giving him automatic authority over the military orders in the pope's name—granted him a key position in Acre. The pope had already written to all the city's factions, to Amalric, to the masters of the military orders, to the leaders of the Venetian and Pisan communities, and to the community of Acre at large, urging them to stand firm in the defense of the Holy Land and to lend support and wise counsel to Hanapes. But it appeared to the patriarch upon arrival that his ability to exert control over the city, despite his sweeping powers of interdiction and his triple authority, was quite limited. His reception was little better than the one Jacques de Vitry had received eighty years earlier. He quickly became aware of the lack of any coherent plan of action or strategy for facing an approaching storm. His reports about the disunity of Acre stunned the pope, who wrote back chiding the authorities there.

At Sicily, the expedition was met by the five galleys of King James—evidently not banned from mounting this token expedition, as Acre's truce with Qalawun had not formally been broken. The fleet, eventually consisting of only thirteen ships, reached Acre in the spring, and Tiepolo and James's galleys departed fairly soon after. "There landed at the gates of Acre 1600 pilgrims and soldiers, aggressive men," some eyewitnesses recorded later.[13] They probably docked on April 2, 1290, Easter Day. This was the traditional time for pilgrims and Western merchants to come to the kingdom of Jerusalem, and Muslim merchants from Damascus would also visit, as if to a trade fair, along with local Muslim peasantry bringing produce to sell. The newly arrived pilgrims, who stepped ashore with a heightened religious zeal to fight for the faith, found themselves in the bustling, confusing metropolis of Jacques de Vitry's description, among unfamiliar-looking people in all kinds of oriental dress, the temptations of a port city, and the presence of Muslims. When no immediate attack from the Mamluks was forthcoming, many of the crusaders sailed home, leaving behind a group of the poorer members of the expedition, who were without funds or purpose. It was a recipe for trouble.

At some time during this trading season, most likely August, in circumstances that have never been clearly established, the ill-disciplined adventurers, "common people" from northern Italy, it was reported, attacked some of the Muslim merchants and killed them.[14] The Templar of Tyre, who was probably on the scene, gave his account:

And when these people came to Acre, the truce which the king had made with the sultan was being well maintained between the two parties, and the poor Saracen peasants came to Acre, bringing their goods to sell, as they had been accustomed to do. It happened, by the workings of the Enemy from Hell, who desires to stir up evil among good people, that the crusaders who had come to do good and to bring their arms to help the city of Acre, brought it to destruction, because one day they rampaged through Acre, put to the sword all the poor peasants carrying their merchandise to Acre to sell—both wheat and other things. These were Saracens from the villages around Acre, and they also killed some Syrians who were of the law of Greece [the Greek orthodox church]. They killed them because by their beards they were mistaken for Saracens.[15]

Inactivity and frustration, drunkenness, the fact that they had not been paid a promised stipend, religious fervor, the desire for action—multiple motives were ascribed. Other variant accounts were given. "They cut down nineteen Saracen merchants in Acre in a place called Lafunda near the exchange," the royal market where the Muslim caravans arrived.[16] Some of the Arab accounts suggested that the culprits were driven by greed, that the merchants had been on their way to Cairo with military slaves from the Black Sea and had been murdered for their goods and the slaves stolen. The citizens and authorities of the town attempted to rescue those being set upon by the mob and secured all whom they could in the royal castle. In yet another version, the ill-disciplined rabble "early in the morning, unable to be restrained by the townspeople and without danger to themselves, left the city armed and with flags unfurled, and made their way to the farms and villages up toward the hills. They indiscriminately killed without pity all the Saracens they came across— men who believed they were peacefully secure—then carried back all the trophies they had with great rejoicing. 'Alas, what grief,'" was the coda to the chronicler's account. "That dance of joy was transformed into mournful danger and sorrowful misfortune for the city of Acre and the Holy Land."[17]

HOWEVER IT HAPPENED, the authorities and established citizens of Acre were aghast. They instantly saw the potential consequences. Word soon reached Qalawun in Cairo, via spies, followed by visible proof. Relatives of the massacred Muslims carried the blood-soaked clothes to Cairo and held them aloft at communal prayers in the mosques. These gruesome relics had an electrifying effect. Qalawun was outraged. In Christian eyes, he had been given a welcome pretext for something he had long intended: "Since the sultan had already planned to harm the city of Acre anyway, he immediately sent his messengers to the lords of Acre, to make it clear that he had a truce with the Christians, and that they had broken it and killed his Saracen peasants," the Templar wrote. "And he required them to make amends and bring to justice those who had done this."[18] The Templar's reading suggests what the authorities in Acre evidently believed: that in the wake of Tripoli, Qalawun's intentions were clear and premeditated. He had both religious and economic reasons for snuffing out the last remnants of the crusader state. Whereas when the truce was signed in 1283, he had expressed the advantages of trade through Acre, now he no longer needed it. The Mamluks had taken both Antioch and Tripoli; Acre remained the sole significant obstacle on the land route along the coast of Palestine. Qalawun already had trading treaties with Genoa, Aragon, and Venice that would comfortably channel Western goods back to Alexandria, away from the Christian port where Muslim merchants were unable to trade safely anyway. There was every reason to destroy Acre.

Back in Acre, young Amalric gathered the leading figures to discuss the crisis. It was widely understood to be a disaster. How to explain it to the sultan and what response to make? There was evidently no appetite for handing over the culprits. Guillaume de Beaujeu suggested an alternative. The Templar, who was not present, gave a hearsay account of the discussions:

> Among the many words spoken between them, my lord the master of the Temple counselled that they should take all the prisoners held in the royal prison and in those of the Temple, the Hospital and of the

Pisans and Venetians, who were condemned to die for their crimes, and say that these were the men who had broken the truce and killed the Saracens. "And thus, by the justice that will strike them—since they are due to die anyway—this will appease the sultan and will check him from harming us." There were some who agreed with this plan, but many others who did not agree at all, and so it turned out that nothing was done, and they framed a reply to the sultan that seemed appropriate. According to what I could learn, they sent word to the sultan that the crusaders who had done the deed were foreigners from overseas, and not subject to their jurisdiction, who they were unable to lay their hands on.[19]

Beaujeu's plan to send Christian prisoners to die at Qalawun's hands could not be stomached. Other sources suggested that even less plausible excuses were advanced. The deaths were the result of a drunken brawl involving both Christians and Muslims. Or, a Christian woman had been caught by her husband in a sexual liaison with a Muslim man; he had killed both of them and a riot broke out. Or again, Muslims themselves had started a brawl. To the sultan, all these explanations were utterly unsatisfactory. The inability of Acre's rulers to act decisively or control people in their own territory merely highlighted the city's weakness.

But had the kingdom of Jerusalem broken the truce? The mere presence of the paltry crusading expedition might have breached it on a technicality: the terms demanded that in the event that "one of the Frankish maritime kings or others should move by sea with the intention of bringing harm to our lord the Sultan," the authorities of Acre were bound to provide two months' notice, which they had failed to do.[20] One man who must have had a shrewd idea of the treaty's stipulations was Beaujeu himself. He had been a signatory to the original document in 1283.

In Cairo, they were also busy scanning the truce's very flexible wording, though it is unclear which version—that of 1283 or the recently re-signed one of 1289. Whichever it was, the truce constituted a sacrosanct and unbreachable contract that Qalawun had sworn by the most sacred formula in the three-times-three names of God:

By Allah by Allah by Allah, in the name of Allah of Allah of Allah, the witness being Allah Allah Allah, great and pursuing, inflicting and bestowing, constructive and destructive, aware of what is revealed and what is concealed, of the secret and the manifest, merciful, forgiving; by the Qur'an and He who revealed it and him to whom it was revealed, Muhammad son of Abdallah, God bless and save him, and by all that is stated therein, chapter by chapter, verse by verse; by the month of Ramadan: I bind myself to uphold this blessed truce agreed between myself and the Commune of Acre and the grand masters who live there.[21]

These words imposed the severest standards of justice on the sultan. At the same time, it seemed likely that Qalawun was keen to find justification for a favorable answer; his reasons were not just the pursuit of jihad. Acre remained an important slave-trading center as well as a place for purchasing arms. It sat astride the north-south trade routes that linked Alexandria to ports further north and the vital supply of military slaves from the Black Sea. The threat to trade from the murder of merchants was extremely serious. Qalawun also called a meeting with his council of emirs and secretaries to discuss the matter.

Surprisingly, many of the emirs believed that the terms had not been breached—that the incident was the result of accidental brawls—and that they were bound by sacred oath to uphold it. Possibly they were also wearied of war and the burdens it imposed. Qalawun was evidently not pleased. He called in Fath al-Din, his chief of the Bureau of Correspondence, on whom fell the burden of delivering a more favorable opinion. The drafting of Mamluk treaties was a family affair: waiting in the wings were his father, Muhyi al-Din, evidently the author of the original truce document, and his nephew Shafi ibn Ali, who left an eyewitness account of the decision-making process. Fath al-Din had been asked,

"Is there any scope (for action) in the truce?"

Fath al-Din glanced at it, and did not find any scope, so then he fetched me and fetched its composer, his father Muhyi al-Din, and gave us the picture, reading the truce to us. His father said: "There is no scope in it, that is the situation."

I did not speak. Fath al-Din turned to me and said, "What do you say?"

Shafi proceeded cautiously, weighing his words to divine the sultan's wishes.

And I said, "We are with the sultan. If he prefers annulment, then it is annulled. And if he prefers it to go on then it continues." So Fath al-Din spoke to me, the essence of which was: "The emirs have grown overbearing and lazy; the sultan prefers annulling it."

I said to him: "We are with the sultan." I pointed to one of the sections of the truce, which was: *And on condition, when strangers arrive with intent to harm the Muslims, the authorities and the governor must protect them from harm to the full extent of their ability. If they are unable, they are to look closely into the matter and make good what was done.*

They [the authorities in Acre] had agreed that this harm to Muslims happened from Franks from abroad. Fath al-Din was delighted with that, and informed the sultan about it, and he started preparations immediately. He went out from the great tent and raised troops to go straight towards them.[22]

7

"My Soul Longed for Jihad"
Autumn 1290–March 1291

Q ALAWUN HAD BEEN intending to join the annual autumn pilgrimage to Mecca but abandoned this to plan for war. Nevertheless, he made pious arrangements for the protection of the pilgrims departing in October, while starting to make preparations against Acre:

> He organised an army to go to the Hijaz [in the Arabian Peninsula] for the pilgrimage to Mecca, and an army to the invasion to overcome the people of Akka [Acre], and many riders to the Hijaz to carry provisions to every needy person, and riders to the people of the House of War to carry weapons and equipment to every warrior. He prepared a banner to go to Mecca the protected by God to increase the two kinds of knowledge, and a banner to the land of the Franks.[1]

At about the same time, the sultan's health started to fail.

Despite this, he continued to mobilize the Mamluk war machine: the gathering of supplies and materials, the raising of troops, the orders to his emirs and vassal tributaries. Fast messengers were dispatched. Carrier pigeons flew. The requirements were both human and material. Muhyi al-Din related that Qalawun

> called all the troops to assemble on the appointed day and spent on the group of emirs sums of money which could not be counted, and

whose benefaction could not be reckoned, and despatched a large part of the great arsenal, the like of which had not been prepared at any time previous, or in any invasion before. He ordered them to proceed, and they went forward. He used a large group of stone-masons and craftsmen drawn from the blacksmiths and carpenters, and money was spent on all. He wrote to all the lands of Syria to bring out catapults, machines, equipment and weapons, and bring out oxen from the lands on account of the [transporting of the] catapults and bring out men with their provisions from every town according to what it could provide.[2]

Supply dumps of food and fodder were established along the five-hundred-mile route through the Sinai desert and up the coast of Palestine to provide for the army from Cairo and its vast concourse of animals. Forty miles south of Acre, and almost under the gaze of the Templar castle of Chateau Pèlerin on the headland at Atlit, the emir Rukn al-Din Taqsu al-Mansuri was putting his men to work felling wood for field fortifications. It was given out that this was in preparation for a campaign in Africa.

The people of Acre should not have been deceived. Al-Fakhri, Guillaume de Beaujeu's mole in the Mamluk court, informed the grand master that Qalawun was preparing for war. As had been the case with Tripoli, this was not believed in Acre's ruling council. Beaujeu's reputation for political machinations, the complexity of his relationship with Mamluk spies and double agents, and presumably past incidences of crying "wolf"—as well as the Mamluks' own strategies of disinformation—meant that these reliable warnings would repeatedly go unheeded.

At some point, it seems that the increasingly concerned Beaujeu sent his own unofficial delegation to Cairo in an attempt to head off war. Qalawun asked for a massive indemnity—a sequin per head of the whole population. This was indignantly refused in council, as it was probably intended to be, and for his pains, some accused Beaujeu of treason.

As if the reality of war threat needed repeating, the Muslim garrison at Jenin, thirty-five miles to the southeast of Acre, was soon tasked with protecting the trade route to Damascus and forcing the people of Acre back within their walls. In the Arabic sources, the emir Sunqur al-Massah was ordered "to ride every day with the soldiery opposite the fortress of Akka [Acre] and keep safe the coast and the merchants fearful of the people of Akka. All the time wars and incidents were taking place between him and the people of Akka, and he was victorious."[3]

By the end of October, Qalawun had all preparations in hand. "It only remained to put his foot in the stirrup. He rode from his castle . . . Aquarius was in the ascendant, Mars was in his glory."[4] A magnificent ceremonial departure from Cairo was staged. "It was a great procession, the like of which had not been seen for pageantry, and numbers, and majesty. The messengers of the kings attended him, he camped by the Gate of Victory—the customary station— and only the journey remained."[5] But the momentum of war was unexpectedly stalled. Qalawun's illness worsened. He wasted away, probably struck down by dysentery. "The advance becomes a delay," wrote Muhyi al-Din.

> This was because our master was overtaken by a disease with which he had been struggling for a time and was resigned to bear. His pain only increased, and the tent ropes were cut, and the Book told of his appointed time. His armies did not protect him, neither his troops, nor his delegations, nor his gatherings, nor his spears, his swords, his weapons, and not his fortresses nor his horses, his strongholds nor his towns. He was taken in the middle of his many machines, his number was him alone, and with this the jungle was stricken by the loss of its lion, and Islam by its support.[6]

Qalawun died on November 10. He had been a great sultan, at least the equal of Baybars in his campaigns against the Mongols and the Christians, and more honorable in his dealings with both friends and foes.

THE CAREFULLY LAID plans for the campaign were thrown into disarray. The Templar of Tyre recounted that when the news reached Acre, the people "had rejoiced greatly and believed themselves saved."[7] They reasoned that it would take a successor a year to stabilize his reign, given the power struggles involved in Mamluk successions. It was a false hope. His son al-Ashraf al-Malik Khalil had been active in managing Qalawun's affairs during his decline, and the day following his death, the twenty-seven-year-old Khalil was proclaimed sultan.

Qalawun's body was carried back to Cairo, there to await later burial in a fitting mausoleum. Khalil had sworn to continue the campaign. In any case, it made all sense to push forward and legitimize his rule in the febrile world of Mamluk politics with a unifying conquest: the momentum of the Mamluk war machine was now almost unstoppable, and it would be perilous for a new sultan to stall. The inheritance of the Mamluk sultanate was not hereditary. Leadership had to be earned. It depended on the support of powerful emirs, and its withdrawal could be swift and bloody.

Khalil was Qalawun's younger and less favored son, and he had enemies. Many had attached themselves to al-Salih Ali, his older brother, and found themselves out of favor at his death, among them Turuntay, the viceroy of Egypt. (The fact that Ali's death was attributed by some to poison at Khalil's hands was due less to its likelihood than to his relative unpopularity.) Qalawun himself had been concerned about Khalil's judgment and had not wanted him to succeed. "I would never give the Muslims a ruler like Khalil," he once remarked.[8]

Nevertheless, the new sultan was brave, energetic, and ruthless. Unlike his father, he spoke and wrote Arabic well, was admired for his mastery of the traditional Mamluk military skills of horsemanship and archery, and led armies in person. He also had expansionist dreams. He was energetic and wasted no time: "He went down from his castle to the camp every day and was informed at the start of it of all matters, and put into order the affairs of the people, and returned to his castle late at night."[9]

On November 18, he arrested Egyptian viceroy Turuntay and put him to death. Khalil also sent posthaste with orders to detain the emir Sunqur al-Massah, skirmishing outside the walls of Acre, on a trumped-up charge of conspiring with the enemy but probably as a supporter of the executed Turuntay. To survive as sultan required striking the first blow. Some emirs were detained, while others were promoted to powerful positions with the bestowing of honorific robes, but dissenters still lingered in the new sultan's circle and army command. Their murmurings would ripple throughout the campaign ahead.

Revising the time table, the armies and tributaries of Syria were ordered to be readied by March for a spring campaign and to provide trebuchets, masons, carpenters, miners, and soldiers. Acre was warned of the blow about to fall. The Templar of Tyre was soon translating into French a letter addressed to his master Guillaume de Beaujeu. It removed any lingering doubts as to Khalil's ambitions. It read:

> The Sultan of Sultans, King of Kings, Lord of Lords, al-Malik al-Ashraf, the powerful, the Dreadful, the Punisher of Rebels, Hunter of Franks and Tartars and Armenians, Snatcher of castles from the hands of Miscreants, Lord of the Two Seas, Guardian of the Two Pilgrim Sites, Khalil al-Salihi. To You the noble Master of the Temple, the true and wise, greetings and our good will. Because you have been a true man, we send you letters of our intentions, and give you to understand that we are coming into your regions to right these wrongdoings. Therefore, we do not want the community of Acre to send us any letters or presents, for we will in no way accept them.[10]

"I took the translation," the Templar went on, "and showed it to my lord the master and to all the lords of Acre. It was made known to the Patriarch and Legate, to the master of the Hospital, Brother Jean de Villiers, and to the commander of the Germans . . . and I showed it to the Pisan consul and to the Venetian bailli, who were completely unwilling to accept that the sultan was coming, almost until he was very close."[11] Given the visible signs over the past few months—the cutting of wood for siege works and the skirmishing outside the walls—such blindness was a willful avoidance of the evidence.

Notwithstanding the sultan's peremptory order to attempt no further diplomatic sweetening, it was decided to make one last initiative to stave off the inevitable. In January, four brave men were dispatched to Cairo to plead the case—the Arabic-speaking Sir Philip de Mainboeuf, a "knight of Acre";[12] Bartholomew Pisan, a Templar brother; a Hospitaller brother, the Catalan Lope de Linares; and a scribe called George. It was far too late. "They came before the sultan, but he refused the letters and their gift, and held the messengers in prison."[13] (The Templar of Tyre recorded that they later perished miserably, but their fates were clearly unknown to him. Some of them were still alive years later. Linares was released in 1306 after fifteen years. Mainboeuf reemerged in 1319. He had been a captive for twenty-eight years.)

Meanwhile, the preparations and the gathering of materials set in motion by Qalawun went on throughout the winter. Since at least the time of Saladin, Islamic armies had mastered the logistical skills and accrued the financial resources to prefabricate and transport large trebuchets to sieges in sections rather than build them in situ from whatever timber was available. Damascus, the arsenal and arms manufacture center of Syria, had become a center for the collection, manufacture, and distribution of catapults, and Baybars had brought these techniques to a high level of development. However, it cost a vast amount in money and human labor to gather and transport the raw materials, and these triumphs of Mamluk logistics were gained at a high price. At the siege of Arsuf in 1265, the components of the trebuchets had to be carried on the men's shoulders over patches of rough terrain. Baybars himself had recorded the difficulty of carrying the siege engines in carts through the mountains of northern Lebanon to attack Akkar in 1271. But trebuchets were an essential component of the siege train, and the Mamluks had the resources to transport very large machines across almost any landscape.

The winter weather was biting by the time the emir Shams al-Din had been dispatched by Qalawun to Wadi al-Murabbib, a valley in the mountains of Lebanon between Acre and Baalbek, to gather long baulks of timber for the siege engines. Here, trees grew to a height of up to thirty feet. It was brutally cold, and the burden of work fell heavily on the co-opted local people, both in taxation and compulsory labor. Shams al-Din himself was "surprised by an extraordinary snowfall. He nearly died. To save his own life, he was compelled to flee precipitously, abandoning his baggage and tents. Everything was buried under snow, and remained there until summer, so that a large part of the equipment was lost."[14] Nevertheless, his suffering work corps somehow managed to transport the timber to Baalbek, where it was used to make the largest trebuchets the Mamluks had ever constructed. Disassembled, these were then transported through the mountains to Damascus by late December.

IN THE COORDINATION of men and materials over vast distances, Mamluk military planning was formidable. Khalil had at his disposal methods of organizing warfare that had been finessed during the previous half century by Baybars and Qalawun. The collection point for the troops and war materials was to be Damascus, but the raw winter weather continued to impede the work. Early in the new year, a detachment was sent to Hisn al-Akrad (Krak des Chevaliers) to collect a giant trebuchet that had been constructed there. The mighty machine was dissembled and its constituent parts loaded onto carts.

Among those who participated in the transport was a young Syrian prince called Abu al-Fida: "There we took delivery of a great mangonel [trebuchet] called 'al-Mansuri' [the Victorious], which made a hundred cart loads. They were distributed among the Hama contingent, and one cart was put in my charge, for at that time I was an emir of Ten."[15] Hauling the components the eighty miles to Damascus and then on to Acre was brutal work:

Our journey with the carts was late in the winter season, and we had rain and snowstorms between Hisn al-Akrad and Damascus.

We suffered great hardship thereby because of the drawing of the carts, the oxen being weak and dying from the cold. Because of the carts we took a month from Hisn al-Akrad to Acre—usually about an eight days' journey for horses. The sultan al-Malik al-Ashraf similarly commanded mangonels to be brought there from all the fortresses.[16]

The exhausting work of hauling the siege machines went on. In February, Khalil sent his representative, the emir Izz al-Din Aybak al-Afram, to Damascus to oversee the construction of the trebuchets and other siege equipment and their conveyance on to Acre. Aybak was the sultan's senior military engineer, a man with twenty-five years of experience, going back to the early campaigns of Baybars, of the construction, supervision, and transportation of siege engines.

At the same time, there was an orchestrated campaign by Khalil to whip up religious fervor, to link his campaign to the pious memory of his father, and to unify the Levant in a holy cause. On the first day of the Islamic New Year, January 4, 1291, Qalawun's body was born in solemn procession by religious figures—sheikhs, dervishes, and qadis (judges)—first to the great al-Azhar mosque in Cairo, then to a newly constructed tomb in his magnificent mausoleum. A week before Khalil was due to depart with the main body of his army, he orchestrated a fervent ceremony and celebration at the tomb. On the night of March 2, there was a complete recitation of the Koran. The following morning, accompanied by the viceroy and vizier, a generous distribution of money and garments was made to the poor, the Koran reciters, and religious establishments. "All this was in the way of the Sultan's farewell to the tomb, because he had decided to embark on the siege of Akka."[17]

THERE WAS A symmetry to the whole arc of the crusades in the religious fervor now gripping the Islamic world. Two hundred years earlier, similar emotions had launched Christian Europe into the Holy Land while Islam was fragmented and disunited. Now it was the pope's pleas for a major crusade that were falling on deaf ears while the Muslim call to holy war proved incendiary. Holy men predicted the fate about to befall the impious Christians. The appeal to join the cause was spread by preaching in the mosques. Volunteers were moved both by the spirit of jihad and, inspired by the spoils from Tripoli, the material rewards.

Khalil set out with his army, on March 6, to cross the Sinai desert. At the moment of departure, the qadi Muhyi al-Din called down curses on Acre and a warning of the catastrophe about to fall. "Oh you, sons of the blond one [Christ], soon will God's vengeance rain down on you, of whom nothing will remain! Already al-Malik al-Ashraf is descending on your shores. Prepare to receive at his hands unbearable blows!"[18] One sheikh was said to have seen in a dream an unknown man reciting verses: "Already the Muslims have taken

Blows about to fall: launching a projectile from a trebuchet. (Oliver Poole, redrawn from *The Illustrations to the World History of Rashid al-Din*, Edinburgh, 1976)

Acre and cut off the heads of the Infidels. Our sultan has led against the enemy squadrons who have crushed beneath their feet veritable mountains. The Turks have sworn on departure not to leave an inch of soil to the Franks."[19] The air swirled with prophecy and fervor.

This excitement and keen anticipation were reflected in the eager response of Baybars al-Mansuri, governor of the strategic fortress of Kerak, taken from the crusaders by Saladin in 1188. Al-Mansuri had been ordered to provide men and equipment for the campaign. He was not expected to participate personally, but the fire of holy war spread throughout the whole society from top to bottom. As he recounted,

> At that time I was at Kerak, and when the order for this invasion reached me, and the decrees of the sultan to prepare the arsenals and the machines arrived, my soul longed for jihad, yearning for it like the craving of the thirsty earth for its rightful duty. I went up to the sultan with that and asked that I should go there to share the recompense for the attack and accompany it, and he allowed me to attend and generously granted permission, and I was like someone who had triumphed in gaining his hope, and whose night had become clear like the morning. I prepared protective arsenals [wooden screens and shelters], useful machinery, dedicated fighting men, and marksmen, stonemasons, raiders and carpenters. I went to meet the sultan and came to him while he had reached Gaza. I met with hospitality and joy and a smile from him, and I travelled with his horsemen to Akka.[20]

THE COLLECTION OF men and matériel was gathering pace: siege catapults, stone balls, naptha, wood for defensive shelters, pit props for mines, food supplies, camels and horses, and specialist troops—miners, stone masons, incendiary experts, catapult crews, shock troops, archers, and provisioning corps. In early March, an advance guard appeared outside Acre, compelling European settlers to abandon villages, cutting and clearing orchards in readiness for the construction of the siege lines and the military encampment. Khahil's intentions were now plainly visible to the people of the city. The troops of vassals and provincial governors were gathering not just from Cairo and Damascus but from as far away as Aleppo, 250 miles to the north; from Hama and Homs on the route from there to Damascus; from Akkar in the Lebanese mountains; from Karak and Tripoli and Hisn al-Akrad. The emir Aybak al-Afram, sent to Damascus to supervise the transport of siege machines, arrived there on March 3, and Khalil crossed the Sinai and collected the Kerak contingent at Gaza, led by its governor, Baybars al-Mansuri. They rode north up the coast with a further consignment of trebuchets prefabricated in Cairo in the baggage train. In the spring of 1291, a vast army was converging.

Damascus was on fire with zeal for war. The city rang with the sound of hammering and sawing: carpenters constructing trebuchets, smiths forging blades and chain mail and horseshoes; the collection of all the paraphernalia for a major campaign: food and fodder, shields, tents, banners, carts and trenching tools; and the gathering of an ever-increasing number of soldiers, horses, camels, and donkeys. In the city's great Umayyad mosque at Friday prayers on March 9, a proclamation was given out that "those who want to fight for the faithful at Acre, in the first ten days of Rabi'I [particularly auspicious as the month of the Prophet's birth] should put themselves to the pulling out of the mangonels and hauling them over the bridges."[21]

There was a huge popular response. In an atmosphere of heightened emotion, the great siege machines, disassembled, were dragged out of the city gates and across the bridges. The volunteers "went out at day break and only returned at midday prayer. Even the jurisprudents, the teachers, the religious scholars, and the deeply pious transported material and helped to drag the trebuchet wood."[22] By March 15, all the component parts of the trebuchets had been moved out, and the first consignment started the eighty-mile haul toward Acre in carts under the command of the emir Alam al-Muzaffar.

Almost simultaneously, various other contingents were assembling at Damascus. On the morning of the twenty-third, the city's governor, the emir Husam al-Din Lajin, left for Acre at the head of his troops. That evening, al-Muzaffar, lord of Hama, reached

Damascus. Three days later, his troops and siege equipment arrived. On March 27, the emir al-Tabakhi, at the head of the Tripoli troops, and those from Hisn al-Akrad, Akkar, Homs, and other places in central Syria, also arrived. The region was witnessing an almost unprecedented mobilization of Islamic armies and people. So great was the popular enthusiasm, it was said that volunteers outnumbered the regular soldiers. One by one, these contingents marched on toward the coast and started to ravage the area around Acre.

Christian sources conjured apocryphal numbers in their assessment of the size of the army and, with grudging respect for the martial display, wrote vivid imaginary accounts of the impact of the troops on the march. They pictured these columns "thirsting for Christian blood,"[23] a terrifying harbinger of apocalypse—barbaric, awe-inspiring, and yet somehow magnificent:

> The sultan progressed towards Acre with the most huge multitude of infidel people, whom none could count, of all races, peoples and tongues, assembled from both east and west. And the earth trembled at the sight of them, with the sound of a vast number of trumpets, cymbals and drums proceeding before them. The sun glittered on their shields like gold as they passed and reflected off the mountains, and the points of their polished spears gleamed against the sun like stars shining in the heavens in a serene night sky. When the army marched, a forest could be seen moving over the earth because of the multitude of spears. They numbered 400,000 soldiers and it was impossible not to admire the sight of so many infidels, because they covered the whole earth, the plains and the hills.[24]

Whatever the truth about its size and appearance, the approaching army represented an extraordinary demonstration of Mamluk military power.

Toward the end of 1290, a sense of urgency finally stirred within the walls of Acre. The call for troops became insistent. Some reinforcements were sent by King Henry from Cyprus. Soldiers were recalled from outlying positions within the kingdom of Jerusalem:

from Chateau Pèlerin, Tyre, Sidon, and Beirut. The grand master of the Teutonic Knights, Burchard von Schwanden, arrived with forty Knights and four hundred other crusaders—and then undercut any positive effect on morale by promptly resigning his office and sailing back to Europe. The funds that the pope had entrusted to Nicolas de Hanapes were put to use for repairing and strengthening walls and outworks, gathering munitions and armaments, and the construction of powerful trebuchets. The patriarch played a central role in maintaining morale with his powerful orations in the city's cathedral, the Church of the Holy Cross, but Acre was still scrambling to complete its preparations as the Mamluk columns closed on the city.

8

THE RED TENT
April 1–9, 1291

SULTAN KHALIL REACHED Acre at the start of April. In one Christian account, "He rested three days with his commanders and with the wise men of his army, organizing the army. On the fourth day, the camps moved, nearing the city up to a mile, where they were set out, with a terrible blast of trumpets, cymbals, drums and the horrible shouting of many different voices."[1] On Thursday April 5, he staged a formal announcement of the siege.

He had chosen a small hill rising 100 feet above the level plain and some 300 yards east of the city as the site for his personal encampment. It was, by all accounts, a pleasant spot, which once possessed "a lovely tower and gardens and vineyards of the Templars," and had a commanding view.[2] The Muslims called it the Tall al-Fukhar, the Christians, Le Touron, and it had historical significance for both. A century earlier, in the summer of 1189, Guy de Lusignan, king of Jerusalem, had commanded the siege of Saladin's Acre from the same hill. Now the wheel of fortune had turned full circle. From here, Khalil could look down over fields and orchards to a long sandy bay directly below him, into which the river Naaman flowed through patches of marshland, and beyond, the ruined citadel of Haifa, desolated by Baybars, on the headland ten miles to the south. To the north lay the double walls and intersecting towers of Acre, laid out like "the shape of an axe" in one description, with its harbor and tightly packed center, its churches and the prominent palaces and fortifications of the kings of Jerusalem, the military orders and the Italian communes rising above the flat-roofed houses.[3] And he could watch his army assembling in front of the city.

The siting and pitching of the sultan's tent was a ceremonial act. Following Mamluk practice, Khalil orientated his ornate pavilion, the *dihliz*, in line with his objective. It was "entirely red, and had its door opened facing towards the city of Acre."[4] The aspect was an indicator of his intentions. "It was the ceremonial practice of the [Mamluk] sultans that the direction in which the door of the *dihliz* faced let everyone know the direction in which the sultan would take the road."[5] Probably the same day, delegates approached the city and offered *aman*, a guarantee of safe conduct and protection for the inhabitants in the event of voluntary surrender. After the steady collapse of crusader strongholds, and the massacre at Tripoli, this was just a formal nod to Islamic law. With their backs to the sea and no other significant footholds left on the shores of Palestine, the defenders knew that this must be a fight to the finish—or they would be departing with the universal condemnation of Christendom clinging to their names. Refusal, if the Franks deigned to respond with more than a shower of arrows, meant that the siege could formally open the following day. It was a Friday, the most holy day of the Muslim week, chosen to underline the sacredness of the cause.

The anonymous Templar of Tyre was among those witnessing the Mamluk deployment. He believed that the sultan's army contained 70,000 horsemen. The corps of royal Mamluks in Khalil's time was perhaps somewhere between 7,000 and 12,000, to which were added the emirs' own Mamluks and a body of free cavalry. Later figures, drawn up in 1315, claimed that the army of Egypt alone numbered 24,000 horsemen (though many of these would travel with two horses, in addition to one or two baggage camels, and so there was considerable scope for miscalculation in surveying a throng of men and animals). Throughout the siege, it is clear that large bodies of cavalry patrolled the Mamluk camp day and night. Alongside the cavalry, the Templar of Tyre put the number on foot at 150,000, both trained and untrained infantry swelled by a vast number of civilian volunteers and the support corps. In all the encounters between the Mamluks and the crusaders, the sheer mismatch of numbers had been a decisive factor. However exaggerated the Templar's estimate of Khalil's army, it is clear that the popularity of the campaign had assembled an enormous force, probably one of unprecedented size.

Despite the discrepancy of numbers, the outcome was not a foregone conclusion. Acre was more populous than any other fortified position the Mamluks had ever tackled. The castles that Baybars had invested rarely held more than a thousand men; Acre was defended by more than ten times that number. The Templar of Tyre estimated that Acre had a population of between 30,000 and 40,000, including women and children; 700 to 800 mounted knights; and 13,000 infantry. It was a mixed force, the heavily armed and armored knights of the military orders and their sergeants comprised elite cavalry units. Each order was recognizable by its distinctive dress: the Templars in their white surcoats with a red cross, the Hospitallers a white cross on red, the Teutonic Knights black on white. Acre's infantry comprised troops from Cyprus, mercenaries, and detachments from Europe. These included experienced crossbowmen (invaluable in siege defense) and a small contingent of technical experts—engineers, miners, and carpenters—essential for constructing defensive shelters, building and repairing catapults, and countermining, should the Mamluks get close enough to tunnel under the walls. The Pisans present in the city were practical mariners, particularly skilled in the construction and operation of catapults. In addition, there were the recently arrived civilian pilgrims and adventurers whose actions had been the cause of the war.

From the ramparts, the Templar could see the pavilions and tents "very close together, stretching from Touron all the way up to as-Sumairiya [just north of the city], so that the whole plain was covered with tents."[6] The army surrounded Acre from sea to sea with its contingents, drawn widely from across the Middle East, arranged in orderly sectors confronting the walls: at the northern tip, flanking a rocky shore, the forces of the Ayyubid vassal al-Malik al-Muzaffar, ruler of Hama in central Syria; in the central section against the city's main gate of St. Anthony, set within a tower, the troops from Damascus under its governor, Husam al-Din Lajin; to their left, those from Kerak under Baybars al-Mansuri; and directly below the sultan's hilltop, his own Egyptian Mamluks, menacing the walls down to the harbor.

Another man closely scrutinizing the Mamluk siege arrangements was the grand master of the Hospitallers, Jean de Villiers, who dated the approach of the sultan a few days earlier. In a letter written afterwards, he described, with grandiose exaggeration, Khalil's dramatic arrival on April 1. He "invested the city of Acre on all sides from one sea as far as the other, between sunrise and tierce [about nine in the morning], and on the other side eastwards as far as the river Euphrates [as far as the eye could see], with all his battering-engines. And so, with numerous engines and a great host he sat down before the city."[7]

If the size of the Mamluk army was routinely overestimated, for those watching on the walls it was still an awe-inspiring sight. They could survey a scene of extraordinary animation: thousands of animals—camels carrying tents, oxen dragging siege machines, Mamluk war horses—and all the resources of the army—cavalry and infantry, carpenters, stonemasons, cooks, holy men, and supply teams bringing fodder, water, and food, as well as an array of outfits and weapons such as helmets, turbans, body armor, shields, and swords. The people of Acre could hear the sounds of an army settling in: the braying of animals, the impact of hammers, the shouting of orders, the calls to prayer, the digging of trenches, the laborious erection of tents and siege machinery, the fluttering of yellow banners, the trumpet calls and thud of drums. "When we settled down there," recorded Baybars al-Mansuri, "they were surrounded from all sides."[8]

Khalil's army could look up at "a town protected by walls, outer walls, towers, moats and strong barbicans . . . triangular in shape like a shield," as one visitor put it a few years earlier.[9] The double line of walls stretched unbroken from shore to shore—a distance of over a mile—pierced at various points by gates and posterns and interspersed at regular intervals by massive square towers. In front was a fosse, a steep-sided, stone-lined ditch forty feet wide. The names of the towers reflected the somewhat piecemeal manner in which they had been constructed and paid for by individual donation or initiative: the tower of the Venetians, of the English, that of King Henry, of the Countess of Blois. Other toponyms were more sinister, reflecting Acre's turbulent past and the legends that clung to it. The Accursed Tower was flanked by the Tower of Blood. Further west, the outer wall's defenses included the Gate of Evil Step.

Well before the late addition of extra defensive measures, however, visitors such as Wilbrand van Oldenburg had praised the "good, large, deep moats, lined with stonework from the bottom, crowned by a double turreted wall, finely arranged in such a way, that the first wall with towers, not higher than the main wall, is overlooked and protected by the second and inner wall, whose towers are high and most powerful."[10] Between the two walls, there was a broad killing field of some forty yards, which also contained a ditch. The sloping ditches were constructed of cut stone, providing a steep escarpment up which an attacker would have to climb to the foot of the walls. The lower, outer wall had towers that were also probably square, spaced at fifty-yard intervals "not a stone's throw distant from one another all around the walls," with additional smaller projecting salients to provide covering fire. The city gates were also set within towers.[11] The intervals between the towers on the inner wall were protected by semicircular bastions. The walls were extremely stout, in Ludolf von Suchem's description, "wide enough that two carts driving along the top of them could easily pass one another," and beyond the outer ditch there were other "divers outer works and defences," terraces probably lined with wooden stockades and fronted by ditches to further slow down an advancing enemy. Acre's defenses were formidable.

According to received Islamic wisdom on the conduct of sieges, collected in the military manual of Ibrahim al-Ansari a century later, a commander should take time to "know the conditions of the fortress, the inaccessible places and those with ease of access; the impossible and the possible places for action . . . [and further] . . . the positions for mining [the walls] and for scaling ropes, siege ladders and grappling irons."[12] From his vantage point and tours of inspection, Khalil had ample opportunity to survey Acre's defenses and run through his strategic options. There were two points of particular interest. Acre was effectively divided into two portions: the old city encircling the port and the newer suburb of Montmusard, both now enclosed in a continuous double wall. The two parts were separated by an internal wall, once the outer wall of the original city. Where the two met, the outer walls took an inward dent to a strategic city gate: that of St. Anthony. About 650 yards further east, the wall took another, sharper right-angle turn down toward the sea. This was Acre's most vulnerable point. It was here that the crusaders had battered the Accursed Tower a century earlier.

The rebuilt Accursed Tower was now shielded not only by an outer wall but also by other fortifications. These included the construction of the barbican of Hugh III—an external defensive structure jutting from the outer wall and linked to it by a walkway—and at the very apex, the nearby tower built by King Henry (the King's Tower), which provided further protection for the Accursed Tower, the entrance into the heart of the city. It was important for Khalil to maintain pressure along the whole wall to spread the defenders thinly, but it was the barbican of Hugh III and the gate of St. Anthony on which his attention would initially focus.

DESPITE THE VAST army that he had assembled and the almost unbroken success of the Mamluks against crusader castles over the past thirty years, there was risk for Khalil in this venture—and his legitimacy as sultan depended on success. The dispatch of an unpopular ruler who lost authority could be sudden and bloody. He had no ships and no ability to seal Acre off against resupply or reinforcement by sea, though he was probably well informed by Muslims who knew the city well as traders and spies about the likely defensive strategy and the response to Acre's appeals for help. Spring seas could be unpredictable, and there was every chance that the weather might disrupt the arrival of any relief from Cyprus.

It was important for the sultan to show a close personal interest in the work in progress. The Mamluk military manual of Ibrahim al-Ansari prescribed that "the commander of the army or one of his army whom he deputized should circumambulate the fortress every day or two" and should "supervise the raising of the mangonels and their firing."[13] Both Saladin and Baybars had understood that personal involvement in the fighting was essential. Baybars had been up close to the walls of Caesarea in 1265 to inspect mining operations from under a wheeled shelter and was nearly killed in the trenches at Arsuf shortly afterwards. The sultan should be visible to his army and rewards given out. Morale was all important if men were to fight and die.

Time was a key factor. The strategy of the Mamluks was to bring overwhelming force against a town to deliver a quick knockout blow. If none of the Christian strongholds that had collapsed like dominoes since the time of Sultan Baybars had survived more than six weeks, this was also probably the maximum length of time that less-committed detachments and volunteers could be reliably retained. Saladin's attempt to take Antioch in 1188 had failed because "the determination of his troops, especially those from far away, had weakened and their zeal for holy war had flagged and they only wanted to return to their countries and rest from fighting."[14] Disease was another factor. In matters of hygiene and camp management—the organization of water supplies and washing facilities, the burial of corpses, the supply of food—Islamic armies were considerably superior to their Christian counterparts, but the vast size of Khalil's force, the growing heat as spring progressed, and the low-lying terrain could provide challenges. The marshes that surrounded Acre were miasmic, as a later traveler, Domenico Laffi, testified. He called Acre "an unhealthy place . . . because of the swamps that surround it . . . our (ships) are unable to stay there throughout the year on account of the bad air and bad conditions during the rainy season."[15] Both armies at Acre in the long siege of 1189–1191 had been ravaged by disease.

THE LOGISTICAL SKILLS of Mamluk armies were considerable but the malign numbers involved in sustaining a lengthy siege gradually stacked up as time dragged on. It has been estimated that a medieval army of 25,000 men required 9,000 gallons of water and 30 tons of animal fodder a day to provision itself. A sixty-day siege would need the removal of a million gallons of human and animal waste and 4,000 tons of solid biological waste. Khalil's army would have multiplied these numbers by at least three. If nothing else, the motivation of the men to wait and die outside castle walls was finite. The vast numbers of volunteers were inspired not only by religious fervor but also by the prospect of booty. They would not be held on the plains of Acre indefinitely.

Seen from his camp, the city's preparations certainly looked thorough: Khalil "found it fortified with all kinds of equipment and siege machines."[16] The defenders had done everything they could within the time available. Jean de Villiers later wrote that "we and all the good Christian people of the city made preparations against them, and we armed ourselves completely, and we put in readiness all the instruments and engines which are intended to protect and defend the city and the bodies of men."[17] Men prepared their equipment: greasing hauberks; cleaning helmets; sharpening swords, knives, and the points of spears; shoeing horses; adjusting shields and crossbows; stockpiling ammunition. The Templar of Tyre also described the defenders preparing their siege engines. They "manned their defences well, and began to raise the alarm, as one must do when one has an enemy."[18]

The city had no seaward defenses, as the rocks and sand banks offshore made an amphibious attack impossible. Instead, the northern end of Montmusard, where the defenses came down to a rocky shore, was protected by an enormous round tower; at the eastern end, where the wall gave way to sandy beach, there was a small tower, then a large spiked iron trellis ran out into the water to prevent any outflanking attack by cavalry riding through the shallows. In the harbor, the Pisans had ships capable of bombarding the shoreline with deck-mounted catapults. Ashore, they had fifteen of these devices, positioned to be fired from just within the inner walls, probably with range finders directing operations from the battlements.

Abutting these inner walls were large, vaulted chambers that served as munitions stores to which the ordinary citizens of the town played an active part in the gathering of weapons, "carrying quantities of rocks, crossbows, crossbow bolts, lances, falchions [single-bladed swords], helmets and mail hauberks, scaled and padded armour, shields with metal bosses and all other type of armour of different sorts."[19] Banners fluttered from the walls, and in all probability, when the gates were finally sealed shut, the defenders employed the conventional ploy of suspending heavy curtains from the outer walls—bales of wool or sheets of leather attached to wooden beams—to muffle the impact of bombardment from stone balls hurled by catapults.

Defensive responsibilities were parceled out in segments. The northernmost section of Montmusard was manned by the Templars, under their grand master Guillaume de Beaujeu and the marshal Pierre de Sevrey, with the support of the leper knights of St. Lazarus; to their right, the Hospitallers commanded a crucial section to the gate of St. Anthony with their master and marshal, Jean de Villiers and Matthieu de Clermont. The Hospitallers alternated shifts with the English Knights of the Order of St. Thomas; from there, it was the responsibility of the Teutonic Knights under Hugo von Boland. The critical King's Tower, the Accursed Tower, and the projecting barbican, where the wall took its sharp turn, were the responsibility of the King of Cyprus's troops under his young brother Amalric, Lord of Tyre and Regent of Acre. The final section, running down to the harbor, was entrusted to the French regiment of Jean de Grailly and the English contingent under Othon de Grandson, with the help of the recently arrived pilgrims and the townspeople.

The seafaring Italians played a sporadic part in the defense. The Venetians and the Pisans provided support at various points. The Genoese hesitated, then declared themselves neutral; in May 1290, they had signed a commercial treaty with Qalawun, which they had no desire to jeopardize. As the Venetians had one too, the commitment of the Italian merchant communes was treated with continuous suspicion, despite a wholehearted Pisan contribution.

The guarding of the walls was to follow a strict rotation in shifts—eight hours on, eight hours off—alternating the responsibilities between two detachments in each sector, which was administered by two rectors. Sources suggest that overall responsibility was shared by a council of war of eight leading figures, including Amalric; the grand masters of the three largest military orders—Villiers, Beaujeu, and Boland; Jean de Grailly, "commander of the men of France and seneschal of the Kingdom of Jerusalem"; Othon de Grandson of the English; and the patriarch, Nicolas de Hanapes.[20]

Despite these apparently logical arrangements, there was no satisfactory, unified defensive plan. The organization of the siege reflected the sectarian history and geography of the city itself, with separate communities each barricaded within their own guarded enclaves, the defense of which they tended to regard as their first priority. The crusading orders were powerful and competing autonomous bodies, answerable to no one but themselves and the pope, in whose name Hanapes, as papal legate, had a nominal jurisdiction. The Italian maritime republics were commercial rivals who had engaged in bitter fighting in the city within living memory and whose priorities excluded a commitment to holy war and frequently included selling war materials to the Mamluks in Egypt.

Over and beyond this there was a deeply established resident civilian population of townspeople and religious orders for whom Acre was their home; vulnerable refugees from Tripoli and other fallen towns; and the rabble of recently arrived crusaders and pilgrims, with little military experience and whose actions had provided the cause of war. The nominal ruler of the kingdom of Jerusalem, the twenty-year-old Henry of Cyprus, delegated his authority over this contentious mass of people to his younger brother Amalric, now aged eighteen or nineteen years old, but his authority was also limited. Throughout the siege, there were scarcely suppressed notes of discord: unequally allocated tasks, arguments about privileges and rank, and unclear command structures. Acre's reputation as a Levantine den of impious sin continued to cling to it during the siege, so that it was said that many closed their eyes to the growing crisis in preference to the delights of port life—the taverns and the brothels.

ISLAMIC ARMIES HAD long and deep experience of siege warfare. As early as the ninth century they were producing military manuals that set out generally agreed procedures for the capture of castles, and by the high Middle Ages their technical and operational management of the investiture of fortified places was highly sophisticated. Despite stunning open-field victories, such as Saladin's at Hattin, the Holy Land under the Mamluk sultans was being wrested back from the Franks, piece by piece, by dynamic, high-intensity sieges. The thirteenth century had witnessed a litany of impregnable places going down one after another: Ascalon, Caesarea, Saphet, Antioch, Chastel Blanc, Krak des Chevaliers, Margat, Tripoli. All fell within a six-week period.

The conventional procedure was first to secure the Mamluk camp against sorties with defensive palisades and ditches. "It must be stressed," al-Ansari wrote,

> that the besieger of the enemy is also the besieged in the sense that he is not secure from their going out against him and their hastening to do so when the opportunity, during the day or night, presents itself to them; for they require victory as much as the besieger desires it over them. Hence it is incumbent upon the commander to be cautious with respect to himself and those of the army with him as much as possible. He should use trenches if there is need of them, and their construction is possible; for this is among the strongest [factors] of resolution and conquest.[21]

To protect the camp against artillery bombardment and counter-attacks, they fronted it with an earth rampart. It was necessary to be on the alert and to keep cavalry posted a bow shot from castle walls against the possibility of sorties. Once securely established, the next step was to find ways of advancing under cover as close to the walls as possible to maximize the effect of their own catapults and pro-jectiles and to start mining operations. Psychological softening up was another key component. The effect of shattering noise—the repeated creak and crash of catapults, the orchestrated thunder of camel-mounted drummers, the cries, shouts, and rhythmic chanting from across the whole battlefield—these could be deeply disheartening to defenders.

Degrading the walls with catapults and sweeping resistance off the parapets with volleys of projectiles was the preparatory stage. Protected by this hale of fire, miners could then work their way under the walls and bring down towers. Once a reasonable breach had been effected, defenders often conceded that further resistance was futile and sued for surrender. Many of the crusader fortresses attacked by Baybars and Qalawun simply gave in with the collapse of a strategic bastion or curtain wall. If not, the day would come for a bloody final assault undertaken before dawn to a barrage of noise. This required any ditch to be filled in sufficiently for men to pass across and the sacrifice of a front line of volunteers or prisoners driven forward from behind. Then a final massacre.

THE ORGANIZATION OF Khalil's army camp evidently took time. Villiers watched the preparations unfold over nine days: "And from the day they came until the Monday after [April 9] they ceased not to take up the ground, some for their engines, some for their defences, some for trenches, some for stockades and to make their other works, and they brought up all their engines and defences round about the walls and set them up against ours."[22]

Khalil's study of Acre's defenses enabled him to site his largest catapults against the most promising objectives. These machines, which had been dragged from Cairo and across the Lebanese mountains, pulled out of the gates of Damascus on a tide of patriotic and religious fervor, dismantled again, hauled another eighty miles and reassembled outside the gates of Acre, represented not just a triumph of Mamluk military organization but a sizeable investment of resources and ergonomic capital. They were irreplaceable, and vulnerable to counter batteries and Greek fire. This was well understood, and they were positioned in line with al-Ansari's advice: "He who has erected them for battling against a fortress should place them in a position which enemy [fire] cannot attain."[23] Each one took two days to erect, position, and prepare for action. They comprised the largest collection of stone-throwing machinery an Islamic army had yet assembled and the ultimate development of mechanical artillery in the crusader era.

During this initial setting up, there was an eerie lull. From the Muslim camp, Baybars al-Mansuri noted an unnerving confidence in the defenders: "They showed great patience and a lack of concern about the siege and did not even close the gates of the city, nor even hang down a defensive screen [against bombardment] in front of the gates."[24] There were, evidently, forays and tentative probing by the defenders while the still-vulnerable camp was being established. The Templar of Tyre noted that the sultan's army "sat before Acre for eight days, doing nothing beyond engaging in sporadic skirmishes between our men and theirs, in which a few died on each side."[25] The Islamic sources gave a more partisan account of something like a tournament between opposing horsemen: the Christians "began to go out to the Muslim military and call their knights to a duel. The troops from the free cavalry and the sultan's Mamluks hastened toward them, and attack and retreat and mutual stabbing took place between them. They kept this up for some days, and the Muslims were victorious, and wounded a number of them and killed a number of them, and every day they returned the losers. They saw the Muslims had the heart they did not have. They ceased fighting and competing, and stood on the gates to protect them, and did not go out."[26] More likely, the Christians were simply outnumbered and common sense prevailed. The gates were sealed shut.

9

"Bolts of Thunder, Flashes of Lightning"

April 10–13, 1291

THE PROFICIENCY AT siege warfare that Khalil's army brought to the walls of Acre, and the technologies that it could deploy, drew on traditions that went back to the very beginnings of Islam. Despite its origins in the deserts of Arabia, the taking of fortified places had been central to the spread of Muhammad's message. The Prophet himself had besieged towns using trebuchets, a technology probably originating in China in the centuries BCE and transmitted to the Middle East via the Byzantines or the Persians. These machines utilized the energy generated by an off-balance beam rotating around a fulcrum to hurl heavy projectiles long distances. Trebuchets were the most powerful form of mechanical artillery ever devised. They had been an essential feature of Baybars's siege trains; by the time of Qalawun, they were being deployed in mass batteries. "There were collected against Acre," wrote Abu al-Fida, who had helped to transport them, "great and small mangonels such as never were collected against any other place."[1] Two years earlier, Tripoli had been taken with the aid of nineteen machines. The devices now being assembled under the gaze of those watching from the walls came to at least seventy-two and possibly as many as ninety-two. Their very presence was a triumph of Mamluk military planning and a testament to the depth of its resources.

The power and variety of the machines that Khalil was preparing to unleash on the stone walls of Acre was impressive. They were of two types. In both, an off-balance beam would be unequally weighted around a pivot and supported on either a stout wooden trestle or a single pole. A sling would be attached to the longer portion of the beam containing the missile—a stone or an incendiary device—and then released. Initially, this was done by human energy. The original trebuchet was a traction machine, which depended on a team of men hauling smartly down on ropes in unison to flip the beam end upwards and release the missile from its sling. Baybars himself had participated in such launching work at the siege of Arsuf. By the end of the twelfth century, the ergonomic efficiency and power of trebuchets had undergone a step change with the creation of a second, larger device that employed the force of gravity to rotate the beam and hurl the projectile. Instead of using muscle power to fling the beam into the air, its short end could be loaded with a heavy counterweight—stones or lead weights in a sack or wooden box. The beam was longer, up to thirty feet, and the heavy wooden frame substantially braced with side supports to resist the greater forces at work. Further modifications included the lengthening of the sling containing the missile, which increased velocity and range, and in some machines a hinged counterweight that could swing from the beam, adding further impetus, in place of a fixed one. The loading and shooting rate of these machines was considerably slower than that of their traction-powered counterparts. A rope winch or human labor would crank the long end of the beam down to the ground, hoisting the counterweight at the other end into the air, and latching it into the firing position. A stone ball was lugged into the pouch of the sling placed within a wooden guide channel in the base of the machine and connected to the beam by a hook that would release the ball at the estimated optimum trajectory to hit a given target. With a release rope attached to the latch, the shooter would retreat a safe distance, give a firm tug to free the trigger, and the counter-weight would crash downward with all the force of gravity, hurling

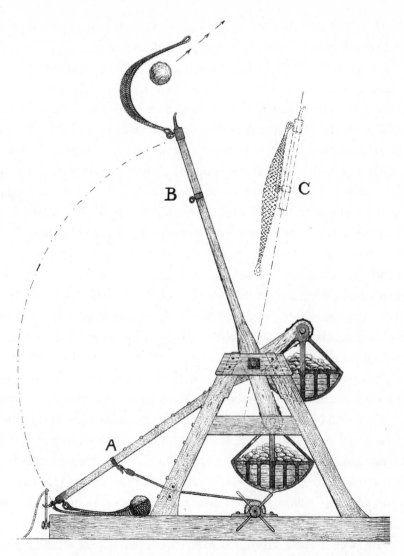

The operation of the counterweight trebuchet. This counterweight is a basket of stones hinged to the beam. In A, the counterweight has been cranked up into the air into the load position by a capstan. The sling with its projectile lies in the bed of the machine waiting the tug on the release rope. At B, the released weight hurtles to the ground with the force of gravity, and the beam flies up and fires the ball from the sling at the chosen trajectory. At C, the beam with its empty sling swings wildly to and fro in the air. (*Sieges of the Middle Ages*, London, 1964)

the throwing arm skyward and releasing the ball toward the walls at frightening speeds, upwards of 130 feet per second.

The skill involved in setting up, range finding, and firing both types of machines was considerable, the result of a long evolution of practical experiments. There were many variables: the size of the stone ball, the length and flexibility of the beam, and the ratio of the relative length of the two parts around the pivot, as well as the length and adjustment of the sling. The faster-firing traction trebuchets called for different resources and skills. To create a continuous bombardment, large consignments of men worked in rotation in teams of up to ten at a time, hauling on ropes in perfect unison. The key figure was the shooter, who directed the team and prepared the ball for launching. This man held the ball in the sling prior to launch. He might be dangling off the ground, pulling the ball down, in order to flex the beam at the moment of launch, or standing on the ground and holding the sling and missile tightly to his chest. It was critical to position these at the correct angle if the ball were not to fly vertically upwards or not launch at all. The shooter required courage, knowledge, and fine judgment. He then gave the order to take up the slack and to haul. The beam whipped up, pulling the ball up out of his hands and releasing it from its sling at the chosen trajectory. The operation of trebuchets also called for considerable logistical and skilled manufacturing support: carpenters and fabricators; quarriers of stone; masons to carve projectiles; and the transport corps, which had hauled the machines to Acre.

The siege of Acre a hundred years earlier had witnessed the power that these machines could unleash and the awe they inspired. Some of the largest had most likely been the relatively novel counterweight devices. According to the Christian chronicles, the Muslim defenders had

> plenty of trebuchets in the city, but one of them was unequalled for its massive construction and its effectiveness and efficiency in hurling enormous stones. Nothing could stand against the power of this machine. It hurled huge stone-shot . . . If the stones met no obstruction

Fragment from a medieval manuscript showing the firing of a projectile from a traction trebuchet. The shooter suspended off the ground from the sling is using his weight to flex the beam and increase velocity and range. The men hidden behind the charging cavalry are awaiting the shooter's order to haul downwards on the ropes and launch the ball out of his hands. (*Sieges of the Middle Ages*, London, 1964)

when they fell, they sank a foot deep into the ground. This machine struck some of our trebuchets and smashed them to pieces or at least rendered them unusable. Its shots also destroyed many other siege machines, or broke off what it hit. It shot with such force, and its blows were so effective, that no material or substance could withstand the unbearable impact without damage, no matter how solid or well-built it was.[2]

The attackers in their turn deployed a machine christened "God's Stone Thrower" that was positioned against the Accursed Tower and was said to have stripped thirty square feet from the top of its adjacent wall. Gravity had brought a considerable acceleration to the propulsion of projectiles even if these descriptions routinely exaggerated their destructive power. Over and above their actual capabilities, the spectacle of the loosed beams rearing wildly to the sky and swinging to and fro like a giant pendulum weighted by its stone box, the emptied sling whipping round, and the anticipated crash of the stone ball into walls, houses, and enemy camps had an immense psychological impact on defenders. Florid Arabic verses fancifully portrayed the trebuchets as instruments in the service of God, comparing the dip and rise of their beams to that of the faithful at prayer: "The prostrate catapults pray and we to God submit."[3]

Using the pulling power of a dozen men, a large traction trebuchet could probably throw an object of up to 110 pounds, though generally they were deployed to hurl smaller projectiles at a rapid rate of fire. The counterweight could hurl further and heavier. There was a trade-off between weight, trajectory, launch speed, and distance, and between all these and rate of fire. At Krak des Chevaliers, Baybars's machines hurled stones of 220 pounds. At Montfort a few months later, stones of 155 pounds had been thrown one-eighth of a mile. Large machines would have required massive counterweights—the most powerful up to ten tons. Counterweight trebuchets also possessed a level of accuracy that made them extremely effective against static targets such as castle walls. They could pepper the same spot repeatedly. A medium-sized machine fired at a wall 200 yards away could reliably group its shots within a seven-yard square. It would be a long time before gunpowder artillery could overtake the effectiveness of these mechanical devices.

Khalil came to Acre in 1291 with catapults of several types: lighter, quick-firing machines designed to rain missiles on defenders and heavier ones to batter walls. Arabic sources listed four different types. The *ifrangi* (the Frankish catapult), of which he had fifteen, was a heavy counterweight device for smashing battlements and the tops of curtain walls, mounted on a trestle frame, capable of hurling massive balls of up to 400 pounds, with counterweights of several tons. Then there were the somewhat lighter, man-operated traction devices—the *qarabugha* (the black bull) and the *shaytani* (the devilish)—probably also trestle mounted. One source lists fifty-two of the latter. There were also small antipersonnel devices on poles, which the Mamluks called the *lu'bah* (the plaything), capable of being swiveled in any direction to pepper defenders with small shot. In addition, some troops hurled stones with hand-held slingshots.

The installation and management of the counterweight Frankish machines, with their sturdy frames and massive counterweights, was time consuming and laborious. The largest might take up to half an hour to crank up, load, and fire, and they could not be quickly resited. The judicious choice of objective at the outset was therefore important. The lighter, man-powered machines could be set up and repositioned more quickly. When a detachment of the Second Crusade besieged Muslim Lisbon in 1147, two traction trebuchets, each operated by squads of a hundred men working in rotation in ten-man teams, were reputed to have fired 5,000 stone shot in the space of ten hours—each machine hammering away at 250 shots an hour. At Acre, Khalil certainly had the human resources to unleash a heavy bombardment.

The logistical demands of artillery warfare also required the supply of a vast number of suitable stone projectiles and the labor to quarry, transport, and shape them. From experience, the Mamluks understood the geological requirements of ballistic ammunition. The walls of Acre were constructed of the local *kurkar*, porous beach sandstone. This rock provided suitable ammunition for antipersonnel machines, but in order to degrade fortifications, it was far more effective to propel stone balls of a harder material than the walls at which they were aimed. Richard the Lionheart was said to have brought granite ammunition with him from Sicily for the first siege of Acre. To obtain rock of suitable density, Khalil sought limestone from other strata and transported it to the firing site. Harder beach rock was sourced from seams up to twelve miles from Acre. From this rock, skilled masons prepared well-formed spherical balls, probably turned on a lathe, in a range of sizes and weights to suit the requirements of various machines, up to giant stone balls of two feet in diameter, 360 pounds in weight. For the counterweight machines, supplies of equally sized spherical ammunition were essential to achieve consistent aerodynamic performance and accuracy.

The Mamluks brought to the walls of Acre a wide range of other siege technologies and skills. These included a highly developed use of fire weapons by specially trained troops adept at the handling of Greek fire—a mixture of crude oil and powdered pine resin, which gave it adhesive properties—that could be projected in different ways. It could be hurled in clay pots from catapults to terrorize both troops and civilian populations and to destroy wooden siege machines and defenses or lobbed over walls by hand in small clay grenades. Specially adapted crossbows also propelled "eggs" of Greek fire and flaming arrows from a greater distance. It is possible that the Mamluks also brought genuine explosives into play at the walls of Acre; the author of a treatise describing the refining of potassium nitrate was living in Damascus at the time of the siege. To get up close to walls, the command of siege craft included the deployment of mantlets—moveable siege shelters—the watchful use of cavalry to deter sorties, and mining. The use of noise—chanting; martial music from drums, trumpets, and cymbals; and full-throated yells— was also a standard technique aimed at keeping defenders in a state of perpetual dread.

Some Islamic sources recorded that it took two days to assemble the war machines out of reach of archers but within open view of the walls. This activity in itself was part of the Mamluks' softening-up process; it was recommended that it "should not be concealed, because by doing it [openly], fright and terror and weakening of their hearts occur."[4] Just the sight of the giant trebuchets had the ability to drain the morale of a besieged stronghold: when King Edward I, erected an enormous machine christened the Warwolf before the gates of Stirling castle in 1304, the Scots tried to surrender before it had fired a single shot. (Having commissioned the giant machine, Edward was not going to let them off that lightly. He wanted to see it in action. He sent the delegation back inside so that he could witness for himself the destructive power of its stone missiles.)

The Arabic-speaking Templar of Tyre watched the developments from the ramparts. He was evidently able to obtain some detailed information on the disposition of Khalil's forces because he recorded not only the position of four particularly large counterweight trebuchets, some constructed from the tall trees of the Lebanon, but also their nicknames. The presence of each of these machines represented a vast amount of human labor, and in them were invested religious zeal and the expectation of victory. Near the northern end of the wall, in the section guarded by the Templars, was positioned an engine called "the Furious." At the far southern end close to the sea, in the section guarded by the Pisans, was the similarly impressive "Victorious," which Abu al-Fida had helped transport through the winter rains. Two more, which he did not name, were positioned against other strategic and vulnerable points—one against the Hospitallers' section, where the wall took an inward turn, menaced the section close to the gate of St. Anthony, the main thoroughfare into the city, another against the exposed protruding right-angled turn, protected by an external barbican, which Khalil had identified as the most promising point of attack, and whose inner defense, the Accursed Tower, gave direct access to the heart of the city.

The spread of these machines from shore to shore suggests Khalil's desire to keep the defenders stretched along the whole perimeter, even if it was in the central sections that his deeper plans lay. The defenders had an unknown but smaller number of trebuchets of their own, the construction and operation of which was largely in the hands of the Pisans. They evidently had some "great machines," counterweight trebuchets that were probably deployed throughout the city within the inner wall to target Khalil's own counterweight monsters, but as the siege progressed, they would run short of suitable ammunition.

By sometime around April 11, the Mamluks' trebuchets were assembled and in position: the stone balls collected in piles, the pulling teams ready, the counterweight machines sited and cranked to fire. Khalil's strategy was to move fast, not to give the defenders a moment to breathe. "When the investment is under way," it was advised in the manual of al-Ansari, "there should be no pause in the discharging of the mangonels against them, and there should be no abating [of fire] in any hour of the day or night. To desist in attack against them is among that which cools fright and strengthens their hearts."[5] While the catapults unleashed a withering torrent of fire, his troops inched forward toward the outer ditch, by night and day, demolishing any outer works in the process. With growing apprehension, the Templar of Tyre watched their method, conducted with extraordinary discipline. Their progress seemed unstoppable:

The first night they set up great barricades and wicker screens and ranged them against our walls. The second night they moved them forward; the third closer still. And so they advanced so far forward that they made it to the edge of the fosse. And behind these barricades they had armed men, dismounted from their horses with bows in hand. And if you want to know how they got so close it was impossible to prevent them, I'll tell you why.

These people had their horsemen fully armed, with their horses in protective armour, spread from one side of the city to the other, that is to say, from one side of the sea to the other, and there were more than 15,000 of them, and they rotated four shifts a day, so that no one was overworked. None of our men sallied out against those behind the screens, because those further back [behind the first enemy line] would have guarded and defended them, and if any of our men had gone out at any time to attack them, the horsemen would have protected them.

So in the end they advanced to the edge of the fosse as I've told you, and those on horseback carried on the necks of their horses four or five bunches of brushwood, and threw them down behind the screens, and when night came they put them in front of the screens and bound them on top with a rope. This pile became like an impregnable wall that no catapult could damage. Some of our medium-sized machines shot and hit the tops of the screens but achieved nothing at all. The stones merely rebounded into the ditch.[6]

The problem for the defenders attempting to destroy these barricades was that the enemy was now sufficiently close to the outer wall to make it impossible for the Christians to deploy their heavy counterweight trebuchets—the angle of trajectory was too great, and there was the chance of misfiring and possibly damaging the wall itself from the inside. Nestled in, these barricades were safe from the heaviest Christian artillery. Instead, from within the inner wall, the crusaders were compelled to use their lighter traction engines, evidently not powerful enough to destroy the invaders' protective wooden wall. Now up to the edge of the fosse, no more than forty yards from the walls and protected by their rampart, the attackers prepared their next initiative:

> After this the enemy drew up their *carabohas* [black bulls], small Turkish catapults operated by hand, which can fire very fast, and these did more damage to our men than the larger engines, since in the sectors where the *carabohas* were firing, none dared to appeared in the open. And in front of the *carabohas* they had made barricades so strong and so high that no one could strike or shoot at those who were firing [the *carabohas*].[7]

Khalil's aim was to neutralize the defense so that the men would be crouching behind their battlements, unable to respond—or be driven off altogether. Particular attention was being paid to the Barbican and the vulnerable King's Tower. Some of the catapults, according to one source, "hurled a bombardment of huge stones against the Tower of the King so that no one dared to remain on top of it."[8]

The defenders were further harassed by teams of archers, armed with their short, powerful composite bows, shooting clouds of "innumerable sharp arrows that came whistling through the air from all directions onto the defenders' heads like heavy rain. These continuous volleys not only dealt death, they poisoned the very air of heaven. Well-armoured soldiers deployed along the ramparts to defend the city were being mortally wounded, while the unarmed were prevented from going to the walls at all."[9] In Christian rhetoric, even God's celestial sphere was being contaminated. The density of this shower shooting, like a meteorological phenomenon, left a deep impression, as if the sky was darkened by such volleys. It was probably Othon de Grandson, fighting for Edward I on the wintry Scottish borders years later, who recalled a blizzard of "little arrows which they call locusts flying in the air thicker than snowflakes."[10] From outside the walls, Baybars al-Mansuri watched as "they sent against Acre stones like bolts of thunder and arrows like flashes of lightning."[11]

This horrible bombardment was part of a coordinated strategy. By keeping the defenders ducking for cover, it allowed the heavy counterweight trebuchets, with their slower rate of fire, to smash away at towers and walls uncontested and strip the ramparts of their battlements. The psychological toll of the heavy catapults was considerable; the impact of massive, carved limestone balls hitting the same spot again and again, "as if by thunderbolts falling from heaven," tinged Christian accounts with the language of apocalypse.[12] One writer ascribed to the Muslims as agents of the anti-Christ an apocryphal 666 siege engines—the number of the beast that comes out of the sea. They conjured similarly bestial images of the terror that their opponents inspired throughout the siege, describing them

> making sallies towards the city for six hours at a time, so that both day and night, there was scarcely any rest for the citizens . . . some bellowing like oxen, others barking like dogs, other voices roaring like lions emitting terrible sounds, as is their custom, and beating enormous drums with twisted sticks to frighten the enemy. Others threw javelins, others hurled stones, others fired arrows and quarrels from crossbows at the Christians who stood defending the weak points of the city's defences.[13]

For the defenders, it was critical to keep Khalil's army well away from the walls, and in this they had already failed. The constant bombardment now enabled him to launch a covert second technique: mining.

Unceasing bombardment: Islamic troops attack city walls with stone missiles and arrows. The horsetail emblem of Turkic tribal warriors protrudes from the trebuchet. (Oliver Poole, redrawn from *The Illustrations to the World History of Rashid al-Din*, Edinburgh, 1976)

The work of tunneling was skilled, dangerous, and time consuming, but it was a critical ingredient of Islamic siege craft and more effective than bombardment in bringing down defenses. For the purpose, Khalil had requisitioned 1,000 miners from Aleppo with a range of specialist skills. This included tunnelers who excavated the mine, carpenters who propped the tunnel, laborers who removed spoil, and men expert in setting up and lighting fires to collapse the foundations. The work commenced under the cover of protecting shelters. The geology of Acre—porous beach rock—made tunneling relatively easy, but it brought its own problems. Careful propping was essential to prevent the tunnels caving in. The miners, armed with single-beaked picks, hacked away in the stifling dark or by the light of smoking torches, passing out excavated material to others behind. Overhead, the bombardment continued.

The aim was to start a tunnel as close to the wall as possible and, in order to limit the work, to make it narrow, usually no more than five feet wide, just enough to allow two men to operate side by side. The tunnel's function was simply to provide access to the exact spot under the edge of a tower or wall where an enlarged chamber would be made to light a fire.

There is no detailed account of the tunneling at Acre in the spring of 1291, but the experience of the subterranean work being undertaken can be reconstructed from the description of a curious Muslim observer of the siege of a crusader fort in 1115:

It occurred to me to enter the underground tunnel and inspect it. So, I went down in the trench, while the arrows and stones were falling on us like rain, and entered the tunnel. There I was struck with the great wisdom with which the digging was executed. The tunnel was dug from the trench to the *bashurah* [the outer wall]. On the sides of the tunnel were set up two pillars, across which stretched a plank to prevent the earth above it from falling down. The whole tunnel had such a framework of wood that extended as far as the foundations of the *bashurah*. Then the assailants dug under the wall of the *bashurah*, supported it in its place, and went as far as the foundation of the tower. The tunnel was narrow, it was nothing but a means to provide access to the tower. As soon as they got to the tower, they enlarged the tunnel in the wall of the tower, supported it on timbers and began to carry out, a little at a time, the bits of stone produced by boring. The floor of the tunnel was turned into mud because of the dust caused by the digging. Having made the inspection, I went on without the troops of Khurasan [the miners] recognizing me. Had they recognized me, they would not have let me off without the payment of a heavy fine.[14]

Once the "room" under the target spot had been excavated, it was the turn of the fire setters to ignite combustible material to collapse the wall:

They then began to cut dry wood and stuff the tunnel with it. Early the next morning they set it on fire. We had just at that time put on our arms and marched under a great shower of stones and arrows to the trench in order to attack the castle as soon as its tower tumbled over. As soon as the fire began to have its effect, the layers of mortar between the stones of the wall began to fall. Then a crack was made. The crack became wider and wider and the tower fell. We had assumed that when the tower fell we would be able to go in and reach the enemy. But only the outer face of the wall fell, while the inner wall remained intact. We stood there until the sun became too hot for us, and then returned to our tents after a great deal of damage had been inflicted on us by stones, which were hurled at us.[15]

Despite the only partial success of this attempt, the effects of tunneling were potentially more dramatic than those of the trebuchets, as Fulcher of Chartres recounted in an attack on King Baldwin II holed up in a castle in 1123. The Muslim lord laying siege

ordered the rock on which the castle was situated to be undermined and props to be placed along the tunnel to support the works above. Then he had wood carried in and fire introduced. When the props were burned the excavation suddenly fell in, and the tower which was nearest to the fire collapsed with a great noise. At first smoke rose together with the dust since the debris covered up the fire but when the fire ate through the material underneath and the flames began to be clearly visible, a stupor caused by the unexpected event seized the king.[16]

Mining was hard to disguise—the erection of covering shelters, the removal of spoil—and vulnerable to sorties, so the barrage of rocks and missiles was essential to sweep the walls of returning fire. The tunnels that Khalil's Aleppo miners were starting to dig were conducted against strategic towers and walls that had been identified at the outset; the corners of square towers were prime targets, considered to fall away more easily than circular towers when undermined. As well as the Barbican and the King's Tower, it seems that Khalil had sufficient resources to snake tunnels outward to the adjacent tower of the Countess of Blois and that of St. Nicolas, and the walls close to St. Anthony's Gate.

It was the unrelenting nature of the attack that wore the defenders down, as it was intended to: the teams of men pulling on the traction trebuchets in unison, the dip and rear of the swinging beams, the crash of rocks into walls, the incessant noise, the whistling shower flights of arrows clouding the sky, the steady advance of the protective screens, the uncertainty about what might be happening underground. The psychological effects of bombardment and the continuous guard duties day and night along the whole length of the wall were attritional on energy and morale. There was to be no let up. Above all, it was about the numbers. The use of troops in disciplined relays allowed Khalil the luxury of applying incessant pressure. As the Templar of Tyre knew, "The Saracens came up every day, because they had so many men."[17] By mid-April, there was already a great deal to concern the defense. It was apparent that sitting tight behind Acre's formidable walls was unlikely to save the city. They had to strike back.

10

SORTIES

April 13–Early May 1291

THE MAMLUKS HAD taken Acre by surprise. Their army had been so well organized, their progress so fast. Within two weeks, the failure of the city's passive defense was clear to all. The ferocity of the bombardment, the menacing advance of the barricades up to the edge of the ditch, and the possibility that their opponents were already mining the walls now required an active response.

The great catapults were irreplaceable. If they could be destroyed and the mantlets burned, this would alleviate the remorseless pummeling and allow their crossbowmen to start picking off the catapult crews and exposing the miners to attack. If nothing else, counterattacks could provide morale-raising release of pent-up frustration among the defenders. It seems that the leading figures in the city made a collective decision. They would take the fight to the enemy, along all sectors of the wall, to unsettle and demoralize their tormentors. One among this inner circle was Nicolas de Hanapes, patriarch of the Latin kingdom of Jerusalem. He was a commanding figure, resolutely committed to providing moral and spiritual encouragement to the defense of the city as the pope's representative. Hanapes was about sixty-five, an old man by the standards of the times, with a lifetime's service behind him. He was the author of a popular work of inspirational teaching, *The Book of Examples from Sacred Scripture*, that drew on the Bible for illustrations for the faithful on how to conduct oneself up to the moment of death. The patriarch was at the heart of the defenders' psychological defense, stiffening their resistance with his unrelenting zeal to fight to the last, and he involved himself in strategic battle decisions too.

It was decided to undertake a concerted series of sorties. The key element was surprise, and the first operation was so unexpected in its tactics that it took the Mamluks off guard. On the night of April 13, a small group of ships loaded with soldiers slipped anchor from the city's harbor. These included a barge, a floating artillery platform armed with a traction trebuchet, which had to be towed. The flotilla circled the sea walls of Acre and closed in on the northern shore, outflanking the right wing of the Islamic army, where the Hama contingent was camped, as Abu al-Fida described it, "beside the sea, with the sea on our right as we faced Acre."[1] The ingenious ship battery had been constructed by the Pisans and was accompanied by a pulling team. Archers, crossbowmen, and foot soldiers filled the other ships, which had been protected against incendiary devices.

The encampment was caught totally unprepared by this amphibious assault. "Ships with timber vaulting covered with ox-hides came to us firing arrows and quarrels," al-Fida recalled. Landing parties came ashore and harassed the camp, whose defenses were orientated toward the city such that its own trebuchets, directed at the walls and which could not be quickly repositioned, were unable to respond. At the same time, a second sortie was launched from the gates. The right wing, unsettled, suddenly found itself under pressure from coordinated fire. Missiles rained onto their camp from all directions: bombardment by rocks from the trebuchet and arrows from both shore parties and from the ships. Al-Fida experienced "fighting in front of us from the direction of the city, and on our right from the sea. They brought up a ship carrying a mangonel which fired on us from the direction of the sea. This caused us distress." Fortune, however, was not on the side of the Pisans. The spring sea was unpredictable in its moods. Al-Fida reported with relief that "there was a violent storm of wind, so that the vessel was tossed on the waves and the mangonel it was carrying broke. It smashed to pieces and was never set up again."[2] The ship-borne initiative had failed.

Coordinated follow-up attacks were planned for both ends of the wall on the night of April 15. One was to be a repeat assault on the Hama contingent. This was to be a joint operation of the Templars led by Guillaume de Beaujeu, French troops under Jean de Grailly, and English ones led by Othon de Grandson. Three hundred men, heavily armed knights and foot soldiers, sallied out from the gate of St. Lazarus, close to the end of the wall. Their principal aim was to burn the great trebuchet, nicknamed "the Furious," with Greek fire. Evidently, silencing it had become a priority. Despite bright moonlight, the element of surprise appeared initially to have been successful. The Templar of Tyre recalled what happened. "The master ordered a Provençal, who was the viscount of the bourg of Acre, to set fire to the frame of the sultan's great engine. They went out that night to the apparatus and the man tasked with throwing the Greek fire was frightened when it came to it, and threw it so that it fell short and landed on the ground and burned out there. All the Saracens who were there were killed, both horsemen and those of foot."[3] Abu al-Fida recalled that the unexpected raid had initially put the sentries to flight, but they rallied. Because of the failure of nerve, the attack had been botched; in the confusion, chaos broke out. The Templars, along with other horsemen, got carried away with the prospect of raiding the camp, "but our men, both brethren and secular knights, went in so far among the tents that their horses got their legs entangled in the guy ropes and went sprawling, and then the Saracens killed them."[4] One unfortunate knight "fell into an emir's latrine and was killed there."[5] In this way, the Templar related,

we lost eighteen horsemen that night—brothers of the Temple and secular knights—but we carried away several shields and Saracen bucklers, trumpets and drums. Then my lord and his men turned back to Acre. As they went they met some Saracens waiting in ambush, but they killed them all because the moon shone bright as day and they could see them very clearly. And as I have told you the lord of Hama was in that area. He rallied his men and they came and intercepted us along the sandy shore, hurling javelins at our men, and wounded some, but they did not dare to closely engage our troops. You should know that they seemed to have something like two thousand horsemen, while on our side of knights and others—brothers of the military orders, *valés* [pages] and turcopoles [local cavalry]—there were scarcely 300.[6]

The Muslims gave other accounts. Abu al-Fida stated that the Franks were routed. In yet another, perhaps more credible, Arabic version, the ambush to trap the returning raiders under an emir called al-Halabi failed. The raiders evidently got wind of it and outwitted the emir: "They realised that al-Halabi had concealed himself and they avoided that route and took another. They found on their way some of al-Halabi's kite shields and rectangular shields and took them."[7] Al-Halabi and his men waited patiently until the dawn broke. Then they heard mocking shouts coming from the walls and saw their stolen shields hanging there as trophies.

Meanwhile, a second operation was under way at the eastern end of the city. The mission was the same: to use fire to destroy wooden siege screens and trebuchets. This was a sector in which the emir al-Fakhri, Beaujeu's informant, played a leading role. According to the Muslim account, he appeared to be expecting an attack. "He was riding with those with him standing outside the camp. When the Franks arrived and approached the camp, they wanted to throw the large consignment of Greek fire they had with them. They followed in the middle of the road until suddenly a cry arose from every side, and arrows rained down on them in the night, and they fled on their heels. No-one turned to look after those with them, and they left behind around twenty knights, and a troop went out and took them prisoner."[8] The Templar of Tyre, evidently not an eyewitness to this, remarked that "the Saracens were aware of them and were on guard, and charged the Christians so fiercely that they turned back without achieving anything."[9]

IT HAD PROVED to be a night of mixed fortunes. Each side counted its trophies and its dead. "When morning came al-Malik al-Muzaffar, the lord of Hama, hung a number of heads of Franks on the necks of the horses which the troops had taken from them, and brought them to the sultan."[10] Doubtless these heads were then mounted on poles in sight of the city. Meanwhile, the shields displayed on the walls of Acre were a visible countertaunt to the whole besieging army. Khalil was furious at this public display: such provocations were bad for morale. He "started to call the emirs and rebuke them for prolonging the siege, and they all agreed on [the need to guard] the catapults."[11] Under their sultan's watchful gaze, the pressure was on to try harder.

But from the defenders' perspective, the fact remained that the sorties had failed to achieve anything substantive. And this raised questions. It seemed as if the enemy were awaiting them. The first cleverly conceived but unlucky amphibious attack had certainly made the Mamluks take notice. Khalil had prudently posted cavalry day and night against further sorties, either in line with the received wisdom that "the besieger of the enemy is also the besieged," or he had been forewarned.[12] Or both. And always, in these raids, the forces were mismatched.

BOTH SIDES HAD concerns about morale, loyalty, and the leakage of information. Khalil could not be certain that all his emirs were supportive. He was particularly worried about the commander of the Syrian forces, the powerful emir Husam al-Din Lajin, governor of Damascus. In addition, Guillaume de Beaujeu, grand master of the Templars, had his own potential ally among the tents ranged outside: the informant al-Fakhri, a close attendant of Lajin, now stationed on the left wing of the Mamluk siege train. As well, al-Fakhri had become an object of the sultan's suspicion; his resolute defense against the recent sortie was perhaps an attempt to demonstrate that his loyalty was not in question.

In fact, Khalil was also receiving covert information from within the besieged city, and he had been forewarned. At about this time, an arrow was fired over the wall. Wrapped around it was a message written in Arabic that was taken to the sultan. It read:

> In the name of God, the Merciful, the Compassionate. The blessings of God be upon our master Muhammad and his family. The only true faith in God's sight is Islam. Oh, sultan of the Muslims, preserve your military from the raid tonight, for the people of Akka have agreed on that, and they intend to attack you, and take care also about your emirs, for they mentioned that some are corresponding against you.[13]

The message was from a clandestine convert to Islam within Acre, and one who was evidently well informed. It heightened Khalil's concern. "When the sultan turned his mind to it, he called his emirs Baydara and al-Shuja'i and read it to them. They all agreed that the orderlies and captains should circulate among the emirs and inform them about this matter as a secret among them. Each emir should keep his position."[14] At least for the moment. The aim was to let the emirs know they were under observation and either bind their loyalty or flush out the dissidents.

It worked. Al-Fakhri had become uncomfortably aware of the sultan's gaze. Either he had turned double agent or, now under suspicion from the letter, he was compelled to show exemplary loyalty by stoutly resisting the attack. His actions suggested complex loyalties. A few days later, feeling the heat, he abruptly left the siege and returned to Damascus. Khalil had much to concern him.

AFTER THE AMBUSHES and the inability to surprise the enemy, the possibility that information was making its way over the wall was evidently also on the mind of Beaujeu and the city's other leading figures. It was decided in confidential conclave that all the forces of Acre should make a further concerted attempt to destroy the tormenting trebuchets and damage enemy morale, this time at the vulnerable central section where the wall took a right-hand turn and command passed from the Syrian army to the sultan's Egyptian army.

The defense of this section of wall was entrusted to the Hospitallers, and it was they who were to lead the sortie, supported by the Templars. It took place on the night of April 18. Fearful of the leaking of information, none were to be told of the mission until the last moment. The night was favorably dark. The Templar of Tyre was on hand to relate what happened, though always with the tendency to inflate the numbers of the enemy:

> Then it was decided that all the lords and mounted forces of Acre should make a sortie in the middle of the night from St. Anthony Gate and fall on the Saracens unexpectedly. This was planned so secretly that no one knew about it until the command "To horse!". And when our troops were mounted and galloped out of the gate, the moon was not shining at all. It was very dark. But the Saracens seemed to be forewarned and created such a blaze of lanterns that it was like daylight among their ranks, and such a detachment fell on our troops—there might well have been nearly ten thousand—and they charged us so fiercely hurling javelins as thickly as falling rain. Our men could not endure this and retreated into the city, with several knights wounded.[15]

It was evident, one way or another, that the Mamluks, illuminating the dark night with bursts of fire, were now fully alert to these sorties.

EASTER WAS APPROACHING and, in an attempt to raise morale before the holy day and aware that hunkering down behind the walls would lead inexorably to disaster, there was a plan to break the stranglehold on the city with a do-or-die attack. In an episode probably related by Othon de Grandson, it was decided on Good Friday to attempt a new strategy:

> When they saw that the enemy was conquering the walls and that it would be impossible to defend the city any longer, they decided by common consent to win God's help with the arms of penance, and having confessed and communicated, to form ranks with the

prisoners of war in front of them and to burst out of the city on the day of our common salvation and give their lives as the Author of life had imperilled His own. And when they had resolved with undaunted hearts and kindled spirits, they sent to the Patriarch, who was in the place, that they might accomplish under his authority, and with his blessing, the purpose which they had begun.[16]

With the inspiration of the risen Christ, they would drive their Muslim slaves and prisoners before them as a human shield and make a concerted attack. However, the initiative was categorically banned by Nicolas de Hanapes the patriarch, who, "broken in spirit and depending on the advice of perfidious persons, replied that none should attempt this, nor open any of the city gates under pain of excommunication."[17]

This blame attributed to Hanapes by Grandson falls at an oblique angle to the generally positive accounts of the patriarch's robust commitment to the defense of Acre. Possibly the use of a human shield on Good Friday was repulsive to holy writ. More likely, Hanapes was concerned that the sorties had proved a futile leaching of manpower, and he was determined to assert his papal authority over the various factions. The criticism says much for the level of discord at the center of the defense. Henceforth, there would be no more sorties. The defenders approached the Easter Day in sober mood. Khalil, meanwhile, had concerns about the security of his rule and the coalition of the emirs assembled for the siege, whom he castigated for insufficient effort.

If the bombardment of the walls went on unabated, so did the work underground. The miners continued digging and propping their way toward the walls from openings shielded by the wooden barricades. Like the crusaders a century earlier, the target was the apex of the vulnerable salient where the Accursed Tower protected the heart of the city.

Within the city, its defenders became increasingly aware of this activity and undertook measures to counter it. The defenders detected and located mining work under the tower of the Countess of Blois—either by the muffled clink of picks working nearby or by placing buckets of water on the ground and detecting vibrations from tell-tale ripples on the surface. They started to dig countermines to intercept the Aleppo miners. Bursting into the chambers, there was nightmarish fighting in the dark, pulling down pitprops to suffocate the invaders. "Our men countermined against them, and fought back fiercely," the Templar of Tyre reported.[18] Yet the work was exhausting and made considerable demands on skilled human labor. The Templar repeatedly emphasized the disparity of numbers. When it came to mining, the Saracens could rotate their men. Working in relays, they could construct more tunnels than the defenders could intercept. And there was danger, too, that the very activity of countermining could further weaken the foundations of the fortifications that the defenders were attempting to protect. Despite their best efforts, the mines advanced and shots continued to rain down.

As APRIL WORE on and apprehension grew, the people of Acre looked with increasing attention toward the sea. They were safe from maritime attacks. The Mamluks had no naval capacity of any note, and the main port of Cyprus, Famagusta, was just 170 miles away— two day's sailing in favorable weather—so that ships could shuttle back and forth supplying the crusader states. There was keen expectation that Amalric's brother Henry, King of Cyprus and Jerusalem, would bring a relief force any day. Others, wealthy townspeople and some of the canny Italian merchants from Genoa, Venice, and Pisa, were sizing up the chance to pay their way out on passing vessels. Acre was the principal trading port of the Levantine coast, a regular destination for the seasonal trading fleets that came twice a year, in the spring and autumn, and the military orders owned their own vessels or chartered them to bring supplies and manpower across the Mediterranean as required.

The spring sea, however, could be violent, and the port of Acre was less than ideal for sizeable ships, particularly in rough weather. The shelter for vessels consisted of a double harbor embraced by breakwaters. The entrance at its mouth was overlooked by a guard post, known as the Tower of Flies; it was positioned at the end of one breakwater and had a commanding view over the bay. Within the enclosing breakwaters, there was an outer harbor and a smaller inner one, protected by a chain "as thick of a man's arm."[19] This defensive boom was itself a relic of crusader ventures. It had once closed the mouth of the Golden Horn at Constantinople and had been sent to Acre by the crusaders who disgracefully sacked the Christian city in 1204. It was in this small inner basin protected by the chain that goods to Acre had to be unloaded. Disembarking, all new arrivals passed into the city through the "Iron Gate," where they paid their customs dues and had access to warehousing facilities. It was here, too, that Acre's naval arsenal was located.

Despite the security that the enclosed harbor provided, the sea run into Acre was tricky even on fair days. Ships approached from the west looking for the landmarks of the Templars' castle and St. Andrew's church, on past the city's most southwesterly point, the ominously named Cape of Storms, and along the southern breakwater. They then had to make an awkwardly sharp turn to negotiate the entrance to the harbor, which was only ninety yards wide, passing under the gaze of the Tower of Flies to starboard.

The reputation of Acre's port was mixed. While the chronicler William of Tyre had praised the sheltering double harbor, which "lying both inside and outside the walls, offers a safe and tranquil anchorage to ships,"[20] the maneuver to enter it was considered difficult and formed the subject of detailed advice in an Italian navigation manual of the period. While conceding that Acre was a good port, its advice, steering via the city landmarks, suggested caution:

> When you approach the said port, go a distance from the city, that is to say from the house of the Temple and from the church of St. Andrew four cables, because of the sandbank that is above St. Andrew, and when you have the house that was that of the constable to the right of the Tower of Flies, you can make your way straight to the port. And when you enter the port, go into it so that you have the city of

Haifa on mid-poop to the east and the Tower of Flies on mid-prow, and so you turn into the port clear of the said sand-banks.[21]

The problem was that when the sea was rough, this maneuver was risky. The pilgrim Theodoric, a century earlier, declared the approach "dangerous of access, when the wind blows from the south, and the shore troubled from the continual shocks which they receive from the waves."[22] Domenico Laffi, an Italian traveler three centuries later, thought the port "insecure and open to winds from the west, which often attain the violence of tempests." The ships with which he was traveling preferred the harbor at Haifa, since it was sheltered from rough weather, "in contrast to that of Acre, the sea-floor of which is sown with rocks so sharp as to tear the cables however strong these may be."[23] The local conditions at Acre were such that the Venetians, ever prudent in matters of trade and navigation, had sent an extra thirty or forty iron anchors for their ships calling at Acre in 1288 as further precaution.

In effect, when the sea was boisterous, it was difficult for ships to call at Acre, and the destruction of the Pisans' ship-mounted trebuchet indicated the difficulties that unpredictable spring weather might bring to resupplying the city or evacuating civilians should the need arise. The inconveniences of its maritime situation were compounded by the comparatively small size of even the outer harbor, which meant that larger vessels preferred to anchor outside, so that goods and people had to be transferred to and fro via smaller vessels—a slow and inefficient process.

All this was in mind during the second half of April as the mood darkened. It seems that supplies of food continued to reach Acre from Cyprus and that the imminent arrival of King Henry had been communicated to the city. But from the start of May, it appears that some of those who had the means to pay their passage on visiting ships were leaving on any that called in to trade. Early confidence had turned to anxiety. "Our people in the city of Acre were thus in great torment and a sorry state," the Templar of Tyre concluded gloomily, "but there was reported to be news that King Henry was about to come from Cyprus bringing great help, and they expected him daily."[24] "They always turned their faces to the sea," recalled Arsenius, a Greek monk, "watching to see if the west wind would carry the sails they were hoping for."[25]

11

Negotiations
May 4–17, 1291

O N Friday, May 4, Henry's fleet of forty ships, carrying the red lions and gold crosses of the regal banner, was finally spotted on the western horizon. Hope rose again. Henry II, the nominal overlord of the kingdom of Jerusalem, in fact had limited power over the interminable squabbles between the city's factions, but he was greeted with rapturous joy. Bonfires, visible to the besieging army, were lit in the streets. There was feasting and the ringing of church bells. The king was twenty years old and epileptic; illness seems to have delayed his departure from Famagusta, but he came with all the troops he could muster and, for spiritual support, the bishop of Nicosia. His forces amounted to a small number of knights and foot soldiers—at the most seven hundred men, too few to materially alter the balance of power. He appraised the situation and injected new vigor into the defense, but any boost to morale was blunted by Khalil's immediate response.

Aware that the joyous clamor reaching his own troops over the wall could lower their own morale, the sultan intensified the bombardment. The crescendo of missiles—the gouts of Greek fire, the shattering of clay pots containing incendiary material lobbed over the wall, the shower flights of arrows, the crashing of catapulted rocks against stone walls—continued unabated. The black bulls also hurled vessels filled with excrement, burning blocks of wood, and fire cauldrons. All the time, behind their protective screens, the Mamluks were getting closer, both below and above ground. The town was well supplied with food, but the defenders' lack of large missiles with which to load their own trebuchets was noticeable, and they were compelled to repair the walls with timber and wads of cotton. Exhausted by the continuous bombardment, the attempts to rebuild walls, and the stamping out of fires, nerves were shredding. The chroniclers give variable accounts of the bickerings inside the city and the lack of coordinated action. They apportioned blame for the dissension in line with their own national and religious interests. From the safety of distance and with the luxury of retrospective blame, the Greek monk Arsenius reserved his fiercest criticism for the Italian merchants. "The Pisans and the assisting Venetians would not endure the religious authority [of the papal legate]," he maintained.[1] While the Venetians almost certainly were less than wholehearted in their participation, the Pisans made unsparing efforts in the operation of their trebuchets. Few escaped Arsenius's withering judgments. He conjured a febrile atmosphere of people dancing on the edge of an abyss. "The crusaders, while we hoped they would give up their souls for the victory of the cross, abandoned themselves to drinking and when the trumpets called people to arms, they were given over to indulgence, ignored the fighting, and did not release their breasts and arms from the embraces of Venus. And what was worse, the brothers of the Hospitallers and the Templars scorned to co-operate with one another, and to take turns [at guard duty] and bear the burdens of fighting."[2] Factually, though, they had at the very least undertaken joint night sorties. The divergence of subsequent accounts only reflected Acre's partisan factions. Where Arsenius reserved his praise for "the illustrious King Henry," the anonymous author of *The Destruction of Acre* heaped multiple accusations on him, and the German Ludolf von Suchem, writing well after the event, would only applaud his fellow countrymen, the Teutonic Knights.

Whatever preexisting frictions there might have been within the city, the deteriorating situation made Henry's task impossible from the start. He may have arrived with a fanfare and a royal flourish, but the young king was a realist. He quickly concluded that his reinforcements were insufficient to sway the tide of events given an unmatchable opponent, and try as he might, he lacked overall authority to heal the city's internal tensions nor was he able to staunch the leakage of people. He decided to sue for peace.

KHALIL POSSIBLY ALSO had some interest in a negotiated outcome, given the stirrings of opposition within the inner circles of Mamluk power. A ceasefire was arranged. For a brief period on May 7, the war machines fell silent and the bombardment stopped. In the compara- tive quiet, Khalil came down from his hilltop position and had a small tent set up outside the walls opposite one of the tower gates, that of the Patriarch close to the sea. Two unarmed envoys emerged—a knight, Guillaume de Villiers, and a Templar from Beaujeu's house- hold, Guillaume de Cafran. They prostrated themselves three times before the sultan. Khalil was blunt. "Have you brought me the keys of the town?" he asked.[3] The messengers replied that Acre could not lightly be given up, but they had come to ask for mercy for its people. It seems that they were offering to pay tribute in order to retain Acre.

Khalil's reply was aimed at a bloodless victory and contained a touch of magnanimity. Negotiated surrender usually meant the de- parture of the people under safe conduct but with almost no posses- sions. He offered more. "I will grant you this much grace, that you only have to give me the stones of the city, and you may carry off everything else, and leave and go away. I will do this for the sake of your king, who has come here and who is a youth, as I once was. But I won't do anything more for you."[4]

Khalil's advisers had been averse to any negotiation from the start. Victory seemed to be at hand—they were on the brink of driving the infidels back into the sea. They begged him not to abandon his father's sacred cause, because "this fortress is one of their great ones, and only these unbelievers remain in all the lands of the coast. It was the firm decision of the martyr, the father of al-Ashraf [Khalil], to conquer it, and the sultan decided at the beginning of his reign to conquer it as his father had decided. Muslims have been wounded, and they have been killed; there is no use in peace, and we are close to conquering it." At the same time, great shouts went up from the Muslim camp as they got word of the sultan's offer. Fired with the popular zeal of jihad, and doubtless with the attraction of plunder, the rank and file who had taken up the cause and followed the army—the common people, the urban mob, and the camel drivers, as well as the Mamluk soldiers—cried out that the siege should continue: "O our master, the sultan in the martyr's tomb would not come to an agreement with those cursed ones!"[5]

The envoys, who had been briefed as to their remit, had little room for maneuver; Henry had evidently drawn a line at surrendering the city. Aware of the opprobrium of the Christian world ringing in their ears at the loss of the last foothold in the Holy Land, they replied that they could not "because the people overseas would regard us as traitors." "Then you should go away," were Khalil's concluding words to the envoys, "because I shall give you nothing more!"[6]

At that moment, any departing niceties were shattered by the crash of a large stone, fired from a trebuchet from the nearby tower gate of the Patriarch. "I don't know by what accident this happened," the Templar of Tyre wrote. "It came so near the tent where the sultan and the messengers were, that the sultan out of instinctive bravado, not wishing to do them any real harm, leaped up, put his hand to his sword, drew it out a palm's length, and cried. 'Ah! You filthy swine, what's to stop me chopping off your heads?'"[7]

One of his emirs, Sanjar al-Shuja'i, prompted him to stay his hand: "Sir, God forbid that you should soil the iron of your sword with the blood of pigs! The traitors are those who fired the shot. You should let these men go, as they are here with you."[8] It was an honest acknowledgment of the terms under which the envoys had come and their innocence of any responsibility.

And so, the Templar concluded wearily, "the messengers returned to Acre, and thereupon the two sides resumed the labour of firing their trebuchets at one another, as enemies are accustomed to do."[9] The brief opportunity for negotiation had come and gone.

If morale and hope were draining away in the Christian camp, Khalil's suspicions of some of the emirs remained, and of two particularly, Alam al-Din al-Hamawi and Husam al-Din Lajin, who had been supporters of the murdered Turuntay, rival for the sultanate on Qalawun's death. The flight to Damascus of Lajin's attendant, al-Fakhri, evidently brought matters to a head. On the day after the failed negotiations, the army was shaken by rumors of trouble in the camp. Khalil had dispatched a fast courier to the governor of Damascus to arrest al-Fakhri. His goods were confiscated, and he was returned under armed escort to Acre.

Lajin knew he too was compromised when someone came to warn him of the sultan's intention to arrest him. Fearing for his life, he loaded his baggage under cover of night and was preparing to flee. His departure was spotted by another emir, Alam al-Dawadari, loyal to the sultan's cause, who was camped nearby. Spurring his horse to a gallop, he rode after the fleeing Lajin, caught up with him, and begged him to return: "Don't be the cause of damage to the Muslim cause. For if the Franks learn that you have taken flight they will become stronger, to our disadvantage, just at the moment that the town is on the point of being taken."[10] Lajin returned. The day after, the sultan ordered Lajin to his presence, gave him robes of honor, and reassured him. This mollifying attitude lasted two days. On the third, he arrested Lajin and sent him under guard to the fortress of Safad. In the long run, Khalil's wariness of Lajin would be confirmed in fatal circumstances.

But the confident shouts of the people and the reasoning that persuaded Lajin back seemed fully justified in the days that followed. Under incessant bombardment, the mines had crept further forward, and with them the mobile wicker screens that protected the troops of Sanjar al-Shuja'i. They inched toward the critical apex of the wall and the projecting barbican of Hugh III. In the week after the failed negotiations, the implications of the Mamluks' advances became clear. On Tuesday, May 8, this barbican, probably now untenable through mining, was abandoned by the defenders. They set fire to it, destroyed the walkway that connected it to the outer wall, and retreated into the King's Tower behind. "The city was in a bad way," recorded the Templar, "because . . . the [outer] wall was mined and the tower [barbican] also."[11] The King's round tower, lynchpin of the defenses on the outer wall and defender of the Accursed Tower on the inner, was now exposed.

This was the start of a disastrous week for the defenders. In the underground chambers they had constructed along this sector, the assiduous Aleppo miners lit fires that weakened the foundations in several places. One by one, the outer facades of towers slumped and walls collapsed. Along the wall from the King's Tower on one side, the tower of the Countess of Blois crumbled; on the other, the English Tower; then further in both directions, sections of the outer wall adjacent to the critical gate of St. Anthony and that of St. Nicholas. The ominous sound of masonry crashing into the ditch outside

The siege of Acre in a manuscript illustration. Miners with picks, protected by archers, undermine the base of the walls. (Oliver Poole, redrawn from *Crusader Manuscript Illumination at Saint-Jean D'Acre, 1275–1291*, Princeton, 1976)

sank spirits in the town still lower. The emir al-Shuja'i's men were also at work mining the King's Tower itself.

As the situation worsened, more were trying to leave the stricken city. Spring was the season when merchant ships put in at Acre; those who could pay their passage, wealthy merchants from the Italian communities and members of the noble classes, were already on their way out as the walls crumbled. By mid-May, 3,000 had left. Many of the old and infirm and the women and children were also evacuated, together with precious holy relics, the city's treasury, and the goods and possessions of citizens. This was done while the weather was still fine and entrance to Acre's port could be easily managed. Most were ferried to Cyprus. According to some sources, this flight was accelerated by King Henry himself in events that ensued, the exact timing and veracity of which is uncertain, but it is clear that on May 15, morale in the city was draining away.

On that day, the efforts of Khalil's miners were rewarded with a key strategic prize. The King's Tower, at the exposed eastern salient of the outer walls, which protected the Accursed Tower, was undermined. Possibly it had been compromised by the defenders' own countermining, but to the dismay of the Templar watching, it was so weakened that "the front face fell forward in a heap into the ditch, so that it was impossible to pass over the top of the stones."[12] This provided a major opportunity for the besiegers but also posed a challenge. The ditch, and the land approaching it, were so strewn with jumbled masonry that no easy attack could be launched to take control of the tower and so penetrate the outer wall, which was still being resolutely and desperately defended, without being dangerously exposed. The practical engineering skills and resources of the Mamluk army improvised an ingenious solution. Baybars al-Mansuri, one of the sultan's emirs, set himself to pondering the problem of how to construct a causeway for a full assault:

Amidst all this I was searching for a place at which opportunity might knock, a corner which might permit a stratagem, but found none. While I was exercising my thoughts and letting my sight and perceptions roam, I suddenly noticed that one of the towers damaged by trebuchets could now be reached. Between this tower and the walls a wide-open space had been uncovered, but, being surmounted by crossbows, could not be traversed unless a screen were erected over the entire area to protect anyone who entered. So I availed myself of some felt, stitching all of it together in the shape of a large cloud, long and wide. Between two posts opposite the dilapidated tower, I placed a pulley rigged with ropes, similar to a ship's. There I hoisted the felt cloud into place as a dam. This was done under the wing of night, unbeknownst to the Akkans, who when they arose in the morning and saw the screen, fired mangonel and arrows against it. When a stone fell into the screen, the felt would slacken beneath it and break its thrust, and the crossbow men could not penetrate it with their arrows. We were able to pass, and found a way to cross, and a wall separated us and the enemy. We started to fill up the ditch which was between the walls using horses' nosebags filled with earth, together with whatever timber made it level so that it became a passable road, and it was a blessed sight.[13]

From within the city, the Templar of Tyre could also observe the speed and efficiency with which the Mamluks capitalized on the situation, which reflected their enterprise, levels of organization, and vast human resources. "The Saracens made small sacks of hemp cloth, filled them with sand, and each horseman carried one on the neck of his horse and threw it down to the men at the barricades who were in that sector. When night fell these men carried the sacks and laid them over the stones and levelled them like a paved road."[14] The way to the stricken tower was now open.

According to the self-congratulating Baybars al-Mansuri, the sultan was delighted with his stratagem. He resolved to launch an all-out assault the following day in two places: at the tottering King's Tower and at the wall to its west, toward the city's main gate, that of St. Anthony.

It was King Henry's troops, displaced from the destroyed barbican, who were now manning these walls alongside those of the Teutonic

Knights. During May 15, a determined attack on this section had been beaten back. Everywhere nerves were strained and men were exhausted. Next morning, confused accounts of a collapse of morale on this sector filtered into the town; conflicting time scales and possibly post hoc blame crept into the Christian chronicles.

The relations between Henry's men and their codefendants seem to have been poor. At sunset on May 15, they had handed over control of the sector to the Teutonic Knights under their grand master according to the eight-hour rotation of shifts. Henry's troops were due to take over again the following dawn. The anonymous author of *The Destruction of Acre*, who drew on eyewitness accounts, claimed that when day broke on the sixteenth, they were nowhere to be seen. The charge was that King Henry, seeing that nothing further could be done to broker a peaceful outcome or gain authoritative control over the city's various factions, had quietly embarked on his ships and fled with the men he had brought, together with a substantial portion of the nobility of the town.

Henry, perhaps realizing that the situation was hopeless and the discord among the defenders so great, reasonably decided that it would be better for the king of Jerusalem to survive another day. He was accused of gross cowardice. "O would that the winds and the sea had sunk them to the depths!" came the chronicler's curse.[15] The truth of this is unverifiable, but the Templar of Tyre, a generally sober eyewitness, claimed that King Henry was still in Acre two days later. Could he have been shielding the monarch out of loyalty? More likely, the events that were about to unfold required both an explanation and a scapegoat, and in the tangled loyalties and partisan accounts that survived the siege, the anonymous author had access to accounts hostile to the king.

Whatever the circumstances, as day broke, the sultan's attack on the section of wall in question—that toward St. Anthony's Gate—appears to have fallen on a weakened defense. The Syrian army, no longer led by Lajin, advanced behind a line of shields, as crossbow bolts, arrows, and javelins rained onto the walls. The assault was well planned, and there were insufficient defenders to resist this tide.

As the wave swept forward, a corps of men filled up the ditch with anything at hand; wood, stones, earth, timber, the bodies of dead horses—all were hurled in to level an approach up the steep slope to the walls rising above them. Ladders were propped against the walls. The defenders bombarded them with rocks, hurled javelins, and fired crossbow bolts. There was hand-to-hand fighting, men hammering at each other at close quarters with swords, clubs, and spears "like smiths beating hot metal . . . so that many died from the blows on both sides."[16] In the din and the carnage, the defenders were unable to sustain the assault "with the advance of a multitude of crossbow men, javelin and stone throwers."[17] The sparsely defended sector was overwhelmed. The survivors were forced a crossbow shot's length back into the city, abandoning their wounded and dead. The critical gate tower of St. Anthony, the entrance into the heart of the city, was now in Mamluk hands, though the gate itself was still sealed shut.

The uproar carried into the city, with a crowd of people fleeing from the front line. Relations between the various factions and military orders remained strained. Some were reluctant to help because they had never participated in the initial breaking of the treaty, others preferred to barricade their own sections, but news of the breach at last stimulated a general call to arms. The Marshal of the Hospital, Matthieu de Clermont, rallied a few knights to arms. Swiftly mounted, they emerged from the nearby gates of the Hospital "armed and plated, heads protected by polished helmets, braceroles fitted round their arms and seated on their war horses with lances raised," in the words of a chronicler, to find themselves engulfed in a rout of fleeing men, "terrified though not yet wounded," impeding their progress. Clermont turned fiercely on the panic-stricken troops abandoning the walls: "Are you mad? Fleeing with your armour intact, your helmets and shields unshattered, your bodies still unwounded? I beg you for the faith of the Church, return to the fight!" Digging his spurs into his horse, Clermont plunged forward into the mêlée, with the hope of personally confronting the sultan. He picked out one of the emirs, "who seemed to be the bravest," pierced him through the chest with his lance, and swept him from his horse. Reaching for his sword, hacking and hewing, chopping off heads, slicing backbones and running through the lightly-armored Muslims, Clermont wreaked carnage. The psychological momentum altered. The Muslims paused, then turned "like sheep fleeing the wolf."[18]

However, Khalil had the resources to launch other coordinated attacks at the same time. Further up the wall, he was now using the causeway of sacks of sand built by the stratagem of Baybars al-Mansuri to attack the stricken King's Tower. Toward the hour of vespers (sunset), his men poured forward. The Templar saw that "half of the vault, on the side facing the town, was still intact," and it was stoutly defended by a large number of men, "but it made no difference, the Saracens took the tower anyway and hoisted the sultan's flag on it. In response we loaded our catapults, positioned them to aim at the tower and fired them. We killed some of the Saracens but were unable to drive them back." The King's Tower was lost. Desperate to prevent any further advance, the defenders had built "a structure of wood, covered with leather, called a cat, and put men inside it, so that the Saracens who had taken the tower could advance no further."[19] This resistance of the men in the cat halted the advance, but the Accursed Tower was now exposed, and the defenders had been pushed back to the inner wall on a long section between the gates of St. Nicolas and St. Anthony. Holding the Accursed Tower was now key to survival.

Meanwhile, Clermont's charge at St. Anthony's Gate, supported by the small band of Hospitaller knights, had had an electrifying effect on morale. The shame-faced rallied; behind the knights, foot soldiers advanced, stabbing the bellies of the attackers' horses with their swords. The intruders turned and ran, pursued from street to street. Those trying to prize open the gate, which was still barred, were repulsed.

As night fell, the sultan abandoned hope of taking Acre that day, and ordered a full retreat by trumpet call. Cries of "Victory! Victory!" echoed through the streets. In a morale-raising show, the defenders advanced out of the gates in armored force with banners unfurled to mop up. Dying Muslims were dispatched on the spot; defenders, some wounded, others lying on the ground too exhausted to move, were taken home. The dead were buried. Clermont had breathed life into the defense. There was a buzz of triumph within the town as word of the stout resistance got about and a spirit of cooperation animated the people.

Late into the night the population worked to help repair the walls as best they could. Baulks of timber and stones were carted up to close the breaches and to make palisades. The enemy dead were thrown out. Weapons were stockpiled on the towers. These included large frame-mounted siege crossbows cranked by a windlass that had great penetrative power, two-feet versions loaded by a foot stirrup, and lighter crossbows, as well as substantial quantities of arrows. Bowmen were detailed to each position and a guard organized. Exhausted by the long, draining day of fighting and repairing, the bulk of the men were sent home for a few hours rest, then ordered to reconvene an hour before dawn at the Hospital.

Underneath the temporary euphoria, the situation was bleak. Casualties had been high, and despite the defenders' best efforts, they were now pinned within the inner walls for a six-hundred-yard stretch from the collapsed round tower of the King to St. Anthony's Gate. Overnight, while they patched up their defenses as well as they could, they could hear the rhymical crash of battering rams destroying sections of the outer walls and collapsing the English Tower, which they were powerless to prevent. By the morning, the breach in the outer wall was some sixty yards wide. "When the tower had been taken," the Templar recalled, "everyone was deeply dismayed and began to place their women and children on the ships."[20] It was doubtless the families of the wealthy who commandeered spaces on board. The poor would have to look elsewhere for salvation. "People were dazed and paralyzed, uncertain what to do."[21]

MAY 17. A Thursday. The start of a grim day, the morning overcast and the sea stormy. An hour before dawn, the leading captains, commanders, and religious authorities were gathered in the Hospital to discuss their predicament. The mood was glum. Khalil now had control of the outer wall along a wide sector, and the continuous whittling away of men left the defense threadbare. There were at best 7,000 able-bodied troops to man a perimeter of over a mile and to confront waves of attack that seemed inexhaustible.

At the meeting at the Hospital, one man stood out. Nicolas de Hanapes rose, motioned for silence with his hands, and delivered a mighty exhortation for faith, resistance, and courage in the name of Christ. To surrender now would be to put themselves in the hands of the infidel. And he stressed the likelihood of the wholesale rape and slavery of the women and children. "For you know that whoever of you was chosen by your Lord to defend his honour fighting against one or many, there is no doubt that we are all men tied to Jesus for the faith that we have in him through which we must be saved."[22] His lengthy peroration ended with the direction to "confess your sins one to another, hoping that through the mercy of God you will be saved and obtain eternal life."[23]

His words, which were followed by a brief mass, lifted the spirits of the people. They took the sacrament, confessed and embraced each other, gave the kiss of peace, and cried. This had a bracing effect on the defense. Those who had been covertly looking for escape on the ships resolved to return to the fight, "their swords sharpened, their lances brandished, and encouraging one another."[24] Hanapes spent his day and far into the night tirelessly touring the front line, inspiring the men to do or die for their faith.

At the walls, there was something of a lull. It was probable that Khalil had been checked by the sight of his men in full flight from St. Anthony's Gate. Given the threats to his authority and the possibility that the enthusiasm of the vast numbers of volunteers might drain away, it was essential that there should be no repeats. On the other hand, his position was incredibly strong. He had control of a significant section of the outer wall, and he used the day to ensure the material conditions for a final breakthrough and to increase the fervor of his men. His main concern was the deep and steeply sloping ten-yard-wide ditch between the inner and outer walls that his men would have to negotiate in order to storm the inner defensive structure. Small diversionary attacks and the continuous play of the catapults were designed to prevent the defenders from relaxation and to limit their interference with his plans. Anything that was available was hauled up to the edge of the inner fosse by camels. Along with earth, stones, and timber, the cadavers of animals and fallen fighters were unceremoniously tipped into the ditch to provide a stable crossing to the foot of the inner walls. An unbearable stench wafted over the walls. At the same time, Khalil prepared the men for the battle. Religious enthusiasm would have been whipped up in the camp by the mullahs passing to and fro among the men. The prayer times were observed with particular devotion, and the sultan offered monetary rewards for acts of bravery in the final assault.

Within the town, the Christians were making their own preparations. They set up their war machines to oppose the gaps by the King's Tower and the English Tower. Swords were sharpened, shields and ammunition collected, guard duties assigned; the enemy dead continued to be thrown over the walls and gaps plugged with whatever materials were at hand. The Accursed Tower had to be held. The people had been inspired to prepare their own civil defense. The maze of narrow, winding thoroughfares, with their blind alleys, internal gateways, small squares, and stout towers—effectively a series of fortified nuclei within the fabric of the city—provided ample possibilities for last-ditch street fighting. Strategic crossroads were sealed with wooden barricades and guarded by detachments of armed men; stones were stockpiled on rooftops to rain down on the heads of intruders.

The attempt to get the women and children away by ship was thwarted by the weather. Acre's port, vulnerable to rough seas, was inhospitable, and luck was not on the city's side. "The weather was very bad," the Templar remembered, "and the sea so rough that the women and children who had boarded the ships could not endure it, and they disembarked and returned to their homes."[25] In the darkness, the defenders went to their positions, the civilians to their houses. Everyone knew that dawn would bring the decisive attack.

12

"SEE THE WOUND!"

Dawn to Noon, May 18, 1291

MAY 18, A Friday, the weather was gloomy and the sea still rough. Khalil's army was readied before dawn and the sultan on horseback a visible presence there to encourage the troops. Holy men and dervishes had been through the camp whipping up spirit for the sacred cause, while Khalil's heralds circulated, promising more earthly rewards. The Templar heard the signal for the advance. With the sound of a great drum booming in the darkness, "which had a great and horrible voice, the Saracens attacked the city of Acre on all sides."[1] If the initial strategy was to compel the defenders to spread their limited numbers along the whole front, Khalil's real focus remained the sector from St. Anthony's Gate to the St. Nicolas Gate, the outer walls of which were in his hands. Opposite the damaging breaches in the wall where the Tower of the English and the Tower of the King had fallen—exposing the pivotal Accursed Tower—the defenders had set up their trebuchets, resolved to mount a spirited defense of the heart of the city.

The noise of the advance, a shock tactic of Mamluk Islamic armies to strike dread into the heart of defenders and to drive fear from those of its own men, was colossal—a mighty wall of sound: three hundred camel-mounted kettle drummers battering out a savage tattoo; the clashing of cymbals; the blare of trumpets; and the screaming and shouting of thousands of men.

On the walls, the defenders waited for the enemy to come in range; trebuchets and crossbows loaded; rocks, crossbow bolts, and arrows

The wall of sound: drums and trumpets to terrify and inspire. (Oliver Poole, redrawn from *Al-Maqamat al-Hariri*, Bibliothèque Nationale de France)

stockpiled; townspeople manning the wooden street barricades and on the roofs of houses ready to rain down missiles. The patriarch tire-lessly exhorted the defenders to be resolute in the name of Christ. "Surround us with your impregnable wall, O Lord, and protect us with your weapons!"[2] Church bells rang.

Khalil's army advanced in well-ordered ranks, each row consisting of 150 to 200 troops specialized in specific fighting techniques. Ahead came the fanatical dervishes and fakirs, shouting out the name of God as they ran wildly forward, impelled by holy zeal and visions of para-dise to die at the foot of the wall and to provide a human bridge over which the soldiers might cross. And prodded forward with them as a human shield, co-opted Christians, subject communities of the sul-tan's realms, who had been compelled to the campaign with a threat and a promise: if they survived with Acre untaken, their taxation would be doubled; if it fell, they and their descendants in perpetuity would be freed from taxation.

Behind these reluctant or zealous suicide troops came a protective phalanx, troops armed with tall, stout, wooden shields to take the first shock. Then the fire troops, men carrying oil kettles and burning torches flaring in the dark, and hurling clay bombs of Greek fire over the walls. They put up a screen of smoke and fire through which the archers in the row behind sent up shower flights of arrows, and crossbowmen stepped forward to loose quarrels. Behind them, the close combat troops, armed with short swords and leather shields to tackle the hand-to-hand fighting. Alongside, men with ladders, hoes, picks, battering rams, and grappling irons rushed forward to scale and dismantle walls. The shield-bearing troops advanced shoulder to shoulder, presenting an unbroken and menacing wall. Unarmed volunteers with simple slingshots peppered those on the walls with small stones. Further back, the trebuchets continued to hurtle rocks into the city.

The defenders, however, had the advantage of height, and some protection from barrels and makeshift battlements, and they were evidently skilled at wall fighting. As the massed wave came on, crossbow bolts wreaked havoc among the front ranks. Aiming down almost vertically on those at the steeply sloping foot of the wall, "they fired volleys of three quarrels at a time into the front line which punctured the shields and pinned them to the shield bearers, and they shot a huge number of quarrels from ordinary crossbows and the powerful siege crossbows that passed clean through many of those who had no protection at all."[3] At the same time, they rained rocks down on the men attempting to dismantle the base of the walls, "so that they were crushed beneath their shields like toads."[4] In this havoc—in which mingled shouts in the names of Christ and Muhammad in French, Arabic, Italian, German, Turkish, English, Catalan, Greek—the defenders tore great holes in the advancing mass.

THE INITIAL ATTACK along the whole perimeter was intended to keep the defenders thinly stretched. It was only diversionary. In the absence of any overall strategic command within the city, it ensured that the considerable fighting skills of the Templars and the Hospitallers remained tied down in the suburb of Montmusard, and as the defenders created initial carnage, Khalil resorted to the second phase of his plan. His aim was to overwhelm the overstretched defense by weight of numbers at the chosen vulnerable spots, and to do this without allowing the enemy to concentrate their men there or to allow them any respite. In what must have been a preplanned maneuver, he quietly and gradually withdrew troops from outlying sectors and "ordered them secretly to the broken wall with all their devices."[5] When they were formed up, they surged forward in a tight phalanx at the signal of the trumpets, totally oblivious to fear, with spades and picks and grappling irons to break through or climb over the walls.

On the walls, the defenders were being worn down by the incessant repetition of dodging missiles, of firing, reloading, and firing again. The resources of the Mamluks seemed limitless. They came on in relays. If checked, "they reformed their ranks and brought up fresh troops, and with the Christians exhausted they applied immense pressure to force a way into the city. With these strategies they could in the twinkle of an eye deny the Christians a moment to breathe."[6] Noise and confusion reigned. "Those [of the enemy] who were hurling Greek fire threw it so often and so thickly," the Templar recalled, "that the smoke was so great that one man could hardly see another."[7] It was impossible to extinguish once it caught. The fear of being burned alive by these roaring balls of fire was always terrifying, and it could be heard coming. Joinville had once vividly described the sound of Greek fire, which "made such a noise as it came that it sounded like the thunder of heaven. It seemed like a dragon flying through the air."[8] The Templar witnessed the equal pressure applied by the bowmen: "Through the smoke, archers shot feathered arrows so densely that our men and mounts were grievously wounded."[9] Exhaustion set in. The supplies of arrows and quarrels were running low. Crossbow fire slackened. They fought on with swords, maces, rocks, and whatever else was at hand.

The breakthrough came in the fiercely contested battle for the Accursed Tower. For a long time, the defenders prevented the Mamluks entering the breaches in the walls by the ruined towers on the outer wall, against which they had positioned their trebuchets. But the supply of projectiles dwindled, and the sheer weight of numbers started to tell. The wooden cat came under intense bombardment and with it the fear of being burned alive. "They all advanced on foot, so many that they couldn't be counted. In the front rank came men carrying great shields. Behind them men who cast Greek fire, and after them men who hurled javelins and shot feathered arrows so thickly that it seemed like rain falling from the heavens. Our men who were inside the cat abandoned it."[10] They withdrew from the Accursed Tower and fell back into the narrow lanes of the city.

It was a decisive moment. The way into Acre lay open.

Some of the king's troops retreated within the inner wall toward St. Anthony's Gate. The attackers were able to flood the space between the two walls and fan out. "They took two routes," the Templar remembered, "since they were between the city's two walls—that's to say, between the first line of walls and ditches, which were called the barbican, and the great [inner] walls and ditches of the city itself. Some of them entered by a gate of the great tower called the Accursed Tower, and moved towards [the church of] San Romano, where the Pisans had positioned their great trebuchets. The others kept to the road [between the two sets of walls] and headed for St. Anthony's Gate."[11]

The loss of the Accursed Tower was critical. One group, making their way toward the Pisan trebuchets, now posed a serious threat to the heart of the town. At the same time, both the gate of St. Anthony and that of St. Nicolas, close to the sea, were coming under increasing pressure. Trumpet calls rang across the city with desperate pleas for reinforcements. At St. Anthony's Gate, so hotly defended two days earlier, the contest was in the balance. There was bloody hand-to-hand fighting for the wall, with the defenders resisting with all their force. For a time, the Christians seem to have driven the intruders back, but many had been drawn off for the defense of the Accursed Tower. Alarmed by the deteriorating situation, the Master of the Temple and of the Knights of St. John hurried to the gate to try to expel the intruders in a contest that was becoming increasingly chaotic. Beaujeu was in such haste that he only had time to don light armor.

> When the master of the Temple, who was at his auberge [headquarters] with the men who were defending it, heard the drum beating, he knew that the Saracens were launching an attack. The master took ten or twelve brothers and his troops and set out for St. Anthony's Gate, between the two walls. He passed the sector guarded by the Hospitallers and he called the master of the Hospital to go with him. The Hospitaller master in turn took some of his brothers with him, and some knights of Cyprus and some local knights, and some footmen. They came to St. Anthony's Gate, where they found the Saracens advancing on foot, and they counter-attacked them.[12]

THIS ACCOUNT, WRITTEN by the Templar of Tyre, strongly emphasized the heroic contribution of the master and his knights and probably distorts any overall assessment of contributions to the final defense. Others were more critical—"he came slowly"[13]—one writer maintained, and the fact that the master had not donned his armor, was unprepared, and appeared to be more concerned with defending his own auberge, which was well away from the walls, suggests the extent to which the defense of the city was hampered by factional self-interest even in its supreme crisis, but Beaujeu himself was probably in his late fifties, conventionally past fighting age, and he did at this moment hasten to the fray.

Matthieu de Clermont, "highly skilled and uniquely physically capable at fighting," again seemed to have distinguished himself in the contest for the Gate.[14] Repeatedly, the Muslims were driven back. "We and our convent [of the Hospitallers]," recorded Jean de Villiers, "resisted them at St. Anthony's Gate, where there were so many Saracens that one could not count them. Nevertheless, we drove them back three times as far as the place, which is commonly called Accursed."[15] Evidently, the Hospitallers were trying to plug the defenses both at this gate and further down the line.

It was essential to push the Mamluk intruders back from the Accursed Tower and hold the inner ring, "but they could do nothing," the Templar explained, "because the Saracens were simply too many. When the two masters of the Temple and the Hospital got there and went into combat, it seemed as if they were hurling themselves against a stone wall." The disciplined battle tactics of the Mamluks were highly effective in small spaces. The numbers now flooding through the narrow lanes proved impossible to dislodge, and the defenders were being whittled away. Jean de Villiers recounted how "in that action [trying to retake the Accursed Tower] and others, where the brethren of our Convent fought in defence of the city and their lives and country, we lost little by little all the Convent of our Religion, which then came to an end."[16]

THE FIGHTING UNFOLDED in a series of confused and bloody snapshots, all seen from the Christian perspective, in which any sequence and narrative is jumbled and incoherent. The hurling of Greek fire was particularly frightening, and its effects appalling. The Templar watched with his own eyes as "one poor English *valé* was so badly hit by Greek fire hurled by the Saracens that his surcoat burst into flames. There was no one to help him. His face was burned, then his whole body. He burned like a cauldron of pitch, and he died there. When this happened he was on foot, as his horse had been killed under him."[17]

Others gave bloody accounts of the hand-to-hand fighting:

You could see many with heads severed from their necks, and from their shoulder blades, hands from arms, other split up to their breastbones, or run through with a spear or swords, or cut in two. Men were dying covered in blood or writhing in pain or with their eyes rolling in their heads, one with his head twisted back and another lying on his stomach, another with his tongue lolling dying in great pain, and others again, though mortally wounded, making feeble attempts to get up again and fight. The slaughter on both sides was so great that it was impossible to step anywhere without treading on corpses.[18]

The death or withdrawal of key figures was the probable cause of the final collapse of morale. Villiers and other Hospitallers trying to stem the advance of the Mamluks had evidently fallen back behind internal street barricades, but here Villiers was "stricken nigh to death by a lance through the barricade."[19] Somewhere near the Accursed Tower, the defense suffered another psychological blow, to which the Templar of Tyre may have been an eyewitness:

> In this place a great disaster happened, one that allowed the Saracens to enter the city more easily and demoralized our people. The occasion was that a javelin was aimed at the master of the Temple [Beaujeu] just as he was raising his left hand. He had no shield, only a spear in his right, and this missile struck him under the armpit and its shaft embedded itself in his body to a palm's depth. It entered through a gap where the armour plates didn't join. This was not his heavy breastplate but light armour for donning quickly at an alarm.
>
> When he realised he was mortally wounded, he turned to go. Some of those there thought he was leaving to save himself. His standard bearer saw him turn and followed behind him, then all his household troops. As he was going, a good twenty crusaders from the Valley of Spoleto [in Italy] saw him departing and cried out: "O sir, for the love of God, don't go! For otherwise the city will certainly be lost!" And he replied to them in a loud voice, so that all could hear: "Sirs, I can do nothing more, for I am dying. See the wound!"
>
> And then we saw the javelin fixed in his body. And at these words he dropped his spear on the ground, his head slumped and he started to fall from his horse. But his household people jumped from their horses and held him up, lifted him down from his horse and laid him on a big wide shield which they found discarded on the ground.

From the Templar's account, it seemed that they carried him away between the inner and outer walls

> with the intention of entering the city through St. Anthony's gate, but they found it closed. They found a small door [in the inner wall]

reached by a bridge over the fosse into the residence of Lady Maria of Antioch. . . . There his men removed his armour, cutting the plates off his shoulders, but could do nothing more because of the severity of the wound. Still in his épaulières [shoulder protection] they covered him with a blanket and carried him towards the seashore onto the beach between the slaughterhouse where they kill animals and the house of the lord of Tyre.

The intention was to get him away by ship.

The Mamluks' advance into the town was now unstoppable. In small spaces, the tactics of their shield-bearing troops provided an unbreachable wall. "The Saracens would pause for a bit, then raise their shields, move forward a little, and when men advanced on them, they immediately locked their shields and stopped. All day they never stopped hurling Greek fire and javelins. This kind of contest continued until mid-morning."[20] They pulled down men on the roofs attempting to bombard them with rocks and pushed forward.

At some point after the withdrawal of the wounded Beaujeu, the defense at St. Anthony's Gate also gave way completely. The Mamluks managed to set fire to the outer face of the gate, while those on the tower above continued to rain down stones and crossbow bolts, but this resistance was unsustainable. "At last," in the words of the Christian chroniclers, "the gates collapsed, and a suffocating multitude of infidels burst in beneath the arch, on horses with their lances, and ran the Christians through."[21]

Unopposed, the walls were scaled, gates were opened, and the incursion turned into a flood. "As men learned what had happened, and saw that the Master had been carried away, each began abandoning his position and set himself to flee. For the Saracens . . . passed through the Accursed Tower and went straight by the church of St. Romano and burned the great trebuchet of the Pisans."[22]

FOR THE WOUNDED Jean de Villiers personally, the situation was critical. He remembered:

A great multitude of Saracens entered the city, on all sides, by land and by sea [along the seashore], moving along the walls, which were pierced and broken, and running through the streets of the city until they came to our barricades . . . We and our brethren, of whom the greater number were sore stricken and wounded to death, resisted them as long as we could. And as some of us were lying thus half-dead and helpless before our enemies, our sergeant and our body-servant came, and carried off ourselves, wounded almost to death, and our other brethren, at great risk of life and limb.[23]

The Hospitallers were being driven back. Villiers was stretchered down to the harbor. Clermont was still managing a rear-guard action along with other small detachments trapped in the city's labyrinth. Elsewhere, organized resistance had turned to flight.

While some of the Mamluks were moving fast into the heart of the city, others were vigorously attacking the gates and walls down toward the harbor. The St. Nicholas Gate was opened from within. "They went down the straight street to the convent of the Teutonic Knights and put to the sword everyone they met on their way."[24] At their hospice near the church of St. Nicholas, the Teutonic Knights were wiped out; at the nearby church of St. Leonard, the English order of the Knights of St. Thomas was overpowered.

While his retinue attempted to evacuate the stricken Beaujeu in choppy seas, a cry went up that the nearby tower gate of the Patriarch, defended by Grandson and Grailly, had fallen, so that the harbor itself risked imminent attack. There was panic among Beaujeu's retainers: "Some of his household threw themselves into the sea to get to the two barques that were there. There were only these because the sea was so wildly tempestuous and the waves so huge that vessels couldn't manage, and because of this many people were lost."[25] It was now a rush for individual survival.

Given the deteriorating conditions, it was decided to abandon the attempt to get Beaujeu away. Terror-stricken and without ceremony, "others of his household carried him to the Temple fortress with the help of other people, and they took him inside—not going through the main gate, which they didn't want to open, but via a courtyard where manure was piled."²⁶

Everywhere people were in full flight, and the flames were spreading into the heart of the city: "The Saracen set light to the siege engines and to the wooden barricades, so that the land was lit up by the fire."²⁷ In places, resistance went on. Some fought heroically to the end, though the balance of praise and blame depends on the slant of individual sources.

Within the confines of the Templars' castle, the dying Beaujeu caught the far-off noise of battle fading in his ears and was shielded from the truth:

> He lingered on all that day without speaking, for after they took him down from his horse he had not spoken, beyond a word to the people in the Temple that on hearing the clamour of people fleeing the slaughter he asked what it was; and they just told him that men were fighting, and he commanded them to leave him in peace. After that he spoke no more, but gave up his soul to God. He was buried before his tabernacle which was the altar where they sang mass. And God has his soul. What great damage his death caused!²⁸

The Temple, a secure stronghold, had become a gathering point for those seeking shelter. "There was the marshal, Pierre de Sevrey, and some brothers of the Templars, and some other brothers lying there wounded, and some secular knights, and women and burgesses and many other people."²⁹

There was, however, still a rear-guard action to be fought. Among those who had fallen back on the Temple in the face of the remorseless advance of the Mamluks was Matthieu de Clermont, Marshal of the Hospital of St. John. He saw Beaujeu lying dead and resolved on one more do-or-die attempt to reverse the tide of events, and "returned to the battle, gathering around him all his brethren, for he would not abandon any of them, and some of the Templars went with him, and they came to a square of the Genoese quarter which was empty of houses, and there Matthieu plunged into combat."³⁰ In this small, closed arena, Clermont, mounted on his warhorse, fought literally to a standstill. His end prompted heroic and possibly creative descriptions of man and beast in their last moments: "His war horse was utterly exhausted and was unable to charge any further. It resisted the spurs and stood in the middle of the street as if rooted to the spot where it was hit by a spear and fell prostrate on the ground. With his horse collapsed he was run through by spears. So the faithful warrior knight of Christ gave up his soul to his creator."[31]

Down on the seashore, the Mamluk cavalry had managed to prize off the latticework spiked iron fence running into the sea, positioned there purposely to prevent horsemen entering the town along the beach. They galloped forward, encircling the defenders from behind.

> Then a great number of Saracens on horseback came in. Sir Jean de Grailly and Sir Othon de Grandson and the men of the king of France put up stubborn resistance, so that there many were dead and wounded. But Sir Jean de Grailly and Sir Othon de Grandson could not withstand the Saracen pressure, and they withdrew from the place and saved themselves, with Sir Jean de Grailly wounded. Henry, King of Jerusalem and Cyprus, when he saw the extent of the catastrophe, came to the Master of the Hospital, and clearly seeing that no strategy or help could now make any difference, they saved themselves and boarded their galleys.[32]

Villiers probably left on these ships. In the blame game that followed the fall of Acre, the chroniclers, from the safety of monasteries and libraries and using the accounts of eyewitnesses, would draw up their own charge sheets of who fought and who ran away, apportioning blame and praise according to national and religious loyalties. But at this point, it was everyone for themselves.

13

THE TERRIBLE DAY

Noon, May 18 to May 28, 1291

"**K**NOW THAT THAT day was terrible to behold," the Templar of Tyre recalled in anguish.[1] There could be no mercy for a city that had not surrendered. Now, with the sultan's army reaching deep into the town and fire raging, all organized resistance collapsed. There was a universal rush down the narrow lanes toward the harbor: "The ladies and the burgesses and the unmarried maidens and other lesser folk ran fleeing through the streets, with their children in their arms, weeping and despairing, and fleeing to the sailors imploring them to save them from death."[2] Villiers recorded no more orderly retreat among the lower ranks of the Hospitallers. "Our serjeants, our yeomen and our hired soldiers and others began utterly to despair, and to fly towards the ships, throwing down their arms and armour."[3]

There were far too few ships, and the sea was rough, churned by the wind, and the shortcomings of the harbor made any attempt at orderly evacuation impossible. Offshore, there were some sailing vessels and transport galleys of the Venetians and six galleys belonging to the papacy and the King of Cyprus. Coincidentally, two Genoese galleys had arrived to trade under their commander Andrea Peleau, and, belying the general reputation of Genoa, these "did a great deal of good, as everyone knows, for they rescued people from the seashore and put them aboard the sailing ships and other vessels."[4] This was difficult and dangerous work, given the weather conditions, which required transfer from rowing boats tossed on the turbulent sea. The Templars and the Hospitallers appear not to have made deep preparations for the possibility of an evacuation, though the Templars had one very large sailing ship there, *The Falco*—described as "the greatest that had been built at that time," most likely capable of taking at least 1,500 people.[5] It was commanded by Roger de Flor, who despite being a member of the Order, had a controversial reputation tinged with accusations of mercenary adventuring and piracy.

It was mainly the wealthy and the titled who got away from a city of fire and slaughter. King Henry and Amalric, Grandson, the wounded Villiers and Grailly, and their men boarded their ships and sailed off to Cyprus. Roger de Flor, in *The Falco*, "brought away ladies and damsels and great treasure and many important people."[6] Quite a lot of this treasure seems to have gone to line his own pocket and earned him a subsequent charge of profiting from human misery: holding these wealthy noblewomen to ransom for their portable jewels and gold as they begged to be saved from the burning city, refusing the poor. Scathing criticism also fell on many of the notables able to pay their way out. The Genoese galley captains alone gained praise for disinterestedly ferrying less well-off citizens out to the sailing ships and saving lives, but the weather and the available shipping meant that only a fraction escaped.

At the water's edge, the scenes became frantic: the wealthy running to the quay offering their valuables to be taken off, the poor with their children begging for pity. Attempts to ferry people out to the merchant vessels tossing offshore in the heavy swell were chaotic. People fought for places in fishing boats and small skiffs. Overloaded, some capsized in the swell. Many of the desperate, caught between the prospect of murder and rape and the sea, tried to swim out to the ships. Women clutching their infants to their breasts waded into the water and drowned. The surface of the sea was reddened with the bodies of the slain. Those left faced the consequences.

Descriptions of the slaughter throughout the city exist in a series of jumbled accounts of terror and self-sacrifice. As awful as anything was the noise: "The terrified wailing of men, women and children, deprived of the chance to flee—some in the middle of eating, were trapped miserably or cornered in the squares, streets, houses and

Death in the sea, from a manuscript illustration of the siege of Acre. (Oliver Poole, redrawn from *Crusader Manuscript Illumination at Saint-Jean D'Acre, 1275–1291*, Princeton, 1976)

corners of the city."[7] All order broke down. It became a case of individual survival. In the words of a chronicler: "The bonds of natural piety were broken. The father didn't think of the son, the brother of the brother, the husband of the wife. A man didn't stretch out his hand to help his neighbour."[8]

Everywhere scenes of terror and confusion: fires raged and screams rang through the streets; "riderless horses, astonished and panicked by the tumultuous noise and the din and shouting from all sides, tore hither and thither through the squares, looking desperately around with gaping eyes as if searching for their lords and owners, until reins were thrown over their necks and they were captured and led away by the enemy."[9] People were suffocated in the crush of the crowds trying to flee toward the harbor. The Templar recalled "the pitiful sight of the little children, knocked down and disembowelled as the horses trampled them. Nor is there a man in the world who has so hard a heart that he would not have wept at the sight of this slaughter; and I'm sure that all Christian people wept who saw these things. Even Saracens, as we discovered later, felt pity and wept."[10] In the midst of this carnival of brutality, some Muslims were apparently moved to tears by the fate of these children, but with nearly all organized resistance gone, general slaughter and pillaging were more the order of the day. The attackers went from house to house rooting out defenders and killing the men. "The slaves, rabble and mob started to plunder."[11] The women and children were prizes, led away in chains or raped. Fighting broke out among the victors:

And when the Saracens came across them, one grabbed the mother, another the child, and carried them away from place to place, and separated the one from the other. In one instance there was a quarrel between two Saracens over a woman and she was killed by them; in another a woman was led away captive, and the infant at her breast was hurled to the ground and the horses rode over it, and so it died. There were some pregnant women caught in the crush who suffocated and died, and the baby in her womb also. And there were cases where a woman's husband or child was lying ill or wounded by an arrow in the house, and she abandoned them and fled, and the Saracens slew them all.[12]

The looting was feverish and spectacular. Despite the apparent removal of much of the city's wealth before the siege, the Muslim sources recorded that, in addition to the human prizes, there were still rich pickings to be had: "treasure, crystal vessels inlaid with gold and pearls which could not be valued, and likewise silver and gold vessels," considerable quantities of Venetian currency and bullion in the form of ingots. In the frenzy to grab, many beautiful works of art were smashed for their raw materials, and Muslims were killed in the competition for loot. The largest rewards fell to the aggressive and the canny: "A number of common people profited from what they bought from the gains of the slaves, the camel-drivers, the rabble and others of the troops and their followers."[13]

AS THE WALLS were abandoned, the sultan's army broke in at more and more points, desperate now to participate in the plunder. When the Templars and Hospitallers moved their forces to try to retake the Accursed Tower, the defenses of Montmusard were denuded of men, and the Hama troops stationed on the right wing swept in. The leper knights of St. Lazarus, left sole guardians of these walls, were all killed.

The churches and monasteries were particularly targeted, both for their wealth and out of hatred of Christianity. Stories would be told of martyrdom for the faith. In the monastery of the Dominicans, as the defense collapsed, thirty monks refused to flee; they were joined by a large number of other friars and were killed saying mass. All but seven of the Dominicans were said to have died. Of the Franciscans, only five survived. Similarly, the Dominican nuns were reported to have been slaughtered in their church singing hymns. Other more apocryphal tales of glorious death circulated in different versions.

There were pockets of valiant resistance. Groups of crusaders fought on. "Completely trapped inside the city in squares and corners they offered armed resistance against the enemy entering and pushed them back . . . men from the religious orders and pious lay people of all social ranks persisted in this exhausting struggle for two days, their numbers slowly being whittled away, weighted down by their heavy armour and weakened by thirst, hunger and stress, until they were all killed in the name of Christ."[14] They were accorded the status of martyrs.

Nicolas de Hanapes lived the dictates of his own *Book of Examples* on how to act up to the moment of death. Determined to keep rallying the resistance and intent on martyrdom, he had to be forcibly carried away to the port, protesting loudly: "I am furious with you, dragging me away against my will, abandoning the flock in my care in such danger of being slaughtered."[15] He was ferried out to a Venetian merchant ship, but was not destined to survive. Accounts of his death vary, emphasizing both his saintliness and the contrasting baseness of behavior in the final collapse. Either the good prelate, solicitous to the last, allowed too many refugees to clamber aboard a small boat so that it capsized and he drowned, or, in an account given by the Templar, "a sailor grabbed his hand, but he slipped and fell into the sea and was drowned. It's not clear if the man who took him by the hand let go of him on purpose because he had put his valuables on the ship, or if his hand slipped because he could not hold on. However it was, the good man died from drowning."[16] It is unlikely that Hanapes had concerned himself with the salvage of his worldly goods.

MANY OF THOSE trapped in the labyrinth of the city and unable to reach the port sought shelter in the city's strongholds—the Templars' castle and that of Hospitallers and the Teutonic Knights, the fortified towers in the Venetian and Pisan quarters, and possibly the royal castle. The Temple, which stood prominently on the seashore, was crammed with survivors. Trapped, they could look out over the water and watch the rescue ships departing. "When all the vessels had put on sail, those of the Temple who had gathered there gave a great cry, and the ships cast off and made for Cyprus, and those good men who were then come into the Temple were left to their fate."[17]

One by one these strongholds were surrounded and were either taken or surrendered. The Hospital, in the middle of the city, surrendered under amnesty on May 20, along with the tower of the Teutonic Knights and probably the royal castle. The fate of the survivors is not certain; some of the nobility were kept alive as valuable assets for future ransom but Abu al-Fida suggests mass beheadings: "The sultan gave the command and they were beheaded around Acre to the last man."[18] The memory of King Richard's treatment of the Muslim garrison a century earlier was widely recalled.

The Temple, however, held out. The Templar of Tyre left a detailed account of its substantial and magnificent fortified complex:

The larger part of the people—men, women, and children—sought shelter in the Temple fortress. There were more than ten thousand people there because the Temple was the strongest place in the city, like a castle, situated on a large site by the sea. At its entrance there was a strong tower, whose walls were twenty-three feet thick, and on each corner of the tower there was a turret, and on each turret stood the figure of a lion with raised paw, gilded and as big as a donkey. The four lions, the gilding and workmanship involved had cost 1500 Saracen bezants. It was a magnificent sight. On the other corner of the site, towards the street of the Pisans, there was another tower and near this tower, above the street of St. Anne was a very fine palace, which was the master's residence. . . . The Temple compound also had another tower overlooking the sea, which had been built by Saladin a hundred years earlier. It was right by the sea so that the waves beat against it, and there were other fine building within the Temple, of which I make no mention here.[19]

Its formidable defenses and situation by the sea ensured that it could not be surrounded and could only be taken with extreme difficulty. The number of those who had taken shelter inside may have been inflated, but by all accounts, the Temple was a substantial complex that could accommodate a large number of people. Despite its strength, the situation of the survivors was hopeless. The position of the Temple on an exposed and rocky coast would have made large-scale evacuation impossible without a guarantee of safe conduct. With the death of Beaujeu, the Order had hastily elected Thibaud Gaudin as his replacement. Under his leadership, Pierre de Sevrey, Marshal of the Templars, parlayed for an amnesty on May 20. The sultan granted it. They could leave under safe conduct and embark to Cyprus without weapons and with one piece of clothing. This was accepted. They were given a white flag to hoist on the walls as a guarantee, and four hundred horsemen, under the emir Sayf al-Din Aqbugha al-Mansuri, entered the compound to supervise the evacuation.

The amnesty relied on mutual trust, but things went horribly wrong. With his troops tempted by the women and children inside, the emir lost control of the situation. "These men saw the great number of people there, and wanted to seize the women who pleased them and violate them. The Christians were unable to tolerate this, drew their weapons, attacked the Saracens, killing and decapitating all of them, so that none escaped alive."[20] The gates were shut, the bodies hurled over walls. "Then the Christians resolved to defend their bodies to the death."[21] They destroyed the banner of truce and threw it from the tower.

In fact, not quite all the Muslims trapped inside were killed. One anonymous survivor told a different story and made a miraculous escape:

The Sultan granted them amnesty through his envoys, the emir Sayf al-Din Baktamur al-Silahdar, Aylik al-Farisi al-Hajib (the secretary), the emir Sayf al-Din Aqbugha al-Mansuri al-Silahdar who was martyred in this tower, and Ibn al-Qadi Taqi al-Din Ibn Razin, who were to administer an oath to the Franks and evacuate them under safe conduct. But the rapacious throng fell upon them and killed one of the envoys (Sayf al-Din Aqbugha). Thereupon the Franks closed the gates and expelled the Muslims. When the tumult first broke out, the emirs left and thereby saved their lives. I, along with a companion named Qarabugha al-Shukri were among the group who went to the tower, and when the gates were closed we remained inside with many others. The Franks killed many people and then came to the place where a small number, including my companions and me, had taken refuge. We fought them for an hour, and most of our number, including my comrade, were killed. But I escaped with a group of ten persons who fled from them. Being outnumbered, we hurled ourselves into the sea. Some died, some were crippled, and some of us were spared for a time.[22]

Each side took the opportunity to accuse the other of bad faith. The Christians were charged not only with massacring the delegation sent to oversee the surrender but also with maliciously hamstringing the horses and mules, though in general, the Muslim sources acknowledge that the breaking of the truce was the result of those sent to manage the evacuation "looting and laying hands on the women and children who were with the Templars."[23]

After the botched amnesty, there was a stand-off. The Templar of Tyre related that "the sultan was angered by this deed, but gave no visible sign of it. Instead he sent again to say that it was the folly of his men and the outrages that they had committed that had been the cause of the slaughter. He held no ill-will against the Christians and they could leave in safety trusting his word."[24] The Muslim sources state that, despite the events of the previous day, it was the Christians who again requested an amnesty, realizing the hopelessness of their situation.

At some point, a small boat managed to come up to the sea wall of the castle, and the marshal persuaded Thibaud Gaudin, the new Master of the Order, to leave with its treasury and a few noncombatants. Gaudin had been reluctant to abandon the castle to its fate. "He saw his position as grandmaster under attack and thought that he ought not to begin his term of office by abandoning the castle. He consulted the brothers, and with their consent went off to Cyprus, promising to send them help from there."[25] He got away first to the Templar castle at Sidon further up the coast. It seems likely that this was the last record of events directly witnessed by the anonymous Templar of Tyre. This most vivid chronicler of the fall of Acre, evidently a man of value to the Order, probably sailed off to safety with Gaudin, carrying with him the story of its fate.

ACCOUNTS OF ACRE's last stand vary. The sultan repeated the same offer of amnesty as before. On May 21, Pierre de Sevrey went out to discuss the surrender with some other knights. They were promptly bound and beheaded in full view of the castle in reprisal for the killing of the emir. The Muslim sources state that he was accompanied by many knights and noncombatants, leaving the wounded inside. When they emerged, "more than two thousand of them were executed and the women and children were taken prisoner."[26] It seems more likely that Sevrey had gone out with just a small delegation to renegotiate terms with the sultan ahead of a final evacuation.

However it exactly happened, Khalil, "when he had the marshal and the men of the Temple in his grasp, cut off the heads of all the brothers and other men. The brothers still inside the tower, those who were not so ill that they could not help, when they heard tell that the marshal and the others had been executed, determined to hold out."[27] They threw five more Muslim captives from the tower and prepared for a last, desperate defense. Despite the reduced number of defenders, storming the fortress was a stiff challenge. Khalil set his miners to work bringing down the fortifications. As the walls crumbled, the defenders retreated into the last tower. By May 28, this final redoubt had been mined on all sides and shored up. All that was necessary was to light the fires underneath. Seeing that further resistance was pointless, the survivors surrendered or were captured. Most of the men were beheaded, with the sultan keeping the most valuable for ransom. The women and children were taken into slavery.

The Chronicle of St. Peter's monastery at Erfurt in Germany gives a different account, written just a few months later, of a last act of defiance: "But when the Templars and the others who had fled there realised that they had no supplies and no hope of being supplied by human help, they made a virtue of necessity. With devoted prayer, and after confession, they committed their souls to Jesus Christ, rushed out strenuously on the Saracens and strongly threw down many of their adversaries. But at last they were all killed by the Saracens."[28]

There followed a dramatic finale. In the Muslim accounts, "when the Franks had come out and most of the contents had been removed, the tower collapsed on a group of sightseers and on the looters inside, killing them all."[29] The Templar of Tyre obtained a version of events to the effect that when "those in the tower gave themselves up, such a great crowd of Saracens entered the tower that the supports [of the mine underneath] gave way, and the tower itself collapsed, and those brothers of the Temple and the Saracens who were inside were killed. In addition, when the tower collapsed, it fell into the street, and crushed more than two thousand Turks on horses."[30] But he could not have been there to see it. Whatever the exact details, the death throes of the Templars' great castle took on dramatic symbolic significance as the final collapse of Christendom's two-hundred-year adventure in the land where Jesus had lived and died.

14

"Everything Was Lost"

S HORTLY AFTER, A boastful and threatening letter to Hethoum, Christian king of Cilician Armenia:

We, Sultan Khalil al-Ashraf, the Great Lord, the wise, the upright, the strong, the powerful . . . who brings justice to the oppressed and downtrodden, the builder of kingdoms, the sultan of Arabia, of the Turks and Persia, the conqueror of the armies of the Franks, the Armenians and the Mongols . . . to the honourable, wise, Hethoum, brave as a lion, of the race of Christ. . . .

We make known to you that we have conquered the city of Acre that was the seat of the true cross. We besieged it for a very few days because their soldiers with all their resources could not defend it, and we took their vast army by siege. We engaged and encircled them. They were unable to withstand us with so many being killed, no matter how many nobles and knights there were, and in one complete hour all of them were captured and swept away. Our glittering swords consumed all the Hospitallers and the Templars, betrayers of the city of Acre and its Franks . . . they did not evade destruction, nor the Teutonic knights. We levelled their churches to the ground, they were slaughtered on their own altars, and the Patriarch himself was delivered into tribulation. And you can see a vast amount of treasure has come into the hands of our men . . . and so many women that they were sold for a drachma a piece. And you can see the towers of Acre have been razed to the ground and turned to a wasteland. . . .

And you should know from the evidence of our letter that the bodies of the slain have been laid low by our siege engines and burned and reduced to dust. And the knights and barons who used to rule over them have been shackled, bound and imprisoned. And you, O King, if you take heed of what happened to Acre, you will be safe. If not, you will weep blood, as they did. . . . And if you comprehend what happened to them, it will be to your advantage to come person-ally with your lords and two years' worth of tribute to our lofty doors, as a man who values his personal safety and his kingdom and does not try to evade our great power. You can be certain that nothing will escape me after the destruction of Acre. I suggest you think and act accordingly, before you fall into a mousetrap.[1]

It was an echo of Baybars's lion clawing the rat.

HETHOUM WAS BEING served notice. It was swiftly followed by an-other letter to him in similar vein, announcing the destruction of the city of Tyre. Tyre was particularly significant, both to the crusaders and to their adversaries. A century earlier, it had represented perhaps Saladin's greatest strategic mistake. After the devastating victory at Hattin, he had chosen to bypass it, leaving the crusaders a coastal foothold that enabled them to claw back territory and remain in the Holy Land for another century. Khalil was determined not to repeat the error. He set about erasing every remaining Christian enclave on the shores of Palestine and the Lebanon. On May 18, Tyre's small garrison, twenty-five miles away, could see the smoke of burning Acre on the southern horizon. Next day, an army appeared before its walls. The city's defenses were formidable, but the garrison was small; the defenders abandoned it without a fight and sailed away to Cyprus. Next it was the turn of the Templars at Sidon, further north, now commanded by Thibaud Gaudin bringing with him the Order's treasury. The emir al-Shuja'i showed up with a huge army, and the Templars retreated to an offshore island. They resisted bravely, but when the Mamluks started to construct a causeway, they sailed away to Cyprus. One after another, the coastal strongholds went: Beirut, Haifa, the Templar castles at Chateau Pèlerin on July 30 and Tortosa on August 3—all were abandoned. By August, the only presence left to Christendom was the Templars' occupation of the tiny island of Ruad, two miles off Tortosa.

Khalil engaged in maximum destruction. Castles were demolished, harbor installations destroyed. The fertile coastal plain was devastated, orchards burned or uprooted, mills demolished, irrigation systems ruined. No beachhead remained for a new crusade. Particular attention was paid to Acre. Much of it was burned and the walls left to fall down. "God is pleased!" wrote the qadi Abu al-Tina.[2] "After the destruction of the walls of Acre, the Infidelity (across the seas) will have nothing to find along our coasts."

Both sides understood the significance of these events. It was all over in the Holy Land. "Thus," wrote the Templar, "as you have been able to learn, was all of Syria lost, and the Saracens took and

The walls of St. Andrew's church, in a drawing by Cornelis de Bruijn, still standing in the seventeenth century despite Khalil's destruction of Acre. (*Reyzen door de vermaardste Deelen van Klein Asia*, Delft, 1698)

destroyed it all . . . this time everything was lost, so that altogether the Christians did not hold a palm's breadth of land in Syria."[3] Islam knew this too. "Because of you," the historian Ibn al-Furat later wrote, praising Khalil, "no town is left in which unbelief can repair, no hope for the Christian religion."[4] He was feted as "the probity of this world and religion . . . the subjugator of crosses, the conqueror of the coastal marches, the reviver of the Abbasid state."[5]

The death toll is impossible to compute. Of those within Acre, round figures of 30,000 were repeated in Christian accounts but are probably far too high. Many women and children disappeared into slavery; the "drachma a piece" trope was a familiar figure of speech in accounts of Islamic conquest but undoubtedly suggests many captives. The Dominican monk Ricoldo de Monte Croce, traveling in the Middle East, heard tell of nuns in the harems of the emirs and officers of Khalil's army, and members of the military orders certainly survived as captives, some of whom were ransomed back. Others were too worthless to be enslaved. "I see old men," he wrote, "young girls, children and infants, thin, pale, weak, begging their bread, and they long to be Saracen slaves rather than die of hunger."[6] Not a few of the survivors converted to Islam. A knight called Pierre was mentioned as being in the Mamluk sultan's service in 1323. The only casualty figures recorded for the Muslims are unbelievably low: seven emirs, six other commanders, and eighty-three regular troops, though the ratio of officers to men in this figure was unusually high. Storming the walls must have taken a toll on both regular troops and the large number of volunteers at the siege, but beyond that, it is impossible to speculate.

There was little soul searching by the victors over the final slaughter. The events of a century earlier were well remembered, and their echo was captured by Islamic writers. "In my view," wrote the Arab chronicler al-Yunini, "this was their reward for what they did when they conquered Akka from the martyred Sultan Salah al-Din [Saladin]. Although they had granted amnesty to the Muslim inhabitants, they betrayed them after the victory, killing all except a few high-ranking emirs. These were sold for so much money that an emir was sold for

50,000 dirhams and more. Thus God requited the unbelievers for what they did to the Muslims."[7] "O you yellow-faced Christians," wrote a poet, "the vengeance of God has come down upon you."[8]

Miraculous correspondences were found emphasizing that this was justice for Richard the Lionheart's massacre. Abu al-Fida, present at the siege and well aware that the final assault had taken place on May 18, 1291 (by the Christian calendar), sought to emphasize the symmetry of events by altering the date by a month to June 1291. "By a strange coincidence the Franks had captured Acre, taking it from Saladin at noon on Friday, 17 Jumada II [July 12, 1191], took the Muslims in it and killed them. God Almighty in His prescience decreed that it should be conquered in this year on Friday, 17 Jumada II [June 17, 1291], at the hands of sultan al-Malik al-Ashraf Salah al-Din. So the conquest was like the day the Franks took possession of it, and likewise the titles of the two sultans."[9]

In the Islamic world, the siege spawned apocryphal stories. One of the emirs charged with demolishing Acre found a lead tablet written in Greek. It was translated in Damascus and read: "Written in the year 222. And recorded on it that men of the community of the prophet of the Arabs shall trample this land. He is a prophet to whom religion and law has been shown, and his religion is the greatest of religions, and his law the greatest of laws, he cleans the earth of unbelief and his law shall remain till the end of time. His community shall possess all the regions of Persians and the Franks and others, and if they enter the year 700 his community shall possess all the lands of the Franks."[10] More likely, the "translator" had sold the emir a fraudulent souvenir.

Khalil's boast to Hethoum about the booty was probably an exaggeration—much had been spirited away—but not an extraordinary one. There were tales of people becoming rich both from treasure and from slaves. "The gain of some of them reached the total of two thousand dinars and more from those who plundered and sold to the common people. A person known as Siraj al-Din Zabyan had a profit in Akka of around one thousand seven hundred dinars and twenty-two thousand dirhams. He arrived at the town in the company of three trains of camels carrying merchandise."[11] There was also a considerable amount of plunder of marble columns and architectural materials, including the magnificent Gothic portal of St. Andrew's church, which was incorporated into a madrasah in Cairo.

On June 7, Khalil left Acre for Damascus. There, he received a rapturous reception:

> The entire city had been decorated, and sheets of satin had been laid along his triumphal path through the city leading to the palace of the governor. The regal sultan was proceeded by 280 fettered prisoners. One bore a reversed Frankish banner, another carried a banner and spear from which the hair of slain comrades was suspended. Al-Ashraf was greeted by the whole population of Damascus and the surrounding countryside lining the route, ulama [legal scholars], mosque officials, Sufi sheiks, Christians and Jews, all holding candles even though the parade took place before noon.[12]

A second, even more opulent parade was held in Cairo for the all-conquering hero. Khalil finished where he had started six months earlier—at his father's tomb, where he gave thanks for his victory. Again, a need for circularity was attributed to these events to link Khalil to the great deeds of Saladin. It provided implicit criticism even of the sultan's worthy predecessors, Baybars and Qalawun. "God saved Akka from the hands of the unbelievers," wrote Baybars al-Mansuri, "by the hand of al-Malik al-Ashraf Salah al-Din [Khalil], in the same way as its conquest was first by the hand of Salah al-Din Yusuf ibn Ayyub [Saladin], and it stayed in their hands one hundred and three years. None of the Ayyubid kings and none of the rulers of the Turkish state after them stood up to return it."[13]

THE BEDRAGGLED REFUGEES who made it to Cyprus were destitute; most brought almost nothing with them, and the influx caused inflation in the island. "Food was very scarce. Even houses which had been rented for ten bezants a year increased in price to a hundred bezants a year."[14] They became at the same time objects of charity—King

Henry provided some measure of poor relief—and contempt. "And all their friends in Cyprus disowned them, nor did they make any friendly mention of them," wrote the Templar of Tyre, who may have personally suffered in this way.[15] Thibaud Gaudin, the new grand master of the Templars, seems to have fallen into deep depression on the island.

It was the Greek monk Arsenius, a pilgrim unwittingly caught up in the siege, who brought the terrible news to the pope in August. He gave a dramatic recounting of the facts and cast blame widely—on the Venetians and the Pisans, on the military orders for discord, on King Henry for fleeing. Even the pope was criticized to his face for his distracted obsession with the question of the ownership of Sicily. "Holy father, if thou hadst not heard our sorrow, out of the bitterness of my heart will I reveal it. Would to God that thou hadst not been so intent on the recovery of Sicily."[16]

ARSENIUS LAID THE blame for the final calamity not only on the sinfulness of people but also on the Vatican's own failure to attend properly to the support of the Holy Land. And, he went on, "it was a real miracle that God did not permit the island of Cyprus to be taken by the infidels"—a gambit that the ambitious sultan was soon considering.[17]

The fall of Acre had been on the edge of possibility for years; it was seen in informed circles as a setback but not a final outcome. It did not stir the level of lamentation that the loss of Jerusalem had a century earlier. If it was God's punishment for sin, the situation might be recoverable. Those, such as the Templar of Tyre, closer to the events and more realistic, knew better. He had firsthand experience of the formidable military skill of the Mamluks. This time, Christendom had lost every foothold on the shores of the Holy Land, and they had all been obliterated. A major crusade for 1293 had been planned by Pope Nicholas IV, but he was dead within the year. Ricoldo de Monte Croce, traveling in Iraq and also fully aware of the power of Islam, read in these events the possibility of the End of Days: "If the Saracens continue to do as they did in two years to

Tripoli and Acre, in several years there will be no Christians left in the whole world."[18]

Survivor blame and survivor guilt inevitably followed. In the accounts that circulated, the crown of martyrdom was bestowed on those, such as Clermont, who went down fighting. Nicolas de Hanapes was the only person in the whole history of the Holy Land crusades to be canonized by the papacy. At the same time, the finger of suspicion was pointed at the leading figures who made it out alive. Like survivors of the *Titanic*, Othon de Grandson and Jean de Grailly were accused of fleeing "with their armour untouched."[19] Grandson was additionally charged with having made off with a considerable amount of money, yet there was evidence that Grailly had been wounded, and on Cyprus Grandson was so poor that the pope ordered the dean of St. Paul's in London to pay him a stipend. Jean de Villiers finished his letter, in which he described briefly the part that the Hospitallers had played, on a keening note that suggests a hinted apology for having survived at all. They had gone down almost to the last man. "God knows it," he wrote, proceeding to explain the circumstances surrounding his personal survival. It had been involuntary and willed from Above; wounded and almost dead, he had been carried off by his servants to a ship. "And so we and part of our brethren escaped, since it pleased God that it should be so, of whom the greater number were sore wounded without hope of recovery, and we had ourselves taken to the island of Cyprus. There we have remained until the date this letter was written in great sadness of heart, overwhelmed with very great sorrow."[20] It was perhaps a particular source of shame to the grand master of the Hospitallers that he had lived when Beaujeu, that of the Templars, had died fighting. In this climate, King Henry, guilty by association, felt obliged to seek pardon from the pope.

Judgment on conduct during the siege remained a burning topic and frequently reflected partisan interests. Generally, the chroniclers tended to favor the Hospitallers in this respect, with the heroically portrayed death of Clermont contrasted with the tardier response of Beaujeu, but retrospective blame would attach to both the orders, in which their discords and self-interest figured heavily. Both were uniquely identified with the Holy Land crusades, particularly the Templars, the original military order with its 172 years of unbroken service in the Holy Land. With the Holy Land lost, their raison d'être was called into question. The military orders were at the heart of the crusading project. They were now vulnerable, open to accusations of selfishness and hypocrisy from all quarters.

In the wake of the fall of Acre, many new crusading strategies were proposed, among them to merge the military orders into one body; to use the total Christian control of the sea to strike at the Mamluks by economic blockade of Alexandria, cutting off its access to goods, military slaves, war materials, and tax revenues from the spice trade; or to forego a general call to crusade in favor of professional forces, centered on the military orders, with national support from the crowned heads of Europe. The most detailed of these proposals was the treatise of Marino Sanudo Torsello, who had visited Acre in 1286. He was deeply knowledgeable about the trade routes that nourished the Mamluk dynasty. His carefully though-out strategy involved a return to the great crusading plans of Louis IX—to strike first at Egypt.

Church taxes were levied to fund such enterprises; successive popes convened councils. For a while, popular enthusiasm for crusading remained high. In 1309, thousands of peasants and townspeople from across Europe made their way to Mediterranean ports to beg for a general crusade, which rapidly petered out for lack of papal support. Crusading required the leadership of great kings. Both Edward I of England and Philip IV of France committed to go but neither made it. There were always higher national priorities—rivalries, wars to fight, disputes to settle. The grand masters of the Templars and the Hospitallers both spurned the idea of a merger. And a maritime strategy depended ultimately on the participation of Venice and Genoa, neither of whom were willing to forego the lucrative trade with the Islamic world. The crusading taxes disappeared into the papal coffers, and lack of coherent secular leadership and political will, and the frightening costs involved, stymied practical action. As one astringent chronicler put it about the papacy of Clement V, at the start of the fourteenth century, "The Pope had the money and his Marquis the nephew had part of it, and the King [of France] and others who had taken the cross did not set out, and the Saracens are still there in peace, and I think they may sleep on undisturbed."[21] By 1370, all concrete plans for recovering the Holy Land were dead.

Yet the dream of Jerusalem died hard. On Cyprus, noblewomen wore black mourning for the loss of the Holy Land for a century. It continued to exert a hold on the chivalric imagination of the aristocracy of Europe, and theoretical schemes for reclaiming Jerusalem continued to be generated for hundreds of years. Manuel I, king of Portugal at the time that Vasco da Gama first sailed to India and a man given to messianic dreams, envisaged a pincer movement against the now dying Mamluk dynasty. He attempted to persuade the kings of England, France, and Spain to embark on a ship-borne Mediterranean crusade to the Holy Land, while a Portuguese fleet would simultaneously attack from the Indian ocean. Not short of ambition, he envisaged a raid on Medina, kidnapping the body of Muhammad and holding it to ransom in exchange for Jerusalem. Such schemes collapsed without a sound. By the start of the sixteenth century, the Ottomans had become the focus of all Christian military effort, and the prospect of retaking the Holy Land had slipped away.

Faced with a challenge to their existence, the Hospitallers cannily repositioned themselves. Retreating from Cyprus, they besieged the Greek Christian island of Rhodes, captured it in 1308, and managed to present themselves as the front line of Christian reconquest, waging piratical war against Islam and for a time maintaining a foothold at Bodrum on the coast of Turkey. As "the shield of Christendom," they survived another five hundred years, first in Rhodes, then at Malta, holding the line against the Ottoman Empire. The Teutonic Knights fell back on their second front, fighting the pagans in northern Europe. The Templars were less swift footed. They no longer had a role; they were distrusted as a state within a state—and they were enviably wealthy. Papal discussions about merging the two orders came to nothing. In France, the heartland of their order, they came under the vengeful gaze of King Philip IV. Their downfall was sudden and dramatic. Under accusations of idolatry, magic, and sodomy, the roundups started in 1307. Show trials and confessions under torture ensured their destruction. The evidence presented of their heroic defense at Acre counted for nothing. By 1314, they were finished, with the last grand master burning at the stake with a defiant shout: "God knows who is wrong and has sinned. Soon misfortune will come to those who have wrongly condemned us. God will avenge our death!"[22] Both Philip and the pope were dead within the year.

The end of the Templars—their redundancy and their problematic status in a Europe gradually coalescing into nation-states—was symptomatic of a gradual alteration in the consciousness of Western Christendom. Among religious men, the collapse of the Holy Land marked something of a spiritual crisis. The belief that Christianity would achieve a final victory over Islam could not be sustained. More broadly, there was a slow shift in faith. People were no longer so easily moved by the simple spiritual fervor that had sparked the early mass crusades, no longer so convinced by the promise of redemption from sin. In any case, the crusading impulse could be fulfilled nearer to home against pagans in the forests of Prussia and Lithuania or against the Moors on the plains and in the mountains of the Iberian Peninsula. Crusading in the Holy Land had become the business of professional armies carried there on the ships of the Italian maritime republics. Neither soldiers nor ships were available. European monarchs were occupied with their own fights. England and France were moving toward a war that would absorb them for a century. The Venetians and the Genoese, whose commitment was always compromised by the lure of trade with the Islamic world, were engaged in long-running trade contests. The papacy itself had been tarnished by its substitute crusades against the Holy Roman Empire in Sicily and by the practice of selling indulgences—payment for remission of sins.

The world of the thirteenth century was different from that of the eleventh. Europe was being gradually lifted out of existential pessimism. A commercial revolution saw money replacing barter, the slow decline of feudal ties, the growth of urban populations, and the invention of new financial instruments—banking, insurance, and bills of exchange—that facilitated the expansion of trade and the improvements in material prosperity that would only be slowed by the Black Death. In Persia, the Mongol dynasty converted to Islam, depriving Christendom of a potential ally. For two hundred years, the spark that Pope Urban had lit burned brightly. The appeal of fighting for the Holy Land had caught the imagination with its heady mix of medieval chivalry, armed aggression legitimized by fighting for Christ, its promises of salvation and redemption of sins, its vivid reimagining of the place of Christ's life. But in the long run, the crusades were unsustainable. Supply lines were too long, support too sporadic, and internal divisions within its kingdoms too great to create long-term strategies and standing armies. Ultimately, defeat was inevitable.

KHALIL'S LETTER TO Christian Armenia was not an idle threat. The following year, he invaded and sacked parts of Hethoum's kingdom; but the king himself avoided the promised fate, and the sultan's bombastic self-belief and vaulting ambition would prove his undoing. He conceived a grand campaign to conquer Baghdad from the Mongols and ordered the construction of a hundred ships for the conquest scheme of Cyprus. Nothing came of either. Such projects alienated leading emirs, who were alarmed by his lack of judgment and perceived him a danger to themselves and the Mamluk state. His suspicions against Lajin at the siege of Acre came home to roost. In December 1293, a group of emirs, including Lajin, hatched a plot to kill him. Now exiled in Cyprus, the Templar of Tyre was able to obtain some kind of account of the event that closed the circle on the fall of Acre:

> And as it happened, one day out hunting, they attacked and killed him. And the one who struck him first was his uncle, Baydara, his mother's brother, but he struck so ineffectively that it wasn't a mortal blow. Then an emir called Lajin struck him, saying to Baydara "You do not strike like a man who wants to be sultan, but I will deliver a manly blow." And he struck him so hard that he was cut in half, and thus was Christianity avenged of the evil that he did.[23]

With Khalil's death, the Mamluk sultanate descended into a period of chaotic bloodshed that made the stable ruthlessness of Baybars and Qalawun seem like a golden age. The sultanate changed hands three times in five years. Lajin himself was sultan from 1296–1298, until the assassin's knife struck him down. Of all the emirs involved in the siege of Acre, it appears that al-Fakhri, Beaujeu's double agent, was one of the most fortunate. Despite Khalil's suspicions, he seems to have died peacefully in his bed in Cairo in 1306. The Templar chronicler vanished in Cyprus, anonymous to the last. His record of events stopped around 1314.

Among the last surviving protagonists of the great event was Othon de Grandson. He died in Switzerland at the age of ninety. He had been in and out of the Holy Land all his life on behalf of his lord and close friend, Edward I of England. In 1271, nearly sixty years earlier—more than a lifetime back by the standards of the Middle Ages—he had fought alongside Edward on his sorties from Acre and had accompanied the Templars and Hospitallers on an ill-fated venture into Christian Armenia to resist the Mamluks in 1292–1293. The mailed figure on his tomb in Lausanne cathedral is the only surviving likeness of any of those who had fought at Acre. And hauntingly, fifty years after the city's fall, the pilgrim Ludolf von Suchem stumbled on two aged woodcutters living near the Dead Sea who spoke French. They turned out to be Templars. They had worked for the sultan, married, and fathered children. They and their families were brought back to Europe and feted at the papal court at Avignon, bewildered and exotic specimens from a lost world.

EPILOGUE

A HABITATION FOR SNAKES

A CCORDING TO THE Syrian nobleman Abu al-Fida, Acre's churches and walls were demolished. The city was razed to the ground. Rocks were dumped in the harbor to render it unusable to ships. The aim was to deny any foothold to future crusader armies, but the destruction was not nearly as complete as was claimed. Christian pilgrims and travelers were still able to make journeys to the Holy Land and to go to Jerusalem, and Acre continued to be visited.

When Ludolf von Suchem passed through in 1340, much was still visible despite the Saracens' attempts "to utterly subvert and destroy down to their foundations all the walls, towers, castles and palaces, lest the Christians should rebuild them. Yet in hardly any places have they been able to beat them down to the height of a man, but all the churches, walls and towers, and very many castles and palaces remain almost entire, and if it pleased God, could with great care be restored throughout to their former state."[1] He was able to describe the city's outline in detail and reconstruct in his mind's eye a nostalgic picture of the city at its peak. A small garrison was stationed there, living off pigeons and partridges that roosted among the ruins. Strangely, as early as 1304, the Venetians had concluded a treaty with the local governor to reside and trade in Acre, though little evidence exists that they did so. Slowly, much of its shattered outline was covered by windblown sand from the long beach, but for hundreds of years the ghostly ruins of its churches and great palaces were still visible as a landmark for passing ships. Like an image of Ozymandias, its remnants fascinated and haunted passing travelers.

James of Verona arrived in 1335, "lamenting and sighing" for what it had been, now a desolate spot, "a habitation only for snakes and wild animals" and a few Saracens, yet he was still able to see "fine towers and many palaces and many large buildings."[2] Successive visitors left valuable, if at times contradictory, accounts of the walls. Francesco Suriano in 1460 described "three sets of walls, an arbalest [crossbow] shot apart, with moats in the form of escarpments built of cut stones, with towers within moats forty paces apart, with very strong forts." Evidence of the siege still lay round about. He saw "a mound half a mile long a short distance from the city as a defence against artillery. And to this day the stones of the bombardment look like a flock of sheep on the ground."[3] Henry Maundrell, who came in 1697, also noted these stone balls scattered on the ground "of at least thirteen or fourteen inches diameter, which were part of the ammunition used in battering the city."[4] Although the place looked devastated to another English traveler, George Sandys, he, too, described it as "strong, double immured, fortified with bulwarks and towers; to each wall a ditch, lined with stone, and under those diverse secret posterns . . . but the huge walls turned topsy turvey, and lying like rocks upon the foundations."[5] Richard Pococke, in 1738, took its fortifications to be quite modern: "a double rampart and a fosse, lined with stone; the inner rampart defended with semi-circular bastions."[6] It was a ghost town of crumbling structures. The cellars of the houses filled up with rainwater so that the whole place gave off a dreadful stench, cloaked at seasons by a thick miasmic vapor. From the late seventeenth century, artists started to come in search of the romantic Orient. In 1682, the Dutch artist Cornelis de Bruijn drew some of the remaining buildings. Three years later, a French artist, Gravier d'Ortières, sent to Acre by Louis XIV, created a panorama of the whole city from the deck of a ship. The long, low profile picks out the prominent remains of a church on the headland; the still impressive bulk of the Hospitallers' palace; towers and arches; and outside the walls, desultory, crumbling ruins stretching to the foot of the hill on which Khalil had pitched his red tent.

Acre from the sea in the drawing of Gravier d'Ortières showing the bulk of the Hospitallers' fortress and the skeleton of the church of St. John. (Bibliothèque Nationale de France)

By the end of the eighteenth century, much of this had gone, been rebuilt, or been refashioned. What was left of the medieval walls was demolished and the stone used to make new buildings and the fortifications that repulsed Napoleon in 1799. New mosques and caravanserais were constructed; the foundations of churches, Italian warehouses, and towers had been subsumed into Ottoman structures.

NOWADAYS, IT IS possible to look down from the impressive ramparts of the old city and imagine the defense and an army encamped outside in the streets of modern Akko, but appearances are deceptive. These walls were built in the late eighteenth and early nineteenth centuries; the medieval walls with their lines of towers, stone-lined ditches, and ominously named towers have vanished. Just tiny stretches at the foot of a wall are still visible. The crusader city is a series of tantalizing fragments over-built with later Ottoman buildings, but the twisting lanes opening onto tiny squares probably follow the crusader footprint, which in turn follow an earlier Arab layout. A chunk of rock by the sea walls marks the sight of the Pisan harbor; another stump standing alone in the sea is all that is left of the so-called Tower of Flies, which guarded the entrance to the port. Acre is a honeycomb of historic structures built one on another—the Arab on the Hellenistic and the Roman, the Crusader on the Arab, the Ottoman on the Crusader. There are deep underground layers. Many houses have arched cellars and undercrofts, with further hollow vaults yet unexplored, evidence of the long accumulation of human habitation. Across the street from where the Templars' castle once stood, a doorway leads down into the darkness, a monument to the wealth of their heyday. A three-hundred-yard stone tunnel, dimly lit, with the whispering sound of running water, passes under the city. You emerge blinking at the far end, close to the port. Up toward the present city walls, portions of the Hospitallers' compound still stand, a warren of pillared halls, vaults, and courtyards; at the entrance lie some of the giant stone balls probably launched by Khalil's catapults.

The impressive castle where the Templars made their last stand has completely gone; instead, a shallow basin of sea in which the outlines of its foundations are just visible. It's a pleasant spot to sit and gaze out at the water and the passing ships, the place where the defenders once looked in vain to the west. From here you can now catch both the sound of church bells and the call to prayer. People come to this sea wall to drink coffee by the lighthouse, to promenade and meet their friends. The sound of Arabic technopop blasts out from speed boats taking tourists on thrill rides around the bay. They churn up dramatic bow waves as they turn. Joy riders scream. After dark, just the slap of water, the fruit stalls still lit, the lighthouse and the moon.

ACKNOWLEDGMENTS

My THANKS ARE due to many people during the writing and production of this book. Firstly to Dan Gerstle who commissioned it, Lara Heimert who ensured a smooth transition, and the team at Basic for their professionalism, enthusiasm, and helpfulness throughout in the making of a better book. Behind them stand ranks of advisers and contributors. I am deeply grateful to my two doughty translators, Martin Dow for access to unreachable Arabic sources and advice and to Steve Elliott for German translations. Ron Morton and Stan and Tom Ginn commented on the manuscript as general readers, while two anonymous academic readers tried their best to correct some of my doctrinal errors over the crusades. Oliver Poole redrew medieval miniatures for the pages of this book with remarkable skill. In Acre, my thanks are due to Danny Syon of the Israel Antiquities Authority for giving me time, good advice, and access to unpublished research and photographs of the archaeology. I enjoyed the friendship and hospitality of Joseph Gable and his family with whom I stayed in Acre and who gave me an insight into life in this most extraordinary of cities. Andrew Abado took me on a fascinating guided tour of its labyrinths. Mike Fulton answered my questions on trebuchets and toned down my wildest imaginings about the power of medieval catapult technology. Denys Pringle explained all that's known of the naming of the Accursed Tower. Andrew Lownie, my agent, continues energetically to promote my work. Lastly, as ever, my thanks are to Jan, a wise voice.

THE EVIDENCE FOR THE FALL OF ACRE

THIS BOOKS RESTS on two centuries of crusader scholarship. The reverberations of the events of 1291 were felt across the whole of Europe, and generations of historians have been assiduous in seeking out reports, letters, chronicles, and church and state records that touch on the final collapse of Outremer as seen from the Christian viewpoint. Despite this, the number of eyewitness accounts is quite small. First and foremost, of course, is that of the so-called Templar of Tyre, on which I have drawn heavily. The Templar remains a fascinating figure in his own right; his mysterious role as an intelligence agent and speaker of Arabic gave him access to inside knowledge both of decision-making processes within the heart of the Acre establishment and of the Mamluk world. He is by turns revealing and knowingly discreet. "I could tell you who they were if I were so inclined." Some of the incidents he describes, such as the horrifying death of an English soldier hit by Greek fire and the mortal wound inflicted on Guillaume de Beaujeu, suggest that he was there as an eyewitness, and yet he gives no hint of personal involvement. Did he fight—there is no indication that he did—or was he just a man of letters? And how did he escape from the burning city? He vanishes from the scene into obscurity. As our most detailed surviving account, he possibly skews the record favorably toward the Templars and exaggerates the importance of Beaujeu's mortal wound to the final collapse.

Alongside the Templar, I have particularly relied on two other anonymous Latin chronicles that seem to have collected the accounts of survivors of the fall: the so-called *Excidium Aconis* (*The Destruction of Acre*), and another simply known as *Thadeus*, after its author. In addition, there are fragmentary letters, such as that of the grand master of the Hospitallers, Jean de Villiers; the report of the Greek monk Arsenius to the pope; and suggestive details from other chronicles and records.

The Islamic version of events has been far less picked over. The pioneering analysis of these in the West is Donald Little's paper reviewing all the available material and constructing a genealogy of reliability and attribution. I have found this an invaluable guide to the Arabic sources and to understanding their perspectives on the events of 1291. But as he points out, while these are highly informative on the "before and after" of the siege—the politics, the decision-making, and the aftermath—they are less helpful on military matters. There are a few precious autobiographical eye-witness accounts; among these are Abu al-Fida's description of dragging the trebuchets to the siege, Baybars al-Mansuri's construction of an ingenious screen to thwart the defenders' catapults from the siege works, and an anon-ymous Mamluk soldier's desperate fight for survival trapped on the Tem-plars' tower at the very end. The narrative and sequencing of events during the siege in the Islamic sources is jumbled and confusing. We learn far more from Christian sources about Mamluk fighting techniques—particularly during the final assault—than we do from the Arabic ones. Nevertheless, by cross-referencing incidents from these sources with those from the Templar and others, I believe it is possible to give a reasonably balanced account.

Beyond the written accounts, there is also the evidence on—and in— the ground. The city of Acre is a fascinating historical site, its layers of occupation lying one on top of another in rich confusion, but as I indicated in the epilogue, it is extremely difficult to understand. A fundamental prob-lem in any account of the events of 1291 that makes continuous mentions of towers and barbicans, the inner and outer walls, and the role of ditches and salients is that we have little reliable information about exactly where they were or what they looked like—beyond an acceptable belief that they would have been in line with the kinds of structures and defensive strategies adopted in many other crusader fortifications in the Holy Land.

For the relative position and identification of the walls and towers, we are largely dependent on the work of Marino Sanudo Torsello, who visited the city in 1286 during the last desperate phase of tower building before the Mamluks came. Maps were drawn in conjunction with his account in various versions, one of which appears on page 15, that enable us to locate the main features, though even these can be misleading. One version of Torsello's map puts the Accursed Tower on the outer wall, though it was quite patently on the inner one, and Torsello himself must have known this as he was in the city when the King's Tower was being constructed to pro-tect it shortly before the fall. The psychological importance of the Accursed Tower, as in the Mathew Paris map on pages 2 and 3, sometimes trumps the facts. The tower in this map is circular. There is good reason to believe that there was a preference for circular defensive structures in strategic locations; though more laborious to build, they were considered harder for miners to bring down than the corners of square towers, but unfortunately, there is no archaeological evidence to go on.

Much of the wall and the towers and stone-lined ditches were still visible well into the eighteenth century, and travelers' accounts of visiting the site, as well as the artists' portrayals, provide valuable evidence even if they are somewhat contradictory. We learn, for example, from the observations of Francesco Suriano that Khalil's army constructed a long earth bank to protect its camp and of the impressive number of artillery balls still littering the site centuries later "like a flock of sheep" that give evidence of the massive work of the trebuchets, but the walls and towers themselves, and the exact course of Acre's outer walls, remain elusive. On my visit to Acre, Danny Syon of the Israel Antiquities Authority showed me the one small stretch of stones at the base of the eighteenth-century city wall that is all that's left above ground of the original crusader structure. Decades of archaeological work have uncovered tantalizing glimpses of walls, ditches and towers, shops, streets, and houses, but the development of the town of New Akko has now covered the ground that was visible in aerial photographs a century ago so that the historic suburb of Montmusard and the line of the walls has completely vanished.

One of the consequences of this has been an ongoing debate among archaeologists and historians about the size of crusader Acre, particularly how far east its outer walls extended toward the Touron, the hill from which Khalil conducted his operations, and at what point these walls met the seashore. There are minimalist and maximalist positions on this. In 1997, Benjamin Kedar made a persuasive case for Acre having been far larger than had been previously thought. Those favoring this view have relied on some archaeological evidence as well as the long panorama of Gravier d'Ortières, drawn in 1689, a section of which is reproduced on page 211. His panorama seems to show the ruins of built structures quite close to the Touron, though it has been countered that there would very likely have been free-standing buildings, bridges, et cetera, outside the city walls, and the accuracy of Gravier's perspective is questionable. In deciding how to brief the necessary map to understand events in the book, I eventually followed the maximalist position as set out in a map by Denys Pringle based on Kedar's work, which elongates the footprint of Acre east toward the Touron, with no certainty, in the absence of archaeological evidence, that it is definitive. All that can be said is that the map at the front of this book is reasonably uncontroversial in relation to the twists and turns of the walls, the relative positions of towers and gates, and the disposition of Mamluk army units in accord with the contemporary sources.

Over decades of archaeological work, during the course of building work and hurried salvage digs, some evidence of the fighting that took place has emerged from the ground: the base of a round tower at the far northern end of the walls beyond which the Pisans must have launched their surprise amphibious attack early in the siege, sections of moat and occasional fragments of tower elsewhere. In 1991, the construction of a courthouse in New Akko gave rise to the discovery and excavation of a square tower, with walls ten feet thick at the base, that had been destroyed by fire. The litter

An excavation outside the walls of the old city uncovers a stock of unused stone trebuchet projectiles ready for firing. (Israel Antiquities Authority)

of burnt beams and smashed pottery bear witness to the final destruction. It has been suggested that this tower was on the outer line of walls near the most vulnerable salient and that possibly it was the Tower of the Venetians. A similar excavation inside the eighteenth-century walls undertaken in 2004 revealed the extensive torching of buildings in direct line of the final Mamluk assault, evidence that "the land was lit up by fire," as the Templar of Tyre put it. A destruction layer of this kind has been discovered at various sites in the city, littered with shattered thirteenth-century pottery and glass, coins, carbonized wood, and collapsed roofs—time capsule evidence that crusader Acre came to an abrupt full stop in May 1291. The forlorn ruins were then covered by windblown sand for hundreds of years until the town was resurrected by the construction of new buildings on top during the Ottoman period.

Archaeologists have also turned up arrowheads, possible fragments of ceramic grenades, and a large number of artillery stones of all sizes. Concentrations of stone balls have been found in various places—some within the city, others outside the likely line of the walls—which appear to have been stores of ammunition ready for firing. Close examination of these projectiles reveals the range of different sizes and their geology from which it's been possible to deduce that the Mamluks sourced stone from a distance away. Some of these are of considerable size, but many of the smaller balls that also must have peppered the walls have not survived or have been incorporated into buildings. Of what is still visible of the city that went down in flames, the most impressive remnants are those of the Hospitallers' compound with its halls and undercrofts, and the finely built tunnel running under the city that possibly connected the Templars' castle with the harbor. Many of the secrets of crusader Acre and its destruction remain buried underground.

A NOTE ON NAMES IN THE BOOK

IN THIS BOOK I have taken some shortcuts with regard to the conventions of personal names with the aim of making it easier for readers to identify the shifting cast of characters that pass through its pages. The names of the Christians generally consist of a personal one, "Jacques," and then their place of family origin, "de Vitry ("of Vitry"). It is usual to refer to them by either their first name or their full name rather than just by the town from which they came. However, in the fast-moving pace of events it is often unwieldy and sometimes confusing to refer to people in this way, so you will find Nicolas de Hanapes, Othon de Grandson, Jean de Grailly, et cetera, frequently cut down to their place of origin. So, Vitry, Hanapes, Grandson, and Grailly appear from time to time, hopefully to give the reader something to cling to as the arrows fly past. On the other hand, I have decided to resist anglicizing their names wherever possible, so Matthieu de Clermont rather than Matthew of Clermont, to give readers a more vivid sense of who these people actually were. I cannot claim complete consistency in this. It might be more accurate to refer to Richard as "Coeur de Lion," as he barely spoke English, and this might give a better sense of who this man was, but I have, of course, stuck with the Lionheart. And Henry of Cyprus is the later ruler of Acre, rather than Henri de Chypre, and so on. My aim throughout has been to try to balance readability against a sense of the past.

With Muslim names, the situation is much more confusing. I'm sure the eyes of Western readers, including my own, tend to glaze over at the introduction of a character called, for example, Sayf al-Din Baktamur al-Silahdar. Baybars's full name is al-Malik al-Zahir Rukn al-Din Baybars al-Bunduqdari. These long name chains often include a reference to their father (as in "ibn"—son of), an occupation ("al-Silahdar"—the emir in charge of armaments), an honorific appellation such as "Rukn al-Din" (Pillar of the Faith), or a reference to their place of origin or one of their masters ("al-Mansuri," from the regiment of the Victorious King, al-Mansur Qalawun). There are several people in this book with the al-Mansuri tag—and one trebuchet!

Mamluks often have a name of Turkic origin. That of the Lion of Egypt, Baybars, actually means something like "great panther." As with the Christians, I have taken a decision to reduce names. After a first introduction, I have stripped names down to a single word where possible: Lajin, Baybars, et cetera, in the hope that readers will be able to cling on in the saddle, so to speak. (Unfortunately, we do get two people with the Baybars name in the book: Sultan Baybars and Baybars al-Mansuri.) With Salah al-Din, I have moved quickly to Saladin. I have chosen not to use diacritics in Arabic names in the main text, as these introduce a further layer of complexity. Overall, my approach to names is not completely consistent, but I hope it will help readers to keep track of who's who and where they come from.

BIBLIOGRAPHY

PRIMARY SOURCES

Abu'l-Fida. *The Memoirs of a Syrian Prince*. Edited and translated by P. M. Holt. Wiesbaden: Franz Steiner, 1983.

Albert of Aachen. *Historia Ierosolimitana*. Edited and translated by Susan B. Edgington. Oxford: Oxford University Press, 2007.

Al-Jazari. *La Chronique de Damas d'al-Jazari*. Edited and translated by Jean Sauvaget. Paris, 1919.

Badr al-Dīn al-Ainī. *Iqd al-Jumān fī Tārīkh Ahl al-Zamān*. Edited by Muhammad Amin. Cairo, 1987.

Bartholomei de Cotton. *Historia Anglicana*. Edited by Henry Richard Luard. London, 1859.

Bartolomeo de Neocastro. *Historia Sicula, 1250-1293*. Edited by Giuseppe Paladino. Bologna, 1921–1922.

Baybars al-Manṣūrī. *Zubdah al-Fikra fī al-Tārīkh al-Hijrah*. Edited by Donald S. Richards. Beirut, 1998.

Bird, Jessalynn, Edward Peters, and James M. Powell, eds. and trans. *Crusade and Christendom: Annotated Documents in Translation from Innocent III to the Fall of Acre, 1187–1291*. Philadelphia: University of Pennsylvania Press, 2014.

Cartulaire Général de L'Ordre des Hospitaliers de S. Jean de Jérusalem. Vol. 3, 1261–1310. Edited by J. Delaville Le Roux. Paris, 1899.

Chronicle of Lanercost, 1272–1346. Edited and translated by Herbert Maxwell. Glasgow: J. Maclehose, 1913.

Chroniques d'Amadi et de Strambaldi. Edited by René de Mas Latrie. Paris, 1891–1893.

Crawford, Paul, trans. *The "Templar of Tyre": Part III of the "Deeds of the Cypriots."* Aldershot, UK: Ashgate, 2003.

Edbury, Peter W., ed. and trans. *The Conquest of Jerusalem and the Third Crusade*. Aldershot, UK: Ashgate, 1998.

Excidium Aconis. In *The Fall of Acre, 1291*, edited by R. B. C. Huygens. Turnhout, Belgium: Brepols, 2004.

Fulcher of Chartres. *A History of the Expedition to Jerusalem, 1095–1127.* Translated by Frances Rita Ryan. Knoxville: University of Tennessee Press, 1927.

Gabrielli, Francesco, ed. *Arab Historians of the Crusades.* London: Routledge & Kegan Paul, 1969.

Ibn 'Abd al-Ẓāhir, Muḥyī al-Dīn. *Tashrīf al-ayyām wa-al-'uṣūr fī sīrat al-Malik al-Manṣūr.* Cairo, 1961.

Ibn al-Athir. *The Chronicle of Ibn al-Athir.* Translated by Donald S. Richards. Aldershot, UK: Ashgate, 2006–2008.

Ibn al-Furat. *Ayyubids, Mamlukes and Crusaders.* Translated by Ursula Lyons and Malcolm C. Lyons. Cambridge, UK: W. Heffer, 1971.

Ibn Jubayr. *The Travels of Ibn Jubayr.* Translated by R. J. C. Broadhurst. London: Jonathan Cape, 1952.

Ibn Khaldun. *The Muqaddimah.* Vol. 2. Translated by Franz Rosenthal. London: Routledge & Kegan Paul, 1958.

Jackson, Peter, ed. and trans. *The Seventh Crusade, 1244–1254: Sources and Documents.* Aldershot, UK: Ashgate, 2007.

Jacques de Vitry. *Lettres de Jacques de Vitry.* Edited by R. B. C. Huygens. Leiden: Brill, 1960.

Jean de Joinville. *Histoire de Saint Louis.* Edited and translated by Natalis de Wailly. Paris, 1874.

Les Gestes des Chiprois. In *Recueil des Histoires des Croisades, Documents Arméniens.* Vol. 2. Paris, 1906.

Les Registres de Nicolas IV. Vol. 2. Edited by Ernest Langlois. Paris, 1905.

Ludolph von Suchem. *Description of the Holy Land, and of the Way There.* Translated by Aubrey Stewart. London, 1895.

Maqrīzī, Aḥmad ibn 'Alī. *Histoire des Sultans mamlouks.* Translated by Étienne Marc Quatremère. 2 vols. Paris: Oriental Translation Fund, 1837–1845.

Maundrell, Henry. *A Journey from Aleppo to Syria.* London, 1810.

Muntaner, Ramón. *The Chronicle of Muntaner.* Translated by Lady Goodenough. London: Hakluyt Society, 1921.

Nicholson, Helen J., trans. *The Chronicle of the Third Crusade: The Itinerarium Peregrinorum et Gesta Regis Ricardi.* Aldershot, UK: Ashgate, 2001.

Paris, Matthew. *Matthew Paris's English History: From the Year 1235 to 1273.* Translated by J. A. Giles. 3 vols. London, 1852–1854.

Pringle, Denys. *Pilgrimage to Jerusalem and the Holy Land, 1187–1291.* Aldershot, UK: Ashgate, 2012.

Rice, David Talbot, and Basil Gray. *The Illustrations to the "World History" of Rashid al-Din.* Edinburgh: Edinburgh University Press, 1976.

Sanudo Torsello, Marino. *The Book of the Secrets of the Faithful of the Cross.* Translated by Peter Lock. Aldershot, UK: Ashgate, 2011.

Shafi 'b. 'Alī. Ḥusn al-Manāqib al-Sirriyya al-Muntaẓa'a min al-Sīra al-Ẓāhiriyya. Riyad, 1974.

Shirley, Janet, trans. Crusader Syria in the Thirteenth Century: The Rothelin Continuation of the History of William of Tyre with Part of the Eracles or Acre Text. London: Routledge, 1999.

Smith, Caroline, ed. and trans. Joinville and Villehardouin: Chronicles of the Crusades. London: Penguin, 2008.

Thadeus. Ystoria de desolatione et conculcatione civitatis Acconensis et tocius terre sancta. In The Fall of Acre, 1291, edited by R. B. C. Huygens. Turnhout, Belgium: Brepols, 2004.

'Umar Ibn Ibrāhīm al-Awsī al-Anṣārī. A Muslim Manual of War. Edited and translated by George T. Scanlon. Cairo: American University at Cairo Press, 1961.

Usāmah Ibn-Munqidh. An Arab-Syrian Gentleman and a Warrior in the Period of the Crusades. Translated by Philip K. Hitti. New York: Columbia University Press, 1929.

Walter de Hemingburgh. The Chronicle of Walter of Guisborough. Edited by Harry Rothwell. London: Royal Historical Society, 1957.

MODERN WORKS

Amitai-Preiss, Reuven. "The Conquest of Arsuf by Baybars: Political and Military Aspects." Mamluk Studies Review 9, no. 1 (2005): 61–83.

———. "Diplomacy and the Slave Trade in the Eastern Mediterranean: A Re-examination of the Mamluk-Byzantine-Genoese Triangle in the Late Thirteenth Century in Light of the Existing Early Correspondence." Oriente Moderno 87, no. 2 (2008): 349–368.

———. Mongols and Mamluks: The Mamluk-Ilkhanid War, 1260–1281. Cambridge: Cambridge University Press, 1995.

Asbridge, Thomas. The Crusades: The War for the Holy Land. New York: Simon & Schuster, 2010.

Barber, Malcolm. The Trial of the Templars. 2nd ed. Cambridge: Cambridge University Press, 2012.

Boas, Adrian J., Archaeology of the Military Orders: A Survey of the Urban Centres, Rural Settlement and Castles of the Military Orders in the Latin East (c. 1120–1291). London: Routledge, 2006.

Chevedden, Paul E. "Black Camels and Blazing Bolts: The Bolt-Projecting Trebuchet in the Mamluk Army." Mamluk Studies Review 8, no. 1 (2004): 228–277.

———. "Fortifications and the Development of Defensive Planning during the Crusader Period." In The Circle of War in the Middle Ages, edited by Donald J. Kagay and L. J. Andrew Villalon. Woodbridge, UK: Boydell Press, 1999.

———. "The Invention of the Counterweight Trebuchet: A Study in Cultural Diffusion." In *Dumbarton Oaks Papers* 54 (2000): 71–116.

———. "The Hybrid Trebuchet: The Halfway Step to the Counterweight Trebuchet." In *On the Social Origins of Medieval Institutions: Essays in Honor of Joseph. F. O'Callaghan*, edited by Donald J. Kagay and Theresa M. Vann. Leiden: Brill, 1998.

Chevedden, Paul E., Les Eigenbrod, Vernard Foley, and Werner Soedel. "The Trebuchet." *Scientific American*, July 1995.

Clifford, Esther R. *A Knight of Great Renown: The Life and Times of Othon de Grandson*. Chicago: University of Chicago Press, 1961.

Cobb, Paul M. *The Race for Paradise: An Islamic History of the Crusades*. Oxford: Oxford University Press, 2014.

Crowley, Roger. *City of Fortune: How Venice Won and Lost a Naval Empire*. London: Farber & Farber, 2011.

———. *Constantinople: The Last Great Siege, 1453*. London: Farber & Farber, 2005.

D'Souza, Andreas. "The Conquest of Akka (690/1291): A Comparative Analysis of Christian and Muslim Sources." *Muslim World* 80, no. 3–4 (October 1990): 234–249.

DeVries, Kelly. *Guns and Men in Medieval Europe, 1200–1500: Studies in Military History and Technology*. Aldershot, UK: Ashgate, 2002.

Dichter, B. *Akko: Sites from the Turkish Period*. Haifa, Israel: Gottlieb Schumacher Institute for Research of the Christian Activities in 19th Century Palestine, University of Haifa, 2000.

———. *The Maps of Acre: An Historical Cartography*. Municipality of Acre, Israel. 1973.

———. *The Orders and Churches of Crusader Acre*. Municipality of Acre, Israel. 1979.

Ellenblum, Ronnie. *Crusader Castles and Modern Histories*. Cambridge: Cambridge University Press, 2009.

Favreau-Lilie, Marie-Luise. "The Military Orders and the Escape of the Christian Population from the Holy Land in 1291." *Journal of Medieval History* 19, no. 3 (1993): 201–227.

Folda, Jaroslav. *Crusader Manuscript Illumination at Saint-Jean d'Acre, 1275–1291*. Princeton, NJ: Princeton University Press, 1976.

France, John, ed. *Acre and Its Falls: Studies in the History of a Crusader City*. Leiden: Brill, 2018.

Fulton, Michael S. *Artillery in the Era of the Crusades: Siege Warfare and the Development of Trebuchet Technology*. Leiden: Brill, 2018.

———. "The Development of Prefabricated Artillery during the Crusades." *Journal of Medieval Military History* 13 (2015): 51–72.

———. "The Siege of Edessa." *Medieval Warfare* 7, no. 1 (2017): 48–53.

Hamblin, William J. "Muslim Perspectives on the Military Orders during the Crusades." *Brigham Young University Studies* 40, no. 4 (2011).

Hartal, Moshe. Introduction to "Excavations of the Courthouse Site at 'Akko.'" *Atiqot* 31 (1997): 1–2.

Hill, Donald R. "Trebuchets." *Viator* 4 (1973): 99–114.

Hillenbrand, Carol. *The Crusades: Islamic Perspectives.* Edinburgh: Edinburgh University Press, 1999.

Holt. P. M. *Early Mamluk Diplomacy (1260–1290): Treaties of Baybars and Qalāwūn with Christian Rulers.* Leiden: Brill, 1995.

———. "Qalawun's Treaty with Acre in 1283." *English Historical Review* 91, no. 361 (October 1976): 802–812.

———. "The Treaties of the Early Mamluk Sultans with the Frankish States." *Bulletin of the School of Oriental and African Studies* 43, no. 1 (February 1980): 67–76.

Hosler, John D. *The Siege of Acre, 1189–1191: Saladin, Richard the Lionheart, and the Battle That Decided the Third Crusade.* New Haven, CT: Yale University Press, 2018.

Housley, Norman. *The Later Crusades, 1274–1580: From Lyons to Alcazar.* Oxford: Oxford University Press, 1992.

Humphreys, R. Stephen. "Ayyubids, Mamluks and the Latin East in the Thirteenth Century." *Mamluk Studies Review* 2 (1998): 1–17.

———. "The Emergence of the Mamluk Army." *Studia Islamica* 45 (1977): 67–99.

Irwin, Robert. "The Mamluk Conquest of the County of Tripoli." In *Crusade and Settlement: Papers Presented at the Society for the Study of the Crusades and the Latin East*, edited by Peter W. Edbury. Cardiff, UK: Cardiff University Press, 1985.

———. *The Middle East in the Middle Ages: The Early Mamluk Sultanate, 1250–1382.* Carbondale: Southern Illinois University Press, 1986.

———. *Mamluks and Crusaders: Men of the Sword and Men of the Pen.* London: Routledge, 2010.

Jackson, Peter. "The Crisis in the Holy Land 1260." *English Historical Review* 95, no. 376 (1980): 481–513.

Jacoby, David. "Aspects of Everyday Life in Frankish Acre." In *Crusades*, edited by Benjamin Z. Kedar, Jonathan Phillips, and Jonathan Riley-Smith. Vol. 4. London: Routledge, 2005.

———. "Crusader Acre in the Thirteenth Century: Urban Layout and Topography." *Studi Medievali* 3, Ser. 20 (1979): 1–145.

———. "L'expansion occidentale dans le Levant: les Vénitiens à Acre dans la moitié du treizième siècle." In *Recherches sur la Méditerranée du XIIe au XVe Siècle.* London: Variorum, 1979.

———. "Montmusard, Suburb of Crusader Acre: The First Stage of Its Development." In *Outremer: Studies in the History of the Crusading Kingdom of Jerusalem*, edited by Benjamin Z. Kedar, Hans Eberhard Mayer, and R. C. Smail. Jerusalem: Yad Izhak Ben-Zvi Institute, 1982.

———. "Pilgrimage in Crusader Acre: The Pardouns d'Acre." In *De Sion Exibit Lex Et Verbum Domini De Hierusalem: Essays on Medieval Law, Liturgy, and Literature in Honour of Amnon Linder*, edited by Yitzhak Hen. Turnhout, Belgium: Brepols, 2001.

———. "Ports of Pilgrimage to the Holy Land, Eleventh–Fourteenth Century: Jaffa, Acre, Alexandria." In *The Holy Portolano: The Sacred Geography of Navigation in the Middle Ages*, edited by Michele Bacci and Martin Rohde. Munich: De Gruyter, 2014.

———. *Studies on the Crusader States and on Venetian Expansion*. Northampton, UK: Variorum, 1989.

———. "Three Notes on Crusader Acre." *Zeitschrift des Deutschen Palästina-Vereins* 109, no. 1 (1993): 83–96.

Jones, Dan. *The Templars: The Rise and Spectacular Fall of God's Holy Warriors*. New York: Viking Books, 2017.

Kedar, Benjamin Z. "The Outer Walls of Frankish Acre." *Atiqot* 31 (1997): 157–180.

Kedar, Benjamin Z., Hans Eberhard Mayer, and R. C. Smail, eds. *Outremer: Studies in the History of the Crusading Kingdoms of Jerusalem*. Jerusalem: Yad Izhak Ben-Zvi Institute, 1982.

Kennedy, Hugh. *Crusader Castles*. Cambridge: Cambridge University Press, 1994.

Khamisy, Rabei G., and Michael S. Fulton. "Manjaniq Qarabugha and Thirteenth-Century Trebuchet Nomenclature." *Studia Islamica* 111, no. 2 (2016): 179–201.

Killigrew, Ann E., and Vered Raz-Romeo, eds. *One Thousand Nights and Days: Akko through the Ages*. Haifa: Hecht Museum, 2010.

King, E. J. *The Knights Hospitallers in the Holy Land*. London: Methuen, 1931.

Little, Donald P. "The Fall of Akka in 690/1291: The Muslim Version." *Studies in Islamic History and Civilization*, edited by M. Sharon. Leiden: Brill, 1986.

Marshall, Christopher J. "The French Regiment in the Latin East, 1254–91." *Journal of Medieval History* 15, no. 4 (1989): 301–307.

———. *Warfare in the Latin East, 1192–1291*. Cambridge: Cambridge University Press, 1992.

Mas-Latrie, M. L. de. *Histoire de L'Isle de Chypre*. Paris, 1861.

Mayer, Leo A. *Saracenic Heraldry: A Survey*. Oxford: Clarendon Press, 1933.

Meyvaert, Paul. "An Unknown Letter of Hulagu, Il-khan of Persia, to King Louis IX of France." *Viator* 11 (1980): 245–260.

Michaud, Joseph Francois. *Histoire des Croisades*. Paris: Furne, 1828.

Morris, Marc. *A Great and Terrible King: Edward I and the Forging of Britain*. London: Hutchinson, 2008.

Morton, Nicholas. *The Teutonic Knights in the Holy Land, 1190–1291.* Woodbridge, UK: Boydell Press, 2009.

Musarra, Antonio. *Acri 1291: La Caduta degli Stati Crociati.* Bologna: Società Editrice Il Mulino, 2017.

Nicholson, Helen. "Images of the Military Orders, 1128–1291." PhD thesis, University of Leicester, 1989.

———. *The Knights Hospitaller.* Woodbridge, UK: Boydell Press, 2001.

———. *The Knights Templar.* London: Sutton, 2010.

———. *Templars, Hospitallers and Teutonic Knights: Images of the Military Orders, 1128–1291.* Leicester, UK: Leicester University Press, 1993.

Nicolle, David. *Acre 1291: Bloody Sunset of the Crusader States.* Oxford: Osprey, 2005.

———. *Crusader Warfare: Byzantium, Western Europe and the Battle for the Holy Land.* London: Continuum Books, 2007.

———. *Crusader Warfare: Muslims, Mongols and the Struggle against the Crusades.* London: Continuum Books, 2007.

———. *Fighting for the Faith: The Many Fronts of Crusade and Jihad, 1000–1500 AD.* Barnsley, UK: Pen & Sword Books, 2007.

———. *Mamluk 'Askari, 1250–1517.* London: Osprey, 2014.

———. *The Mamluks, 1250–1517.* Oxford: Osprey, 1993.

———. *Medieval Siege Weapons (2): Byzantium, the Islamic World & India AD 476–1526.* Oxford: Osprey, 2003.

Northrup, Linda S. *From Slave to Sultan: The Career of Al-Manṣūr Qalāwūn and the Consolidation of Mamluk Rule in Egypt and Syria (678–689 A.H./1279–1290 A.D.).* Stuttgart: Franz Steiner Verlag, 1998.

Prawer, Joshua. *The Latin Kingdom of Jerusalem: European Colonialism in the Middle Ages.* London: Weidenfeld & Nicolson, 1973.

———. "Military Orders and Crusader Politics in the Second Half of the XIIIth Century." In *Die Geistlichen Ritterorden Europas,* edited by Josef Fleckenstein and Manfred Hellmann. Sigmaringen, Germany: Thorbecke, 1980.

Pringle, Denys. *The Churches of the Crusader Kingdom of Jerusalem.* Vol. 4. Cambridge: Cambridge University Press, 2009.

———. "Town Defences in the Crusader Kingdom of Jerusalem." In *The Medieval City under Siege,* edited by Ivy A. Corfis and Michael Wolfe. Woodbridge, UK: Boydell Press, 1995.

Rey, Emmanuel Guillaume. *Étude sur la Topographie de la Ville d'Acre au XIII Siècle.* Paris, 1879.

Riley-Smith, Jonathan, ed. *The Atlas of the Crusades.* London: Times Books, 1991.

———. *The Knights of St. John in Jerusalem and Cyprus, c. 1050–1310.* Vol. 1 of *A History of the Order of the Hospital of St. John of Jerusalem.* London: Palgrave Macmillan, 1967.

————. *The Knights Hospitaller in the Levant*, c.1076–1309. London: Palgrave Macmillan, 2012.

Röhricht, Reinhold. *Geschichte des Königreichs Jerusalem*, 1100–1291. Innsbruck: Wagner, 1898.

Runciman, Stephen. *A History of the Crusades*. 3 vols. Cambridge: Cambridge University Press, 1964.

Sadeque, Syedah. *Baybars I of Egypt*. Dacca: Oxford University Press, 1956.

Schein, Sylvia. *Fideles Crucis: The Papacy, the West, and the Recovery of the Holy Land, 1274–1314*. Oxford: Oxford University Press, 1991.

————. "The Image of the Crusader Kingdom of Jerusalem in the Thirteenth Century." *Revue belge de Philologie et d'Histoire* 64, no. 4 (1986): 704–717.

————. "The Patriarchs of Jerusalem in the Late Thirteenth Century." In *Outremer: Studies in the History of the Crusading Kingdom of Jerusalem*, edited by Benjamin Z. Kedar, Hans Eberhard Mayer, and R. C. Smail. Jerusalem: Yad Izhak Ben-Zvi Institute, 1982.

Schlumberger, Gustave. *La Prise de Saint-Jean-d'Acre en l'an 1291 par l'armée du Soudan d'Égypte*. Paris: Plon, 1914.

Shagris, Iris. "The Fall of Acre as a Spiritual Crisis: The Letters of Riccoldo of Monte Croce." *Revue belge de Philologie et d'Histoire* 90, no. 4 (2012): 1107–1120.

Smail, R. C. *The Crusaders in Syria and the Holy Land*. London: Thames and Hudson, 1973.

Stickel, Edwin. *Der Fall von Akkon*. Frankfurt: Peter Lang, 1975.

Thorau, Peter. *The Lion of Egypt: Sultan Baybars I and the Near East in the Thirteenth Century*. London: Longman, 1992.

Tschanz, David W. "History's Hinge: Ain Jalut." *Aramco World* 58, no. 4 (2007).

Tyerman, Christopher. *God's War: A New History of the Crusades*. London: Allen Lane, 2006.

Ziadeh, Nicola A. *Damascus under the Mamluks*. Norman: University of Oklahoma Press, 1964.

NOTES

All the quotations in the book are from primary sources. References are from books as listed in the bibliography. The following abbreviation is used:

GDC: *Les Gestes des Chiprois*. In *Recueil des Histoires des Croisades, Documents Arméniens*. Vol. 2. Paris, 1906.

PROLOGUE

1. Pringle, *Pilgrimage to Jerusalem and the Holy Land, 1187–1291*, 127.
2. Asbridge, *The Crusades: The War for the Holy Land*, 453.

CHAPTER 1: THE SECOND CITY OF JERUSALEM

1. Jacques de Vitry, *Lettres de Jacques de Vitry*, 77–97.
2. Jacoby, "Aspects of Everyday Life," 82–83.
3. Ibn Jubayr, *The Travels of Ibn Jubayr*, 318.
4. Pringle, *Pilgrimage to Jerusalem and the Holy Land, 1187–1291*, 62–63.
5. Hillenbrand, *The Crusades: Islamic Perspectives*, 222.
6. Hillenbrand, 204.
7. Nicholson, *The Knights Templar*, 85.
8. Irwin, "The Mamluk Conquest of the County of Tripoli," 6.
9. Ibn Khaldun, *The Muqaddimah*, 257–258.
10. Ibn Khaldun, 257–258.
11. Thorau, *The Lion of Egypt*, 17.

CHAPTER 2: DEATH ON THE NILE

1. Jean de Joinville, *Histoire de Saint Louis*, 82.
2. Jean de Joinville, 86.
3. Jean de Joinville, 88.
4. Crowley, *City of Fortune: How Venice Won and Lost a Naval Empire*, 37.

5. Asbridge, *The Crusades: The War for the Holy Land,* 552.

6. Jean de Joinville, 90.

7. Jackson, *The Seventh Crusade,* 131.

8. Jean de Joinville, *Histoire de Saint Louis,* 98.

9. Jean de Joinville, 100.

10. Jackson, *The Seventh Crusade,* 141.

11. Jackson, 139.

12. Jackson, 139.

13. Jean de Joinville, *Histoire de Saint Louis,* 112.

14. Jean de Joinville, 115.

15. Jean de Joinville, 115.

16. Jean de Joinville, 116.

17. Jean de Joinville, 118.

18. Shirley, *Crusader Syria in the Thirteenth Century,* 95.

19. Jackson, *The Seventh Crusade,* 144.

20. Shirley, *Crusader Syria in the Thirteenth Century,* 96.

21. Jackson, *The Seventh Crusade,* 144.

22. Jackson, 145.

23. Shirley, *Crusader Syria in the Thirteenth Century,* 97.

24. Jean de Joinville, *Histoire de Saint Louis,* 120–122.

25. Jean de Joinville, 120–122.

26. Jean de Joinville, 124.

27. Jean de Joinville, 124.

28. Jean de Joinville, 126.

29. Jean de Joinville, 128.

30. Jean de Joinville, 130.

31. Jean de Joinville, 132.

32. Jean de Joinville, 158.

33. Jean de Joinville, 160.

34. Jean de Joinville, 166.

35. Jean de Joinville, 164.

36. Jackson, *The Seventh Crusade,* 161.

37. Jean de Joinville, *Histoire de Saint Louis,* 160.

38. Jean de Joinville, 164.

39. Jean de Joinville, 174.

40. Jean de Joinville, 176.

41. Jean de Joinville, 269

42. Jackson, *The Seventh Crusade,* 102.

43. Jackson, 144.

44. Jackson, 160.

45. Jean de Joinville, *Histoire de Saint Louis,* 192.

46. Jackson, *The Seventh Crusade,* 167.

47. Jackson, 170.

Chapter 3: Between the Mamluks and the Mongols

1. Jean de Joinville, *Histoire de Saint Louis*, 178.
2. Jean de Joinville, 267.
3. Tschanz, "History's Hinge: Ain Jalut," 24.
4. Shirley, *Crusader Syria in the Thirteenth Century*, 117.
5. Jackson, *The Seventh Crusade*, 495.
6. Paris, *Matthew Paris's English History: From the Year 1235 to 1273*, 251.
7. Jackson, *The Seventh Crusade*, 505.
8. Tschanz, "History's Hinge: Ain Jalut," 24.
9. Thorau, *The Lion of Egypt*, 76.
10. Amitai-Preiss, *Mongols and Mamluks: The Mamluk-Ilkhanid War, 1260–1281*, 41.

Chapter 4: The Lion of Egypt

1. Thorau, *The Lion of Egypt*, 105.
2. Hillenbrand, *The Crusades: Islamic Perspectives*, 237.
3. Ibn al-Furat, *Ayyubids, Mamlukes and Crusaders*, 58.
4. GDC, 756.
5. Amitai-Preiss, "The Conquest of Arsuf by Baybars: Political and Military Aspects," 68.
6. Ibn al-Furat, *Ayyubids, Mamlukes and Crusaders*, 70.
7. Amitai-Preiss, "The Conquest of Arsuf by Baybars: Political and Military Aspects," 73.
8. Ibn al-Furat, *Ayyubids, Mamlukes and Crusaders*, 75.
9. Ibn al-Furat, 77–78.
10. Ibn al-Furat, 78.
11. Hillenbrand, *The Crusades: Islamic Perspectives*, 230.
12. Hillenbrand, 231.
13. Ibn al-Furat, *Ayyubids, Mamlukes and Crusaders*, 89–90.
14. GDC, 764–766.
15. Ibn al-Furat, *Ayyubids, Mamlukes and Crusaders*, 123–125.
16. Ibn al-Furat, 116.
17. Ibn al-Furat, 148.

Chapter 5: A Puppy Yelping at a Mastiff

1. Prawer, "Military Orders and Crusader Politics in the Second Half of the XIIIth Century," 217.
2. Morris, *A Great and Terrible King: Edward I and the Forging of Britain*, 69.
3. Asbridge, *The Crusades: The War for the Holy Land*, 641.
4. Psalms 137:5.

5. Crowley, *City of Fortune: How Venice Won and Lost a Naval Empire*, 27.

6. Gabrielli, *Arab Historians of the Crusade*, 318–319.

7. Kennedy, *Crusader Castles*, 162.

8. Morris, *A Great and Terrible King: Edward I and the Forging of Britain*, 99.

9. Morris, 99.

10. GDC, 793.

11. Ludolph von Suchem, *Description of the Holy Land, and of the Way There*, 50–53.

12. Ludolph von Suchem, 50–53.

13. Jean de Joinville, *Histoire de Saint Louis*, 277.

14. Pringle, *The Churches of the Crusader Kingdom of Jerusalem*, 24.

CHAPTER 6: WAR TO THE ENEMY

1. GDC, 802.

2. GDC, 798.

3. GDC, 802–803.

4. Abu'l-Fida, *The Memoirs of a Syrian Prince*, 14.

5. GDC, 803.

6. GDC, 803–804.

7. GDC, 804.

8. Abu'l-Fida, *The Memoirs of a Syrian Prince*, 15.

9. Abu'l-Fida, 15.

10. Holt, *Early Mamluk Diplomacy (1260–1290): Treaties of Baybars and Qalāwūn with Christian Rulers*, 91.

11. Holt, 73.

12. Holt, 135.

13. *Excidium Aconis*, 49.

14. GDC, 805.

15. GDC, 805.

16. Sanudo Torsello, *The Book of the Secrets of the Faithful of the Cross*, 367.

17. *Excidium Aconis*, 50.

18. GDC, 805.

19. GDC, 805.

20. Holt, *Early Mamluk Diplomacy (1260–1290): Treaties of Baybars and Qalāwūn with Christian Rulers*, 84.

21. Gabrielli, *Arab Historians of the Crusades*, 331.

22. Shafi 'b. 'Alī, *Ḥusn al-Manāqib al-Sirriyyah al-Muntaza'a min al-Sīra al-Ẓāhiriyya*, 285–286.

Chapter 7: "My Soul Longed for Jihad"

1. Ibn 'Abd al-Ẓāhir, *Tashrīf al-ayyām wa-al-'uṣūr fī sīrat al-Malik al-Manṣūr*, 177.
2. Ibn 'Abd al-Ẓāhir, 177.
3. Badr al-Dīn al-Ainī, *Iqd al-Jumān fī Tārīkh Ahl al-Zamān*, 55.
4. Ibn 'Abd al-Ẓāhir, *Tashrīf al-ayyām wa-al-'uṣūr fī sīrat al-Malik al-Manṣūr*, 178.
5. Ibn 'Abd al-Ẓāhir, 178.
6. Ibn 'Abd al-Ẓāhir, 178.
7. GDC, 807.
8. Nicolle, *Acre 1291: Bloody Sunset of the Crusader States*, 22.
9. Ibn 'Abd al-Ẓāhir, *Tashrīf al-ayyām wa-al-'uṣūr fī sīrat al-Malik al-Manṣūr*, 178.
10. GDC, 807.
11. GDC, 807.
12. GDC, 807.
13. GDC, 807.
14. Maqrīzī, *Histoire des Sultans mamlouks*, 109.
15. Abu'l-Fida, *The Memoirs of a Syrian Prince*, 16.
16. Abu'l-Fida, 16.
17. Little, "The Fall of Akka in 690/1291: The Muslim Version," 70.
18. Schlumberger, *La Prise de Saint-Jean-d'Acre en l'an 1291 par l'armée du Soudan d'Égypte*, 29.
19. Schlumberger, 29.
20. Baybars al-Manṣūrī, *Zubdah al-Fikra fī al-Tārīkh al-Hijrah*, 278.
21. Al-Jazari, *La Chronique de Damas d'al-Jazari*, 4.
22. Al-Jazari, 4.
23. *Excidium Aconis*, 64.
24. *Excidium Aconis*, 64–65.

Chapter 8: The Red Tent

1. *Excidium Aconis*, 68.
2. GDC, 808.
3. Dichter, *The Maps of Acre: An Historical Cartography*, 32.
4. GDC, 808.
5. GDC, 808.
6. GDC, 808.
7. King, *The Knights Hospitallers in the Holy Land*, 301.
8. Baybars al-Manṣūrī, *Zubdah al-Fikra fī al-Tārīkh al-Hijrah*, 278.
9. Dichter, *The Maps of Acre: An Historical Cartography*, 45.
10. Dichter, 47.

11. Ludolph von Suchem, *Description of the Holy Land, and of the Way There*, 50–51.

12. 'Umar Ibn Ibrāhīm al-Awsī al-Anṣārī, *A Muslim Manual of War*, 116–117.

13. 'Umar Ibn Ibrāhīm al-Awsī al-Anṣārī, 118.

14. Kennedy, *Crusader Castles*, 100.

15. Dichter, *The Maps of Acre: An Historical Cartography*, 33.

16. Chevedden, "Black Camels and Blazing Bolts: The Bolt-Projecting Trebuchet in the Mamluk Army," 250.

17. GDC, 807.

18. GDC, para. 485.

19. *Excidium Aconis*, 60–61.

20. Marshall, *Warfare in the Latin East, 1192–1291*, 82.

21. 'Umar Ibn Ibrāhīm al-Awsī al-Anṣārī, *A Muslim Manual of War*, 118.

22. King, *The Knights Hospitallers in the Holy Land*, 301.

23. 'Umar Ibn Ibrāhīm al-Awsī al-Anṣārī, *A Muslim Manual of War*, 117.

24. Chevedden, "Black Camels and Blazing Bolts: The Bolt-Projecting Trebuchet in the Mamluk Army," 251.

25. GDC, 808.

26. Badr al-Dīn al-Ainī, *Iqd al-Jumān fī Tārīkh Ahl al-Zamān*, 57–58.

CHAPTER 9: "BOLTS OF THUNDER, FLASHES OF LIGHTNING"

1. Abu'l-Fida, *The Memoirs of a Syrian Prince*, 16.

2. Chevedden, "The Invention of the Counterweight Trebuchet: A Study in Cultural Diffusion," 96.

3. Badr al-Dīn al-Ainī, *Iqd al-Jumān fī Tārīkh Ahl al-Zamān*, 61.

4. 'Umar Ibn Ibrāhīm al-Awsī al-Anṣārī, *A Muslim Manual of War*, 117.

5. 'Umar Ibn Ibrāhīm al-Awsī al-Anṣārī, 117.

6. GDC, 808–809.

7. GDC, 809.

8. *Chroniques d'Amadi et de Strambaldi*, 221.

9. Thadeus, *Ystoria de desolatione et conculcatione civitatis Acconensis et tocius terre sancta*, 101–102.

10. *Chronicle of Lanercost, 1272–1346*, 79.

11. Baybars al-Manṣūrī, *Zubdah al-Fikra fī al-Tārīkh al-Hijrah*, 279.

12. "as if by thunderbolts falling from heaven," Thadeus, 101.

13. *Excidium Aconis*, 65.

14. Usāmah Ibn-Munqidh, *An Arab-Syrian Gentleman and a Warrior in the Period of the Crusades*, 100.

15. Usāmah Ibn-Munqidh, 102–103.

16. Kennedy, *Crusader Castles*, 104–105.

17. GDC, 810.

CHAPTER 10: SORTIES

1. Abu'l-Fida, *The Memoirs of a Syrian Prince*, 16–17.
2. Abu'l-Fida, 17.
3. GDC, 810.
4. GDC, 810.
5. Abu'l-Fida, *The Memoirs of a Syrian Prince*, 17.
6. GDC, 810.
7. Badr al-Dīn al-Ainī, *Iqd al-Jumān fī Tārīkh Ahl al-Zamān*, 60.
8. Badr al-Dīn al-Ainī, 59.
9. GDC, 810.
10. Abu'l-Fida, *The Memoirs of a Syrian Prince*, 17.
11. Badr al-Dīn al-Ainī, *Iqd al-Jumān fī Tārīkh Ahl al-Zamān*, 60.
12. 'Umar Ibn Ibrāhīm al-Awsī al-Anṣārī, *A Muslim Manual of War*, 118.
13. Badr al-Dīn al-Ainī, *Iqd al-Jumān fī Tārīkh Ahl al-Zamān*, 59.
14. Badr al-Dīn al-Ainī, 59.
15. GDC, 810.
16. *Chronicle of Lanercost, 1272–1346*, 80.
17. *Chronicle of Lanercost, 1272–1346*, 80.
18. GDC, 807.
19. Jacoby, "Aspects of Everyday Life in Frankish Acre," 14.
20. Dichter, *The Orders and Churches of Crusader Acre*, 102.
21. Jacoby, "Aspects of Everyday Life in Frankish Acre," 11.
22. Jacoby, 11.
23. Dichter, *The Orders and Churches of Crusader Acre*, 32–33.
24. GDC, 810–811.
25. Bartolomeo de Neocastro, *Historia Sicula, 1250-1293*, 132.

CHAPTER 11: NEGOTIATIONS

1. Bartolomeo de Neocastro, *Historia Sicula, 1250-1293*, 132.
2. Bartolomeo de Neocastro, 132.
3. GDC, 811.
4. GDC, 811.
5. Little, "The Fall of Akka in 690/1291: The Muslim Version," 174.
6. GDC, 811.
7. GDC, 811.
8. GDC, 811.
9. GDC, 811.
10. Al-Jazari, *La Chronique de Damas d'al-Jazari* 5.
11. GDC, 811.
12. GDC, 811.
13. Badr al-Dīn al-Ainī, *Iqd al-Jumān fī Tārīkh Ahl al-Zamān*, 279–280.

14. GDC, 811.
15. *Excidium Aconis*, 69.
16. *Excidium Aconis*, 71.
17. *Excidium Aconis*, 71.
18. *Excidium Aconis*, 73.
19. GDC, 811–812.
20. GDC, 812.
21. *Excidium Aconis*, 76.
22. *Excidium Aconis*, 78–79.
23. *Excidium Aconis*, 80.
24. *Excidium Aconis*, 80.
25. GDC, 812.

CHAPTER 12: "SEE THE WOUND!"

1. GDC, 812.
2. *Excidium Aconis*, 84.
3. *Excidium Aconis*, 82.
4. *Excidium Aconis*, 82.
5. *Excidium Aconis*, 83.
6. *Excidium Aconis*, 86.
7. GDC, 812.
8. Jean de Joinville, *Histoire de Saint Louis*, 112.
9. GDC, 812.
10. GDC, 812.
11. GDC, 812.
12. GDC, 812.
13. *Excidium Aconis*, 89.
14. *Excidium Aconis*, 90.
15. King, *The Knights Hospitallers in the Holy Land*, 302.
16. GDC, 812.
17. GDC, 812–813.
18. *Excidium Aconis*, 88–89.
19. King, *The Knights Hospitallers in the Holy Land*, 302.
20. GDC, 813.
21. *Excidium Aconis*, 86.
22. GDC, 814.
23. King, *The Knights Hospitallers in the Holy Land*, 302.
24. GDC, 814.
25. GDC, 814.
26. GDC, 814.
27. GDC, 814.
28. GDC, 813–814.

29. GDC, 815–816.
30. *Excidium Aconis*, 91.
31. GDC, 814.
32. GDC, 814.

Chapter 13: The Terrible Day

1. GDC, 814.
2. GDC, 814.
3. King, *The Knights Hospitallers in the Holy Land*, 302.
4. GDC, 815.
5. Muntaner, *The Chronicle of Muntaner*, 468.
6. Muntaner, 468–469.
7. Thadeus, *Ystoria de desolatione et conculcatione civitatis Acconensis et tocius terre sancta*, 102–103.
8. Thadeus, 103.
9. Thadeus, 125–126.
10. GDC, 815.
11. Badr al-Dīn al-Ainī, *Iqd al-Jumān fī Tārīkh Ahl al-Zamān*, 61.
12. GDC, 814.
13. Badr al-Dīn al-Ainī, *Iqd al-Jumān fī Tārīkh Ahl al-Zamān*, 61–62.
14. Thadeus, *Ystoria de desolatione et conculcatione civitatis Acconensis et tocius terre sancta*, 108–109.
15. Thadeus, 90.
16. GDC, 805.
17. GDC, 805.
18. Abu'l-Fida, *The Memoirs of a Syrian Prince*, 17.
19. GDC, 814–815.
20. GDC, 816.
21. GDC, 816.
22. Nicolle, *Acre 1291: Bloody Sunset of the Crusader States*, 83.
23. Little, "The Fall of Akka in 690/1291: The Muslim Version," 175.
24. GDC, 816.
25. GDC, 817.
26. Little, "The Fall of Akka in 690/1291: The Muslim Version," 175.
27. GDC, 817.
28. Nicholson, *The Knights Templar*, 86.
29. Nicolle, *Acre 1291: Bloody Sunset of the Crusader States*, 84.
30. GDC, 816–817.

Chapter 14: "Everything Was Lost"

1. Bartholomei de Cotton, *Historia Anglicana*, 215–217.

2. Nicolle, *Acre 1291: Bloody Sunset of the Crusader States*, 89.

3. GDC, 818.

4. Shagris, "The Fall of Acre as a Spiritual Crisis: The Letters of Riccoldo of Monte Croce," 1118.

5. Nicolle, *Acre 1291: Bloody Sunset of the Crusader States*, 89.

6. Prawer, *The Latin Kingdom of Jerusalem: European Colonialism in the Middle Ages*, 456.

7. Little, "The Fall of Akka in 690/1291: The Muslim Version," 177.

8. Nicolle, *Acre 1291: Bloody Sunset of the Crusader States*, 89.

9. Abu'l-Fida, *The Memoirs of a Syrian Prince*, 17.

10. Badr al-Dīn al-Ainī, *Iqd al-Jumān fī Tārīkh Ahl al-Zamān*, 62–63.

11. Badr al-Dīn al-Ainī, 62.

12. Nicolle, *Acre 1291: Bloody Sunset of the Crusader States*, 87–88.

13. Baybars al-Manṣūrī, *Zubdah al-Fikra fī al-Tārīkh al-Hijrah*, 280.

14. GDC, 818.

15. GDC, 818.

16. Schein, *Fideles Crucis: The Papacy, the West, and the Recovery of the Holy Land, 1274–1314*, 113.

17. Schein, 113.

18. Schein, 126.

19. "with their armour untouched," *Excidium Aconis*, 90.

20. King, *The Knights Hospitallers in the Holy Land*, 302.

21. Housley, *The Later Crusades, 1274–1580: From Lyons to Alcazar*, 30.

22. Jones, *The Templars: The Rise and Spectacular Fall of God's Holy Warriors*, 397–378.

23. GDC, 821.

EPILOGUE: A HABITATION FOR SNAKES

1. Ludolph von Suchem, *Description of the Holy Land, and of the Way There*, 60.

2. Pringle, *The Churches of the Crusader Kingdom of Jerusalem*, 25.

3. Pringle, 27.

4. Maundrell, *A Journey from Aleppo to Syria*, 106.

5. Maundrell, 106.

6. Maundrell, 28.

INDEX

Credit: Oliver Poole

Roger Crowley was born in 1951 into a naval family and educated at Cambridge University. The author of numerous bestselling books, including *1453* and *Empires of the Sea*, Crowley lives in Gloucestershire, UK.